The Advocates of Poetry

The Advocates of Poetry

A READER OF
AMERICAN POET-CRITICS
OF THE MODERNIST ERA

Edited by

R. S. GWYNN

The University of Arkansas Press
FAYETTEVILLE

1996

Copyright 1996 by R. S. Gwynn

All rights reserved
Manufactured in the United States of America

00 99 98 97 96 5 4 3 2 1

Designed by Alice Gail Carter

⊗ The paper used in this publication meets the minimum requirements of the American National Standard for Permanence of Paper for Printed Library Materials Z39.48-1984.

LIBRARY OF CONGRESS CATALOGING-IN-PUBLICATION DATA

The advocates of poetry : a reader of American poet-critics of the modernist era / edited by R.S. Gwynn.
p. cm.
Includes bibliographical references (p.).
ISBN 1-55728-426-1 (cloth : alk. paper)
1. American poetry—20th century—History and criticism—Theory, etc. 2. Modernism (Literature)—United States. 3. Poetics.
I. Gwynn, R. S.
PS310.M57A48 1996
811'.509—dc20 96-22484
CIP

R. P. BLACKMUR: "Lord Tennyson's Scissors: 1912–1950" from *Language as Gesture: Essays in Poetry,* copyright © 1952 by Richard P. Blackmur and renewed 1980 by Elizabeth Blackmur, reprinted by permission of Harcourt Brace & Company.

LOUISE BOGAN: "Some Notes on Popular and Unpopular Art" from *Selected Criticism.* Noonday, 1955. Reprinted by permission of Ruth Limmer, literary executor of the Estate of Louise Bogan.

KENNETH BURKE: "Freud—and the Analysis of Poetry" from *The Philosophy of Literary Form,* 3d ed. University of California Press, 1973. Copyright © 1973 by The Regents of the University of California. Reprinted by permission.

JOHN CIARDI: "How Does a Poem Mean?" from John Ciardi and Miller Williams, *How Does a Poem Mean?: An Introduction to Literature,* 2d edition. Copyright © 1975 by Houghton Mifflin Company. Reprinted with permission.

ROBERT HAYDEN: "'How It Strikes a Contemporary': Reflections on Poetry and the Role of the Poet" from *Collected Prose,* ed. Frederick Glaysher. University of Michigan Press, 1984. Reprinted by permission of the Estate of Erma Hayden, literary executor Maia Patillo.

RANDALL JARRELL: "Poets, Critics, and Readers" from *Kipling, Auden & Co.: Essays and Reviews 1935–1964.* Copyright © 1980 by Mrs. Randall Jarrell. Reprinted by permission of Farrar, Straus & Giroux, Inc.

ELDER OLSON: "The Lyric" from *On Value Judgments in the Arts and Other Essays.* University of Chicago Press, 1976. "The Lyric" was originally published in *Poetic Theory, Poetic Practice: Papers of the Midwest Modern Language Association,* ed. Robert Scholes. Reprinted by permission of the Midwest Modern Language Association, Thomas E. Lewis, executive director.

JOHN CROWE RANSOM: "Wanted: An Ontological Critic" from *Beating the Bushes.* Copyright © 1941 by New Directions Publishing Corp. Reprinted by permission of New Directions Publishing Corp.

DELMORE SCHWARTZ: "The Isolation of Modern Poetry" from *Selected Essays of Delmore Schwartz,* ed. Donald A. Dike and David H. Zucker. Permission to reprint granted by Robert Phillips, literary executor for the Estate of Delmore Schwartz.

ALLEN TATE: "Tension in Poetry" from *Essays of Four Decades.* Chicago: Swallow, 1968. Reprinted by permission of Helen H. Tate.

ROBERT PENN WARREN: "Pure and Impure Poetry" from *New and Selected Essays.* Random House, 1989. First published in the *Kenyon Review,* Spring 1943, OS Vol. 5, no. 2. Copyright © 1943 by the *Kenyon Review.* Reprinted by permission.

YVOR WINTERS: "The Audible Reading of Poetry" from *The Function of Criticism,* Ohio University Press/Swallow Press, 1957. Reprinted with the permission of The Ohio University Press/Swallow Press, Athens.

Respectfully dedicated to the memory of

CLEANTH BROOKS

American Man of Letters

1906–1994

Acknowledgments

Thanks are due the Faculty Senate of Lamar University for granting a semester's leave to work on this manuscript. I am also indebted to John Idoux, Kendall Blanchard, and Robert Moulton, Lamar administrators past and present, for their support of faculty research projects. My gratitude also goes to Tim Summerlin, late chair of the Department of English and Foreign Languages, and Sallye Sheppeard, current chair, for their unstinting patience and generosity. Cindy Colichia, departmental secretary, and Geri Dauphine, student assistant, performed many thankless chores, and Amber McClintock, who served as my editorial assistant, provided invaluable help in completing this project.

CONTENTS

INTRODUCTION

THE ADVOCATES OF POETRY

The remarkable flourishing of American poet-critics that occurred in the first half of the twentieth century is without precedent in literary history. To be sure, the role of the poet-critic is an old and honorable one, stretching as far back in English literature as Daniel, Campion, and Sidney and accommodating later figures as diverse as Dryden, Pope, Wordsworth, Coleridge, and Shelley, and, on this side of the Atlantic, Emerson and Poe. In the second half of the last century Matthew Arnold perhaps best established the paradigm of poet-critic, advancing the modest requirements that "criticism must be sincere, simple, flexible, ardent, [and] ever widening its knowledge" in an effort to become, in his own italicized phrase, *"a disinterested endeavour to learn and propagate the best that is known and thought in the world."*[1] Arnold set the standards for the generation of American poet-critics collected here, the eldest of whom was born in 1888, the year of Arnold's death, and the youngest in 1916, when world events made it no longer possible to ignore the full implications of what the word *modern* would come to mean.

The roots of the modern American poet-critics' family tree lie, of course, in Pound and Eliot, expatriates whose self-conscious efforts to be both modern and deracinated now wear a slightly comic aura. Pound's enthusiastic endorsement of the young Eliot to Harriet Monroe speaks with awe of the fact that he had managed to "modernize himself on his own," that is, without the generous assistance of his elder countryman. Pound's own criticism bears the marks of his eccentric character; it is intensely didactic, even evangelical, in its efforts to educate his provincial countrymen as both poets and readers. Eliot's aim is similar, though his Americanism was subsumed beneath the role he was to play to perfection for the rest of his life, and his manner was less strident than Pound's, if equally insistent that only a new kind of reader would be fully capable of appreciating the new poetry. We know more than the writers of the past, he says, and that is because they are part of what we know. And the criticism of Pound and Eliot became a large part of what modern American poet-critics knew and built upon.

Because I have attempted to give this collection a unity that is not only indicative of an extended generation of poets but also of a tradition of homegrown pragmatism, I have begun not with Pound and Eliot but with an American contemporary, John Crowe Ransom, whose poetry and criticism I regard only slightly less highly than I do his skills in literary leadership. I have also been guided by a desire to return some important poet-critics to accessibility. Essays such as Pound's "A Retrospect" or "The Wisdom of Poetry" or Eliot's "Tradition and the Individual Talent" are widely anthologized, and collections of the prose of both writers remain in print; on the other hand, samples of the criticism of many important poets are found now with increasing difficulty. Ransom was born in the same year as Eliot and, like him, was in the years immediately preceding World War I a sojourner at Oxford, where both poets studied philosophy. But Ransom came home and never left again. His career was spent in the provinces, first in Nashville and later in Gambier, each of which he managed to establish as an important center of what Pound would have called a "vortex." As Emerson said a century before, "If the single man plant himself indomitably on his instincts, and there abide, the great world will come round to him." And come it did, first to the pages of the *Fugitive* and later to those of the *Kenyon Review*. The first volume (1939) of the *Kenyon Review* included work by John Peale Bishop, R. P. Blackmur, Yvor Winters, Dylan Thomas, Muriel Rukeyser, Allen Tate, and three unknown poets still in their twenties—John Berryman, Randall Jarrell, and Robert Lowell.

Lowell, born in 1917 and a typical rebellious child of equally strong-willed literary parents, expressed what it was like for a poet of his generation to go through the rites of passage in an era when the poet was *expected* to be a critic as well:

> When I was twenty and learning to write, Allen Tate, Eliot, Blackmur, and Winters, and all those people were very much news. You waited for their essays, and when a good critical essay came out it had the excitement of a new imaginative work.[2]

This situation no longer exists. True, a good number of contemporary poets write excellent criticism, if we are to judge by the overall quality of the fifty-odd volumes in the University of Michigan's Poets on Poetry Series. Unfortunately, the excitement that Lowell mentioned occurs today only infrequently. A few years ago Dana Gioia published an essay called "Can Poetry Matter?" in the *Atlantic Monthly,* and that event elicited one of the largest mail responses from readers in the magazine's history. But this intrusion of serious criticism of poetry into the consciousness of the general reading public, the elusive "common reader" for poetry, remains an anomaly; the real action, so to speak, lies elsewhere. That "elsewhere" is among the academic theorists who have in recent years dominated American literary discourse.

In 1988 the *Dictionary of Literary Biography* published two volumes dealing with prominent American critics of this century. The first of these covered the years from 1920 to 1955; the second, from 1955 to the present. Comparing their contents reveals much about the diverse directions that American literary criticism has taken over the last four decades. Other than the expected numerical shifts in gender and in the ethnic backgrounds of the critics—in the earlier volume all were male and, with only two exceptions, white—the tables of contents reveal, significantly, that in the first volume over one-third of the twenty-five critics were also practicing poets. In the second, which covered twenty-seven writers, the number of poet-critics had dwindled to only one, Adrienne Rich. Whereas many of the critics in the first volume had no advanced degrees—one of the most influential, R. P. Blackmur, had no university diploma at all—and made their livings to some extent outside the academy, virtually all of the younger group hold Ph.D.s and occupy senior positions in English departments. The elder group had some public visibility as well, occasionally appearing as media commentators and consultants to book clubs; their publications might have found no large fund of general readers, but they were not confined solely to appearances in scholarly journals and academic books of interest only to the specialist. Finally, and perhaps most tellingly, the second volume concludes with a twenty-page appendix covering the "Critical Terms, Schools, and Movements" which in the texts of the articles form a labyrinth of terminology that readers will presumably find unnegotiable without a glossary. The first volume contains no such apparatus, nor does it have much need of one.

What are the implications of these differences? It has become perhaps too easy to leap to dire conclusions about the state of health of our literary culture, especially in the manner of neo-conservative commentators like John Leo, Hilton Kramer, or Roger Kimball, who find the proceedings of the annual convention of the Modern Language Association roughly comparable to the preposterous goings on in Swift's Grand Academy of Lagado. Still, it should be apparent to anyone who has been attuned to American literary culture for more than a few years that a significant power shift has occurred. Joseph Epstein, in a widely discussed 1988 *Commentary* article called "Who Killed Poetry?", laments contemporary poetry's retreat from the general public consciousness as it becomes more closely identified with and controlled by university creative writing programs. To an even greater degree, serious criticism of poetry has constricted its focus to a far narrower realm, that of the academic specialist. In 1837

Emerson warned his nascent American scholars against becoming merely "the restorers of readings, the emendators, the bibliomaniacs of all degrees"; today he might instead indict those who would make their life's work the deconstruction of *all* readings rather than the restoration of a single usable one.

The academy has always been an easy target, especially for those who toil outside its gates, but of late the wailing and gnashing of teeth have resounded from somewhat closer quarters. Here is one complaint from *inside* the cloister, commenting sourly on what has been labeled the "school of resentment" in academic criticism:

> What interests me more is the flight from the aesthetic among so many in my profession, some of whom at least began with the ability to experience aesthetic value. In Freud, flight is the metaphor for repression, for unconscious yet purposeful forgetting. The purpose is clear enough in my profession's flight: to assuage displaced guilt. Forgetting, in an aesthetic context, is ruinous, for cognition, in criticism, always relies on memory. Longinus would have said that pleasure is what the resenters have forgotten. Nietzsche would have called it pain; but they would have been thinking of the same experience upon the heights. Those who descend from there, lemminglike, chant the litany that literature is best explained as a mystification promoted by bourgeois institutions.
>
> This reduces the aesthetic to ideology, or at best to metaphysics. A poem cannot be read as a poem, because it is primarily a social document or, rarely yet possibly, an attempt to overcome philosophy. Against this approach I urge a stubborn resistance whose single aim is to preserve poetry as fully and purely as possible. Our legions who have deserted represent a strand in our traditions that has always been in flight from the aesthetic: Platonic moralism and Aristotelian social science. The attack on poetry either exiles it for being destructive of social well-being or allows it sufferance if it will assume the work of social catharsis . . . .[3]

Rueful words indeed. And that they should come from Harold Bloom, a critic at home in the most prominent center of contemporary academic theory, is indeed ironic, for many would have heretofore identified Bloom's own post-Freudian criticism, with its concomitant baggage of arcane terminology, as precisely the sort of thing he seems to be attacking. Still, one welcomes allies wherever they are to be found.

If Bloom's tone is one of resigned sadness, that of Louis Simpson, one of the most lucid and reliable of contemporary poet-critics, is outwardly hostile and, I would venture, more typical of the distrust, if not disgust, with which many poets view the situation of contemporary academic criticism:

> People with a love of poetry are desperately needed at the present time in departments of English, languages, and comparative literature, for those departments are being taken over by those who have no love of literature. Indeed, as they have proudly and repeatedly proclaimed, they wish to use literature only as a means of demonstrating critical theories. Jacques Derrida and Paul de Man had no respect for authors; in fact, they told us that authors are irrelevant. It is language that writes, not an author. Stanley Fish tells us that the aim of teaching is to advance oneself in the profession. The followers of these successful theorists are even less attached to literature; Derrida, de Man, and Fish had at least read the authors they set out to deconstruct, but these have only read critical theory. They are like the followers of Marx who do not take into account the results of Marxism in practice. Perfecting a theory is all that matters; whether or not it can be applied concerns them not at all.[4]

One could simply label this sort of thing alarmist overreaction, a crank letter to town hall from a prosperous suburban compound. Still, I would argue that Simpson's feelings are widespread among poets themselves; the most blistering (and most hilarious) attack on current literary theory was poet David Lehman's demolition of Paul de Man in his *Signs of the Times.*

But in fairness, let one of the current theorists speak for himself:

> Perhaps the closest we teachers of language and literature can come in our everyday work to glimpsing what we

> have erased, forgotten, or even forgotten that we have forgotten is in that most ordinary of experiences for the literary scholar, the act of holding a book in one's hand and reading, that is, confronting face to face the materiality of the inscription. The trouble is that the inscription makes the matter invisible once more. We do not see the paper for the words. Another way to put this is to say that reading is always theoretical. Theory, even a theory of the material base, is precisely a clear seeing that turns the material base, this particular piece of paper here and now, into a generalized and generalizable abstraction. The triumph of theory is the resistance to reading in the sense that theory erases the particularity of the unique act of reading, but reading itself is always theoretical in the sense of performing the erasure and forgetting before we know what is happening and without our being able to know. So even the most vigilant and theoretically enlightened reading is the resistance to reading. Nevertheless, a rhetorically sophisticated reading is our best hope at least of remembering that we have forgotten and that we must forget. For this reason I affirm that the future of literary studies depends on maintaining and developing that rhetorical reading which today is most commonly called "deconstruction."[5]

The speaker is J. Hillis Miller, at the time president of the Modern Language Association. I will forego comment on the murkiness of the ideas and expression and note merely that "the particularity of the unique act of reading" is precisely what drew every poet with whom I have ever spoken of the matter into the foolhardy endeavor in the first place. In essence, the experience is always the same: one hears a voice speaking across distance and time and wishes to speak in a like manner to others. Poetry is, at heart, always Emily Dickinson's "letter to the world." I cannot believe that Miller understands this, much less sympathizes with it. For him,

> deconstruction and literary theory generally are the only way to respond to the actual conditions—cultural, economic, institutional, and technological—within which literary study is carried on today. Literary theory is the only way to avoid the sequestering of literature within an aestheticism of

> "organic form" that deprives the study of literature of any effective purchase on our society.[6]

It is as if, in a bizarre role-reversal, Miller and his followers have leapt clear-eyed from a Thomas Hart Benton mural to confront an indolent collection of Aesthetes, intent only on depositing the ashes of a burning culture in well-wrought urns.

Ridicule is easy enough, but for the present the power, the "purchase," rests in hands like Miller's. Again, here is Bloom on the subject:

> Finding myself now surrounded by professors of hip-hop; by clones of Gallic-Germanic theory; by ideologues of gender and of various sexual persuasions; by multiculturalists unlimited, I realize that the Balkanization of literary studies is irreversible. All of these Resenters of the aesthetic value of literature are not going to go away, and they will raise up institutional resenters after them.[7]

Lately, theoretical criticism has become so dominant that a bewildering variety of critical strategies has become institutionalized everywhere, even in the freshman English classroom. I say "even" because if there is any place where theory must seemingly yield to the practical concerns of getting students to explain "who-did-what-to-whom" with a worn number-two pencil, it is in the "Intro Lit" class. Nevertheless, theory has entrenched itself even here, a fact that should come as no surprise when one considers that the majority of freshman classes are taught by graduate students and lecturers fresh from the graduate schools. For their convenience and that of their students, there are many "Critical Approaches to . . ." collections available to introduce the fledgling critic to structuralist, deconstructionist, new historicist, feminist, reader-response, and other strategies of analyzing a text. While such approaches may be valuable in demonstrating to students that there is more than one way to examine literature, I am not convinced that it is necessarily a good idea to launch them on an ideological deep-space mission before ascertaining that the students have first carefully read the instruction manual. Still, it is not my purpose here to launch a Quixotic assault on methods that have now been passed on to the third generation of teachers and academic critics; the citadel of the theoretician, like that of the quantum physicist, can be breached only by those armed with other theories. The academic followers of the New Criticism, in the 1940s and 1950s, occupied their own cloud castle, and their insistence on certain critical procedures, with dire warnings against "fallacies," provided the current generation of theorists with an orthodoxy against which to rebel.

In invoking the bogeyperson of "an aestheticism of 'organic form,'" J. Hillis Miller is obviously referring to this earlier generation, familiarly known today as Formalist or New Critics. It is with this group that most of the poet-critics collected in the present volume have been identified, yet it should be noted that by the time the term New Criticism became well established it had already moved into purely academic circles, attracting critics like Cleanth Brooks, William Wimsatt, and Monroe Beardsley to its orbit. Over the years, several misconceptions about New Criticism have arisen. For one, it has become a commonplace to speak of the exponents of formalist criticism as if they possessed unanimity of approach. One should bear in mind that when Ransom wrote *The New Criticism* (1941) his use of "new" was followed by a list of synonyms: "unsure, inconsistent, perhaps raw." The basis of this so-called "new criticism" (Joel Spingarn had used the same term as early as 1911) was rather general, resting primarily on avoiding two "specific errors of theory" for which Ransom occasionally faulted the four critics (Richards, Empson, Eliot, and Winters) under discussion. The first was "making literary judgments in terms of the feelings, hopes, emotions, and attitudes of poems instead of in terms of their objects," all of which share the error of separating a poet's content—personal or moral—from its formal structure. The second was exercising "plain moralism, which in the new criticism would indicate that it has not emancipated itself from the old criticism." Ransom's own call for an "ontological criticism" concludes the book, and in it he formulates his definition of a poem as "a loose logical structure with a good deal of local texture." If his proposal is indeed for a radically "new" kind of criticism, in light of subsequent developments in the field it seems a modest proposal indeed:

> It is my feeling that we have in poetry a revolutionary departure from the convention of logical discourse, and that we should provide it with a bold and proportionate designation. I believe it has proved easy to work out its structural differentiation from prose. But what is the significance of this when we have got it? The structure proper is the prose of the poem, being a logical discourse of almost any kind, and dealing with almost any content suited to a logical discourse. The texture, likewise, seems to be of any real content that may be come upon, provided it is so free, unrestricted, and large that it cannot properly get into the structure. One guesses that it is an *order* of content, rather than a *kind* of content, that distinguishes texture from structure, and poetry from prose. At any rate, a moral content is a kind of content which has been suggested as the peculiar content of poetry, and it does not work; it is not really peculiar to poetry but perfectly available for prose; besides, it is not the content of a great deal of poetry. I suggest that the differentia of poetry as discourse is an ontological one. It treats an order of existence, a grade of objectivity, which cannot be treated in scientific discourse.[8]

The passage appears difficult but, at heart, is simple enough; if we judge a poem on the basis of its paraphrasable content, we are judging not *poem* but a prose replica of only its most basic structure. We must come to a poem with a perspective that is ontologically different from that which we bring to prose, and we must not bring preconceptions about content, especially moral content, to our reading. To try to separate the moral or prose content from a poem is impossible because doing so destroys the very "poemness" (to coin an ontological term) that gives it value as an aesthetic object.

What is perhaps the best-known formulation of this method is to be found in the contemporaneous work of two of Ransom's students, Cleanth Brooks and Robert Penn Warren, an alliance between an academic and a practicing poet that perhaps still represents how the two worlds of criticism, the theoretical and the practical, may come together. At about the same time that Ransom was sharpening his own views, the first edition of *Understanding Poetry* (1938) appeared, a textbook that was to have more influence on the teaching of poetry than any other and one that has spawned a host of imitations in the ensuing decades. In their "Letter to the Teacher" Brooks and Warren identify three "temptations to make a substitute for the poem as the object of study":

1. Paraphrase of logical and narrative content.
2. Study of biographical and historical materials
3. Inspirational and didactic interpretation.[9]

To this might be added a fourth, the sort of vague impressionism that leads to subjective responses about the "beauty" of a poem or the universality of its sentiment without ever citing specific evidence from the text to support those responses. While Brooks and Warren clearly wished to separate the language of poetry from the language of scientific discourse, it is equally clear that their method aspired to the empirical and inductive. The poem was an organic whole, but in order to be understood in its totality it would have to be separated into its individual components, showing how each contributed to unity of the work. The kinds of "close reading" and attention to specific detail that this method demanded have become perhaps the most lasting legacy of *Understanding Poetry.*

Brooks and Warren were scions of the same generation that stood in rebellion against the attitudes and styles of the Victorian era. In their criteria for poetic interpretation they wished to avoid and perhaps reverse the errors of their forebears. Paraphrase was and remains a valuable tool for critical analysis; indeed, any explication must hinge on it to some degree. But how was the reader to paraphrase the "logical and narrative content" of the last lines of *The Waste Land* or the opening of Canto 2? Clearly, modernist dislocations and juxtapositions went far beyond the paraphrasable. Similarly, biographical and historical approaches to poetry were the legacy of the cult of the individual in Romantic and post-Romantic poetry; if, as Goethe said, his lyrics were fragments of a single great confession, then the critic's chief job must be to reassemble the fragments into a coherent version of the artist's life—and times as well. When Brooks and Warren were writing, Vernon L. Parrington's *Main Currents in American Thought,* that monument to both the "great man" and the socio-historical approaches to literature, was still only a decade old and unassailed in its supreme position as a history of American literary and intellectual culture. As for the other two "temptations," we need look only as far as early modernist poets like MacLeish or Williams to gauge early modernist attitudes toward high-toned didacticism or sentimental notions of the beautiful and true. "A poem should not mean / but be" or "No ideas but in things" were the aesthetic battle cries of a new age.

But now that age is no longer new. *The Waste Land* has passed into the public domain, and even "post-modernism" is crowding middle age. Culture and taste generally run in cycles, and I would suggest that the extreme applications of contemporary literary theory have ironically brought us back to a situation analogous to the one which Ransom, Brooks, and Warren were reacting against. The deconstructionist eschews "understanding" poetry and provides, instead of a paraphrase of logical and narrative content, what amounts to an anti-paraphrase, a demonstration of how the indeterminacy of language itself eventually confounds its attempts to signify anything beyond itself. Consequently, deconstructionist readings of poems often take the form of restatements of their contents, albeit restatements that seem far from what common sense might dictate. What a New Critic might have seen as necessary poetic tension, the centrifugal and centripetal forces that hold a poem together, the deconstructionist perceives as manifestations of phenomenological chaos theory.

In the same vein, the old-fashioned biographical and historical approaches have been replaced by new ones which, in their own ways, aim at the remarkably similar ends. Biographical criticism attempted to link every poem to a specific incident in the poet's life; thus, a poem like Poe's "To Helen" could only be understood by discovering the identify of the woman in the poet's past who had inspired him. The new brands of biographical criticism appear to have much the same goal in mind. Just as Freudian criticism seems, on the whole, more interested in the artist than in the art, much contemporary feminist criticism, to cite one example, retains the apparatus of Freudian psychoanalytical criticism even if it rejects its key assumptions; that is, the poem is seen not as an object worthy of study in itself but as a means to an end, a key to unlocking the life of the poet. Thus, with the incursions of other types of gender-based theory, the spinster Emily Dickinson (perhaps even secretly married) has had to make way for the gay Emily Dickinson, the masturbatory Emily Dickinson, and the incest-survivor Emily Dickinson to swell the already swollen ranks of all the other Emily Dickinsons who have been martialed for inspection over the years.

Similarly, the new historicism, with its focus on race, class, and gender, employs general methods like those of the old historicism, which focused instead on politics, economics, and sociology. The pressure on poets and critics to be multiculturally and politically correct has produced a new didacticism, where *poets* (often more important in an age of celebrity than the *poems* they create) may be damned or praised solely on the basis of their moral pronouncements on sexism, racism, homophobia, or other ills of society. Even individual taste is suspect. Reader-response theory, which flies in the face of what an older generation learned to avoid as the "affective fallacy," openly invites subjective responses that blind the eyes like a cloud of gnats, blurring everything in the buzz of a new, improved brand of impressionism. "And palm for palm, Madam," Mr. Stevens might well repeat, "we are where we began."

In gathering the essays that make up this book, I have tried to keep several considerations in mind. One was to include only those poets who exhibited a serious and sustained involvement with criticism and who could be termed men or women of letters in the fullest sense. Wallace Stevens, to mention one notable case, certainly displays flashes of brilliance in his critical writings, but these pieces were produced for infrequent occasional presentation; Stevens may indeed be a serious critic, but his criticism was not a sustained effort. William Carlos Williams may have been somewhat more sustained in his efforts, but I find in his criticism much of the "village explainer" (and *complainer*) that Gertrude Stein early saw in Pound. For slightly different reasons, I decided not to include a sample of the criticism of Marianne Moore, which, fascinating as it may be as an extension of her methods of poetic collage, consists almost entirely of assemblages of quotations from the books under review. Critics like Charles Olson strike me as so far out of the mainstream that I leave it to others to champion their causes. I have tried to indicate a distinct line of descent from Ransom through Jarrell and Ciardi, the former a student of Ransom's and the latter an important editor in his days at the *Saturday Review* whose own contribution to this book, the last collected here, seems to me one of the best practical expositions of a method shared by most of his colleagues.

More troublesome for me to ponder was that the proportion of poet to critic in individual cases would vary widely. Ransom, like Eliot, represents the ideal of how a poet may combine two (or *three*) equally distinguished careers. In some other instances, like those of Blackmur and Burke, the critic far overshadows the poet; in others, the criticism plays a lesser role in an otherwise notable career. Also, I wished to include essays that, if not purely theoretical, at least would possess sufficient general interest to suggest an overall approach to *poetry* rather than to specific poets and poems. In the cases of Louise Bogan and Randall Jarrell, I worked with the realization that their most representative work is to be found in their lively and often irreverent reviews of new books of poems. As good as their general observations about the art may be, they never attain the level of the reviewing these two poet-critics did for popular magazines and quarterlies.

My chief aim has been to demonstrate that poet-critics occupy a uniquely valuable position not only in literature but in the arts in general. The advantage that they possess is obvious; their knowledge comes from the *inside*. The complaint may quickly arise that in the other arts we do not necessarily expect the artists to have the final word on their own media. True, we do not expect painters or composers to be the most reliable critics of their respective art forms for the simple reason that their primary medium is not language; indeed, many of them have proven virtually incoherent in attempting to explain what lies behind their work. Oddly, novelists and playwrights, whose primary medium is prose, have not contributed much to the canon of literary criticism. In this century, only Henry James and George Bernard Shaw and a handful of others seem likely to be remembered for their critical writings. The poets, on the other hand, have consistently distinguished themselves in criticism. Of all of the literary critics of the nineteenth century, I would suspect that the four still most widely read are Coleridge, Arnold, Emerson, and Poe—all poets. Why is this so? One answer is simple: we read their criticism as an adjunct to the poetry. But the other is more speculative. The poet brings the dyer's hand of the creator to the critical task, knowing that a poem is not a tabula rasa or a nexus of historical forces or a stifled cry for empowerment; each poem, as Emerson put it, "adorns nature with a new thing." If the poet-critic occasionally intrudes with sprayer and pruning shears it is only to make sure that nature is "to advantage dress'd" when a reader approaches.

In making my selections I tried to imagine a common reader, one who was willing to stand up to the challenges that poetry and the serious discussion of it present, and who wishes to be rewarded for his or her efforts, not further perplexed by them. However difficult one might sometimes find the poet-critics included here, it should be borne in mind that many of them, like Eliot, wrote for the book pages of daily newspapers and that others published in mass-circulation magazines aimed at an audience which Mr. Arnold would have immediately recognized as potentially fertile soil—"Philistine" was no easy term of dismissal for him. I likewise tried to think of the needs of contemporary students, whose literary education so often takes place on a darkling plain where schools of theory contend so heatedly that the original object of contemplation, the poem itself, may be totally obscured. Theory may occasionally have been useful to these poet-critics, but their main concerns are the practical tasks of elucidating the difficulties of poetry for readers who bring to poetry, first, a *desire* to better understand what has initially intrigued them. If, in doing so, they helped to train those readers to cope with the greater difficulties that modernist poetry presented, they were in fact cultivating an audience for their own work and that of their contemporaries. Admittedly, a note of special pleading sometimes creeps in, but it is, I think, a bias that promotes the self-rewarding pleasures of reading poetry and understanding, in Ciardi's phrase, *how* it means.

If poetry must, first, give pleasure, those whom I call the advocates of poetry largely devoted themselves to demonstrating that both the source and destination of that pleasure are aesthetic ends, not the advancement of social or moral agendas. Jarrell puts it this way:

> The work of art, Rilke said, says to us always: *You must change your life*. It demands of us that we too see things as ends, not as means—that we too know them and love them for their own sake. This change is beyond us, perhaps, during the active, greedy, and powerful hours of our lives; but during the contemplative and sympathetic hours of our reading, our listening, our looking, it is surely within our power, if we choose to make it so, if we choose to let one part of our nature follow its natural desires.

The critical testaments of these advocates of poetry are most eloquent in their implicit respect for the poet, for the reader, and, most important, for poetry itself. We need their advocacy still, perhaps as never before in the history of the art.

NOTES

1. Matthew Arnold, *Essays in Criticism: First Series* (New York: Macmillan, 1903), 38.

2. *Writers at Work:* The Paris Review *Interviews,* Second Series, ed. George Plimpton (New York: Viking Press, 1963), 339.

3. Harold Bloom, *The Western Canon: The Books and School of the Ages* (New York: Harcourt, 1994), 17–18.

4. Louis Simpson, *Ships Going into the Blue: Essays and Notes on Poetry* (Ann Arbor: University of Michigan Press, 1994), 159–60.

5. J. Hillis Miller, "Presidential Address 1986. The Triumph of Theory, the Resistance to Reading, and the Question of the Material Base," *PMLA* 102 (1987): 289.

6. Miller, 290.

7. Bloom, 517–18.

8. John Crowe Ransom, *The New Criticism* (Norfolk, Conn.: New Directions, 1941), 280–81.

9. Cleanth Brooks and Robert Penn Warren, *Understanding Poetry* (New York: Holt, 1938), iv.

The Advocates of Poetry

JOHN CROWE RANSOM

WANTED: AN ONTOLOGICAL CRITIC

I

A poem differentiates itself for us, very quickly and convincingly, from a prose discourse. We have examined some important new critics who sense this fact but do not quite offer a decisive version of what the differentia is.

It is not moralism, for moralism conducts itself very well in prose, and conducts itself all the better in pure or perfect prose. And the good critics who try to regard the poem as a moral discourse do not persuade themselves, and discuss the poem really on quite other grounds.

It is not emotionalism, sensibility, or "expression." Poetry becomes slightly disreputable when regarded as not having any special or definable content, and as identified only by its capacity for teasing some dormant affective states into some unusual activity. And it is impossible to talk definitively about the affections which are involved, so that affective criticism is highly indistinct.

Much more promising as a differentia is the kind of structure exemplified by a poem. The good critics come round to this in the end. But it is hard to say what poetry intends by its

---

Reprinted from John Crowe Ransom, "Wanted: An Ontological Critic," in *Beating the Bushes: Selected Essays, 1941–1970* (New York: New Directions, 1972), 1–46.

odd structure. What is the value of a structure which (a) is not so tight and precise on its logical side as a scientific or technical prose structure generally is, and (b) imports and carries along a great deal of irrelevant or foreign matter which is clearly not structural but even obstructive? This *a* and *b* formulation is what we inevitably come to if we take the analysis our best critics offer. We sum it up by saying that the poem is a loose logical structure with a good deal of local texture.

It is my feeling that we have in poetry a revolutionary departure from the convention of logical discourse, and that we should provide it with a bold and proportionate designation. I believe it has proved easy to work out its structural differentiation from prose. But what is the significance of this when we have got it? The structure proper is the prose of the poem, being a logical discourse of almost any kind, and dealing with almost any suitable content. The texture, likewise, seems to be of any real content that may be come upon, provided it is so free, unrestricted, and extended, that it cannot properly get into the structure. One guesses that it is an *order* of content, rather than a kind of content, that distinguishes texture from structure, and poetry from prose. At any rate, a moral content is a kind of content which has been suggested as the peculiar content of poetry, and it does not work; it is not really peculiar to poetry but perfectly available for prose. I suggest that the differentia of poetry as discourse is an ontological one. It treats an order of existence, a grade of objectivity, which cannot be treated in scientific discourse.

This should not prove unintelligible. We live in a world that must be distinguished from the world, or the worlds, for there are many of them, which we treat in our scientific discourses. They are its reduced, emasculated, and docile versions. Poetry intends to recover the denser and more refractory original world which we know loosely through our perceptions and memories. By this supposition it is a kind of knowledge which is radically or ontologically distinct.

2

I have failed to find a new critic with an ontological account of poetry. But I almost thought I had found a new philosopher, or aesthetician, with one. It would have been Mr. Charles W. Morris, of the University of Chicago and the *Encyclopedia of Unified Science.* I had his name at first in the title at the top of this paper. But I could not study his aesthetic achievement very long without seeing that, though he got to the point where one further step would have taken him into an ontological conception of poetry, he held back and did not take that step; either as if he lacked the speculative curiosity to go further, or as if the prospect ahead of him impressed him vaguely as dangerous, probably threatening some disparagement of the paramount prestige of science.

The writings of Mr. Morris which bear on our discussion are, first, the presentation of his now-famous semantic system, *Foundations of the Theory of Signs,* in Vol. 1, No. 2, of the *Encyclopedia;* and, applying his new semantics to art, the two essays, "Science, Art and Technology," in the *Kenyon Review* of Autumn, 1939, and "Aesthetics and the Theory of Signs," in the *Journal of Unified Science,* Vol. 8.

Mr. Morris as a semanticist finds that all discourse consists in signs, and that any sign functions in three dimensions. There is the *syntactical* dimension, involving all of what we should call its logic; there is the *semantical* dimension proper, involving the reference of the sign to an object; and finally the *pragmatical* dimension, involving whatever reference there may be in the sign, implicit or explicit, to its psychological, biological, and sociological uses. I cannot here enlarge upon this outline. There IS no shortcut to Mr. Morris's knowledge; his own account will need to be read, and then reread. I think it will appear to the reader that he has a genius for fixing sound distinctions, and imposes order on a field that has hitherto been filled with confusion. I have but one source of hesitation. I do not quite sense the coordinate equality, as a component in the sign-functioning, of the pragmatical dimension with the other two.

It is like according a moral dimension to poetry because there are some poems which not only present their own content but in addition moralize about this content. We may reflect that they need not do so, and that many other poems do not, and that the moral value we may find for the poem seems somewhat external to the poem itself. But at any rate Mr. Morris makes the pragmatical dimension quite distinct from the others, if not subsidiary, and that is something. Science, in Mr. Morris's view, need not be very conscious of any pragmatics; and so it may be, in our view, with art; really it is technology, or applied science, that is decidedly pragmatical.

For Mr. Morris not only distinguishes three irreducible dimensions of meaning, but finds as well three irreducible forms of discourse: science, art, and technology. These seem to him to emphasize respectively the semantical, the syntactical, and the pragmatical dimensions. To us, as I have just remarked, art may seem specially affiliated with science, and further away from technology, in not having any necessary concern with pragmatics or usefulness. But in another sense it is closer to technology and further from science. We recall our old impression, perhaps we recall our knowledge of the Greek philosophers, the effect that art, like technology, is concerned with making something, as well as knowing something; while pure science seems concerned only with knowing something. And what poetry makes—and the word means a making—is the poem, which at least in respect to its meter is a peculiarly novel and manufactured form, and obviously a rather special unit of discourse.

With regard to the credibility of aesthetic discourse, Mr. Morris pronounces handsomely enough: like scientific discourse, it is objective, and knowledge-giving. He says:

> It is true, I believe, that the aesthetic sign, in common with all signs, has all three dimensions of sign-functioning; such a position seems a wise corrective to the common but too simple view that the artist simply "emotes" or "expresses himself" without any concern for actuality.

But if art as knowledge seems to Mr. Morris capable of the same sort of validity that science has, and at times to be indistinguishable from science in this respect, it has a remarkable differentia, and is forever unlike science, in the following respect. The sign which science employs is a mere sign, or "symbol," that is, an object having no other character—for the purpose of discourse at least—than that of referring to another object which is its semantical object. For example, symbols are algebraic characters; or words used technically, as defined in the dictionary, or defined for the purpose of a given discourse in the discourse itself. But the aesthetic signs are "icons," or images. As signs they have semantical objects, or refer to objects, but as iconic signs they also resemble or imitate these objects.

The significance of this distinction that immediately flashes upon us, though it does not seem to be noticed by Mr. Morris, is that the object symbolized by a scientific sign would seem to be abstract, as, for example, a single property or aspect of objects, whereas the object symbolized by an iconic or aesthetic sign must be a whole object. And even if both seem to refer to the whole object, and the same object, there is a difference; if, for example, the scientific sign is of "man," the iconic sign is of "this particular man." By general convention the man of scientific discourse is the definable and "essential" man, whose definition involves a single set of values which are constant and negotiable for logical discourse. The man of the iconic sign is evidently imitable, or imaginable, but not definable. In brief, under the iconic sign the abstract item is restored to the body from which it was taken.

The iconic character of aesthetic signs is given by Mr. Morris in a rather matter-of-fact sort of testimony; yet it is almost the more impressive just because he does not draw the exciting implications. It amounts to a late restoration of the old doctrine of art as "imitation," to which Plato and Aristotle adhered, but which most modern aestheticians have abandoned as something absurdly simple. "Imitation" is a commonplace locution, but may be thought unworthy of the aesthetic occasion; yet I can imagine our aestheticians solemnly accepting the doctrine of "icons" because it sounds technical; actually of course it is one of the two ordinary terms in which the Greeks rendered the idea of imitation. And since Mr. Morris is affiliated in the project of the *Encyclopedia* with naturalist, positivist, and pragmatist philosophers, I think of this enlightened testimony as another evidence of what I have hoped for: the capacity of radical modernist philosophy to apprehend and testify to kinds of truth that do not necessarily suit its own preoccupations, which are scientific ones.

It is sometimes difficult to say what is being "represented" by an aesthetic icon; in music, for example, or in a poem which makes discourse without very often referring specifically to concrete material objects. We think of "reflective" poetry which is truly poetry, and is imaginative, and yet probably a little deficient in brilliant object-images. Mr. Morris makes no question but that any variety of poetry employs iconic signs. (He offers at one point an analysis of "abstract" painting for the purpose of showing that it denotes ultimately the structure of the natural world.)

It is less difficult, and I believe Mr. Morris does not remark this problem, to see how the poem, which is a discourse in words, may offer icons as easily as painting does. The icons here are in the mind, they are the mental images evoked. The technical use of language by the poet is one that lifts words out of their symbolic or definitive uses into imaginative or image-provoking uses.

3

And that is almost as far as Mr. Morris goes. He claims that art is especially interested in the syntactical dimension of discourse, but offers almost no study of how art makes a syntax out of its peculiar mixture of pure symbols and liberal iconic signs. That would become a study of almost monumental significance. Is its validity comparable with that of science? Is its syntactical validity comparable with its own semantical validity, which Mr. Morris is good enough to accept as beyond question?

Science deals exclusively in pure symbols, but art deals essentially, though not exclusively, in iconic signs. This makes at once a sharp formal or technical distinction between the two forms of discourse; but one would think it must become also a philosophical distinction. Mr. Morris elicits chiefly the consequence that no treatment of the arts can be included within the *Encyclopedia of Unified Science.* Only semeiotic, the theory of signs, which makes its own entry as prefatory to the body of the work, may remark for the sake of formal exclusion upon the contrasted arts. But one might think that semeiotic required a closer and therefore surer study of the arts than that; for example, a study of the question why science did not choose, or had not the constitutional capacity, to employ iconic signs also; and, of course, of the ontological question itself, respecting the grades of content that the two discourses handled through their different sorts of signs, and the elemental or categorical nature of scientific knowledge as determined through the comparison with aesthetic knowledge.

In the independent essays outside the *Encyclopedia* Mr. Morris does offer some results of his own study. They seem to me inadequate. For example:

> The view proposed is that the aesthetic sign designates the value properties of actual or possible situations and that it is an iconic sign (an "image") in that it embodies these values in some medium where they may be directly inspected (in short, the aesthetic sign is an iconic sign whose *designatum* is a value). To give content to this statement it would be necessary to analyze in detail the notion of value and the characteristics of iconic signs, but this is neither practical nor advisable in the present context. For whatever theory of value be maintained, it must be recognized that objects have value properties among their total set of properties (an object can be insipid, sublime, menacing, oppressive, or gay in some contexts just as it may have a certain mass or length or velocity in other contexts) and that aesthetic media, since they themselves are objects, can embody certain value properties (a small piece of cork could hardly be sublime, but it could be insipid or even gay).

Here it seems to me that Mr. Morris in effect is about to recant from his doctrine of the icons. The icon here is only a medium denoting, by embodying, a value; but that is more than a symbol does; he should say that the icon is a body imitating some actual embodiment of the value. And what value? I do not think he makes it clear, even with the help of his illustrations, how an icon embodies a value-property, or what sorts of values aesthetic discourse ordinarily is interested in. Certainly it sounds as if the aesthetic value-properties were quite different from the scientific ones; gaiety and sublimity, among others, for aesthetic value-properties, mass and velocity for scientific ones. It is rather suspicious that several of the aesthetic value-properties mentioned might be said to be affective ones, whereas the scientific value-properties mentioned are objective physical ones; so that Mr. Morris's aesthetic theory looks at this point like another version of affective or psychologistic theory. But we require much more detail from him about all this.

Briefly, may we say that the observations of Mr. Morris are promising, and even exciting: aesthetic discourse is objective knowledge, and its constituent signs have the remarkable character of being icons. But the sequel is disappointing. An icon merely embodies some certain value-property or other; that is all we are told about its operation. And as to the human significance, the usefulness or pragmatical function, Mr. Morris's imagination is again very timid. For example:

> . . . the scientists may be helped in the scientific study of values by the vivid portrayal of the value whose conditions he endeavors to trace.

And similarly:

> The technologist in turn can only be grateful for the vivid presentation of the values whose status in nature he attempts to control.

The artist is pictured here as furnishing the icons which embody the precise and single scientific values, not the values causing the massive affective states referred to in the previous quotation. But his virtue seems to lie solely in the technical assistance, or else the moral encouragement, which his icons lend to the scientist and technologist in their need.

The aesthetic project has turned out rather small and ignominious after its fine beginnings in Mr. Morris's hands.

We might sketch here, though tentatively and rudely, a really ontological argument, such as Mr. Morris's preliminaries seemed to invite.

The validity of a scientific discourse depends in part, we should say, on its semantical purity. That is, each symbol should refer to an object specifically defined, or having a specific value-aspect, for the discourse; and throughout the discourse it should have exactly that reference and no other. The reference of a single symbol is limited, and uniform.

In aesthetic discourse, however, we replace symbols with icons; and the peculiarity of an icon is that it refers to the whole or concrete object and cannot be limited. As Mr. Morris says, an icon "embodies" the value-property that is the object of discourse. But "embodies" is a great word, and Mr. Morris ought to accept its consequences. Certainly he offers no rule as to how the value-property may be isolated in the body of the containing icon, or placed in the center, or otherwise made to stand out so that we shall be sure to attend to it rather than to the containing body.[1]

The icon is an individual, therefore indefinable; that is, it exceeds definition. In the play, the icon is our image of Prince Hamlet, and it is never twice the same, so that the rule of consistent definitive reference is abrogated with each reappearance. An individual has too many properties, and too many values. If a kind of discourse is accredited (and given a semantical bill of health) which proposes to deal in particulars, as one must propose to do which deals in icons, then it is removed far indeed from scientific discourse; it decidedly invites philosophical attention, and one must be prepared to make dispositions which are heroic, because in the present state of theory they will be novel.

The syntactical dimension is imperiled, upon the introduction of icons into discourse, along with the semantical. It will be impossible for discourse to compel its icons to function in the strict logic which we have learned to expect from the symbols. The logic of art will probably be variable in the degree of its validity, but always in degree lower than that of science. At the same time we shall probably incline to assert that it will have no validity at all unless it holds itself together at least in part by true symbols. So the aesthetic discourse will be discovered, one expects, making digressions from its logic with its icons at local points; or perhaps maintaining itself on the whole in terms of valid symbols, but occasionally and suddenly building a routine symbol out into the icon denoting the full body of the object of which the symbol denotes only a single value-property. But the semantics and the syntactics of art together invite the most exacting study if we care to identify them really.

In scientific discourse we deal with a single value-system at a time. In art only the paraphrase, of which Mr. Morris gives an adequate account, and which is the "moral," the theme, or the argument of the discourse, offers the single-value system; the work itself goes beyond its paraphrase into the realm of the natural objects or situations themselves, which are many valued.

Art as a discourse, indeed, is anomalous, and all but incredible; a discourse which looks legitimate so long as it looks merely scientific, but every moment or so turns up its icons, in which it hardly seems that discourse could take place.

Science, as Mr. Morris says, is statemental, and its statements have predictive value. But art employs icons, which being individual are contingent and unpredictable. Art seems to permit us to predict only some order of unpredictability.

But principles of this sort are ontological. The world of predictability, for example, is the restricted world of scientific discourse. Its restrictive rule is: one value at a time. The world of art is the actual world which does not bear restriction; or at least defies the restrictiveness of science, and offers enough fullness of content to give us the sense of the actual objects. A qualitative density, or value-density, such as is unknown to scientific understanding, marks the world of the actual objects. The discourse which tries systematically to record this world is art.

As to the pragmatics of the poetic act, or its "psychological, biological, and social" motivation, I have almost nothing to suggest. It seems very idle to assume, as Mr. Morris does in effect, that the pragmatical intention of art is the same as that of science; we would ask him why scientists should not commit themselves then to aesthetic as well as scientific discourse. But the psychologists have not furnished us with decisive motivations for this as for many other acts. It is an act of knowledge. The scientific and aesthetic ways of knowledge should illuminate each other; perhaps they are alternative knowledges, and a preference for one knowledge over the other might indicate an elemental or primary bias in temperament. But even if the pragmatical sanction behind the act has to be improvised, and psychologically is less than regular, nevertheless it seems certain that the act is imperative.

4

At this point I venture to abandon the framework of Mr. Morris's speculations. They have provided considerable moral reinforcement for the inquiry. I wish to start a little further back in the ontological analysis of the poem.

The critic of a poem knows that the labor of composing it was, at the least, a verbal exercise in search of a language which on the one hand would "make the sense," and on the other hand would "make the rhythm," and if it liked would even "make the rhyme." He knows it so well that perhaps he is past being curious about the fact.

But it is still strange to us, who are not agreed on any standard version of the natural history of the form, that poetry should ever have coveted a language that would try to do not one hard thing but two hard things at once. Extravagant exercises with language are not the rule by which the logical men have arrived at their perfections of thought. But the composition of a poem is an operation in which an argument fights to displace a meter, and the meter fights to displace the argument. It would seem that the sacrifices made on both sides would be legible forever in the terms of peace, which are the dispositions found in the finished poem, where the critic must analyze them if he thinks they further the understanding of poetry. Most critics seem to think it does not, for they do not try the analysis, nor the philosophical speculations it might suggest. On the contrary, it is common for critics to assume that a good poet is in control of his argument, and that the meter has had no effect on it, or if anything points its logic all the better, and that the form of the argument is perfect.

If the unsatisfactoriness of poetic theory, which strikes us so painfully, is due to the absence from it of radical philosophical generalities, the fault must begin really with its failure to account for the most elementary and immediate aspect that formal poetry wears: its metrical form. The convention of the metrical form is thought to be as old as the art itself. Perhaps it is the art itself. I suggest that the meter-and-meaning process is the organic act of poetry, and involves all its important characters.

Let us suppose a lady who wishes to display a bowl of fruits upon her sideboard says to her intelligent houseboy: "Go to the box of apples in the pantry and select and bring me a dozen of the biggest and reddest ones." The box contains a hundred apples, which vary both in bigness and in redness. And we will suppose, as it is easy to suppose, that there is no definable correlation between the bigness and the redness; a big apple is not necessarily a red one, and vice versa. The boy interests himself in the curious problem, and devises the following solution.

He ranges the apples first in order of their bigness, and denotes the biggest as B_1, the next as B_2, and so on down to B_{100}. Then he ranges the apples in order of their redness, and denotes the reddest as R_1, the next reddest as R_2, and so on to R_{100}. Then for each apple he adds the numerical coefficient of its bigness and the numerical coefficient of its redness; for example, the apple which is tagged B_1 is also tagged R_{36}, so that its combined coefficient is 37. He finds the twelve apples with the lowest combined coefficients and takes them to his mistress.

She will have to concede, as he has conceded, that objects systematically valued for two unrelated properties at once are likely not to be superlative in both properties. She will not secure the perfection of her object in one aspect if she is also trying to secure its perfection in another aspect. She has committed herself to a two-ground basis of selection, and her selections on the one ground have to accommodate themselves to her selections on the other ground. It is a situation in which some compromises are necessary.

But she may find an unexpected compensation. In regretting the loss of certain nearly solid-red apples, which are denied to her because they are little, she may observe that the selected apples exhibit color patterns much more various, unpredictable, and interesting. She finds pleasure in studying their markings, whereas she would have obtained the color-value of her solid-red apples at a glance.

I am sorry to think that no such compensation appears for her putting up with second-best apples in the respect of size; which is a stupid category. But I am afraid the analogy of the bigness-redness relation in apples does not represent sufficiently the meter-meaning relation which we are to examine in poetry.

5

Much more difficult than the selection of apples that shall be both big and red is the composition of a poem on the two-ground basis of (1) an intended meaning and (2) an intended meter. In theory the feat seems impossible, unless we are allowed to introduce some qualifications into the terms. It is true that language possesses two properties, the semantic and the phonetic; that is, respectively, the property of referring under fairly fixed conventions to objects beyond itself, which constitute its meaning, and the property of being in itself a sequence of objective physical sounds set to an elementary music.

I assume that there is hardly necessity for an extended argument to the effect that a perfect metrical construction, of which the components were words selected from the range of all actual words, and exclusively for phonetic effects, would not be likely to make noteworthy sense. It would be nonsense. Nor for another argument to show that a pure logical construction would not be likely to make meter. The latter case we have with us always, in our science, in the prose of our newspapers and business correspondence, in our talk. Even so, there might be some instruction in considering for a moment such a little piece of mathematical discourse as this:

$$(a + b)^2 = a^2 + 2ab + b^2$$

Here the mathematician is saying exactly what he means, and his language is not metrical, and we can discover if we try that he does not want any poet to meter it, on the matter-of-fact ground that the poet would have to take liberties with his logical values. At once a question or two should present themselves very vexingly to the nebulous aesthetician: What sort of liberties does the poet take with a discourse when he sets it to meter? And what sort of discourse is prepared to permit those liberties?

An argument which admits of alteration in order that it may receive a meter must be partly indeterminate. The argument cannot be maintained exactly as determined by its own laws, for it is going to be undetermined by the meter.

Conversely, a metrical form must be partly indeterminate if it proposes to study an argument. It is useless to try to determine it closely in advance, for the argument will undetermine it.

The second principle, of the two just stated, may seem the less ominous. To most poets, and most readers, the meaning is more important than the meter.

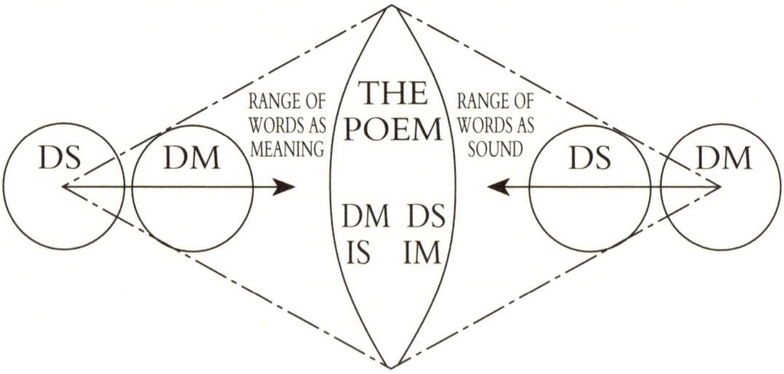

Let DM stand for determinate meaning, or such of the intended meaning as succeeds in being adhered to; it may be fairly represented by the logical paraphrase of the poem. IM stands for indeterminate meaning, or that part of the final meaning which took shape not according to its own logical necessity but under metrical compulsion; it may be represented by the poem's residue of meaning which does not go into the logical paraphrase. DS stands for the determinate sound-structure, or the meter; and IS stands for whatever phonetic character the sounds have assumed which is indeterminate.

In theory, the poem is the resultant of two processes interacting upon each other; they come from opposite directions. On the one hand the poet is especially intent upon his meter, DS, which may be blocked out as a succession of unaccented and accented syllables arranged in lines, perhaps with rhyme endings; but there is DM, a prose discourse, which must be reduced into the phonetic pattern; his inclination is to replace its words with others from the general field of words which suit the music, and without much regard for their logical propriety. But he is checked on the other hand where he starts with firm possession of DM, a prose meaning, but has to assimilate it to DS, the sound-pattern that he has chosen; his inclination is to replace the required metrical sounds with others that suit his logic and are not quite so good for the sound structure.

Actually, a skillful piece of composition will have many stages of development, with strokes too subtle and rapid to record, and operations in some sort of alternation from the one direction and the other. The poet makes adaptations both of sound to meaning (introducing IS) and of meaning to sound (introducing IM). Both adaptations are required for the final version of the poem.

6

The most interesting observation for the critic, perhaps, is that the poem is an object comprising not two elements but four; not merely a meaning M, but DM, that part of a meaning which forms a logical structure, and IM, a part which does not belong to the structure and may be definitely illogical, though more probably it is only additive and alogical; and not merely DS, a sound-pattern, but IS, a part of the total sound effect which may be in exception to the rule but at any rate does not belong to it. These elements are familiar enough to the poet himself, who has manipulated them. Frequently they are evident to the critic too. They should be, very substantially; they can be distinguished to the extent that he is capable of distinguishing them. Logically they are distinct elements, now, in the finished poem, though it may not be possible to trace back the precise history of their development under the tension of composition.

I cannot but think that the distinction of these elements, and especially of DM and IM, is the vocation par excellence of criticism. It is more technical than some other exercises which go as criticism, but more informed. It brings the criticism of poetry to somewhat the same level of professional competence that of the discussions which painters sometimes accord to paintings, and that which musicians accord to music; which means, I think, an elevation of our normal critical standard.

If a poet is a philosopher, explicitly or implicitly, treating matters of ethical or at least human importance—and it is likely that he is that—the discussion of his "ideology" may be critical in every sense in which one may be said to criticize systematic ideas; but the ideas of the poet, struggling but not quite managing to receive their really determinate expression, are only his DM, and a better version is almost certain to be found elsewhere in prose, so that their discussion under the poem is likely to be a tame affair. Few poets serve, as Wordsworth and Shelley may be thought to do, as texts for the really authoritative study of ideas; mostly they serve amateur ideologists for that purpose, or serve distinguished critics who fall back upon this sort of thing because nothing is quite prescriptive in their vocation. The more interesting thing to study is the coexistence and connection of DM and IM—the ideas and the indeterminate material in which they are enveloped. This kind of study is much severer, but its interest is profounder and more elemental than the merely ethical; it is an ontological interest.

Possibly an examination of poetry along these lines might finally disclose the secret of its strange yet stubborn existence as a kind of discourse unlike any other. It does not bother too much about the perfection of its logic; and does bother a great deal, as if it were life and death, about the positive quality of that indeterminate thing which creeps in by the back door of musical necessity. I suggest the closest possible study of IM, the indeterminate meaning.

But there are two kinds of indeterminacy in IM, and I wish to show how the poet in metering his argument yields reluctantly to the first, as to an indeterminacy that means only inaccuracy and confusion, and then gladly to the second, as to an indeterminacy that opens to him a new world of discourse.

First, he tries to shift the language within the range of a rough verbal equivalence, and to alter DM no more substantively than necessary. A given word will probably have synonyms. The order of words in a phrase may be varied. A transitive predication may be changed to a passive; a relative clause to a participial phrase. In the little words denoting logical connections and transitions a good deal of liberty may be taken without being fatal; they may be expanded into something almost excessively explicit, or they may be even omitted, with the idea that the reader can supply the correct relations. A single noun may become a series of nouns, or nearly any other element may be compounded, without introducing much novelty. Epithetical adjectives and adverbs may be interpolated, if they will qualify their nouns and verbs very obviously. Archaic locutions may be substituted for contemporary ones. A poet is necessarily an accomplished verbalist, and capable of an almost endless succession of periphrases that come nearer and nearer to metered language until finally he achieves what he wants; a language that is metrical enough, and close to his intended meaning.

Mr. C. D. Abbott at the library of the University of Buffalo is collecting a very large number of work sheets from living poets, with the idea of securing an objective exhibit of the actual process of perfecting poems by revision. The most immediate use of these manuscripts that will suggest itself will surely be the critical study of the way poets tinker with given phrases in order to adapt them to the metrical pattern. Presently there should be a voluminous bulk of evidence on this point. But anybody who has tried versification can predict the sort of evidence that will turn up. Meanwhile we may see what evidences there are in the final poems themselves.

Wordsworth would probably be cited by the historian as one who metered his language with more method than inspiration, especially in his longer work. Here is a passage from the *Prelude,* where he is talking about the power of poetry, and its habitation in a place called "the mystery of words":

> . . . there,
> As in a mansion like their proper home,
> Even forms and substances are circumfused
> By that transparent veil with light divine,
> And through the turnings intricate of verse
> Present themselves as objects recognized
> In flashes, and with glory not their own.

It is easy to find disagreeable lapses of logic here. There are the painful inversions of order, clearly in the interest of metric: *light divine* and *turnings intricate.* The line *As in a mansion like their proper home* is certainly a curious involution for *As in a mansion which is their proper home.* The third and fourth lines are not transparent for us like the veil talked about: Does the veil possess and give off the divine light? And if not, how does it circumfuse the forms and substances with it? The brevity of statement is either a laziness on Wordsworth's part, or it is a recourse to elliptical expression invited by metrical exigencies. But at this point all our little objections pass into a big and overwhelming one: there is really in this passage scarcely any specific discourse of respectable logical grade. We do not know what any of these pretty things is, or does. No prose would be cynical enough to offer so elusive a content. The mansion, the forms and substances, the magic veil, the divine light, the movement of the turnings, the flashes and the borrowed glory—these look like responsible and promising objects, but none of them establishes a sufficient identity when they all assemble together. The poet became a little paralyzed, we may imagine, when he took pen in hand to write a poem; or got that way after going a certain distance in the writing of a long one. I go beyond the direct evidence here, but I assume that making distinguished metrical discourse was such a job, and consisted in his own mind with so much corruption of the sense at best, that he fell into the habit of choosing the most resounding words, and stringing them together as the meter dictated. This is not unusual in Romantic poetry. The point to make about Romantic poetry now is not the one about its noble words, but a negative and nasty one: the noble words are almost absurdly incoherent. (But I realize that my tone is too severe.)

Pope was not a Romantic, and I suppose the language has known no poet more nice in his expression. I quote:

> Close by those meads, forever crowned with flowers
> Where Thames with pride surveys his rising towers,
> There stands a structure of majestic frame,
> Which from the neighboring Hampton takes its name.
> Here Britain's statesmen oft the fall foredoom.
> Of foreign tyrants and of nymphs at home;
> Here thou, great Anna! whom three realms obey
> Dost sometimes counsel take—and sometimes tea.

With so great a master of language, it is a little dangerous to insist on the exact place where the meter coming in drove some of the logic out. But the superiority of his logic over Wordsworth's is not so overwhelming as it seems; for the most part it is merely that his improvisations are made to look nearly natural, as if he thoroughly intended them all the time, and meter had nothing to do with them. The *flowers* is arrived at gracefully, but the chief source of any "inevitability" claimed for it is the fact that it rhymes with *towers,* which is more important to the discourse. In four lines we come to Hampton Court, where will presently appear Belinda, whom we have left traveling in her boat on the Thames. Hampton Court has a location with respect to the Thames which we need to know, under the principles of the logical or narrative argument; and at Hampton Court assemble the royalty and the fashionable gentry, whom we must know too; these are among the necessary moves. Hampton Court is close by those *rising towers* which are London-on-Thames, and that is enough as to its location; it is a matter of course that it will be close by the meads, since the towers will rise out of the meads by the river rather than rise out of the river. If we should invert the two lines, as follows,

> Near where proud Thames surveys his rising towers,
> And where are meads forever crowned with flowers,

something would happen not only to the euphony of the language but to the respectability of its logic, for then it would be plain that the meads-and-flowers line is chiefly useful for filling up a couplet. But the next couplet lacks honest logical economy too. The *structure of majestic frame* is nothing but a majestic structure, with a rhyme tag added, and the account of the naming of Hampton Court is a metrical but logically gratuitous expansion of the simple recital of its name. The other two couplets both employ rhyme words, and contexts to assimilate them, which are so incongruous that they have to be employed in discourse as the occasions of wit. As logicians we need not take much stock in wit as forwarding argument, even when it is free from suspicion as a device to look after difficult rhyme pairings; it supposes such a lack of an obvious logical relation between two things that any technical bridge of connection must be accepted. No honest "argument" prefaced to a poem would cover the poet's witticisms. We condemn Romantic poets for injecting their burning sentiments into an objective argument, but other poets are given to wit, which is likewise at the expense of argument and logic.[2] A final remark will sound a little captious. Hampton Court is in mind, but the word "Court" is not used and possibly its absence troubles the poet; at any rate if he does not have a court he supplies the short passage with three royalties. There is the lady of the meads, a figurative queen, with a crown of flowers; Thames, a figurative patriarch, and at least a prince with all his rising towers (though a little while earlier there was a feminine character of the same name upon whose "silver bosom" Belinda rode in her boat); and actual Queen Anne. It seems an excessive profusion of royalties.

There are certainly readers of the Binomial Theorem who are prohibited by conscience from the reading of poetry; we have just been looking at some of the reasons. On these terms meter may be costing more than it is worth. Milton thought of the possibility, and went so far as to renounce its most binding device, the rhyme; it is employed by

> Some famous modern Poets, carried away by Custom, but much to their own vexation, hindrance, and constraint to express many things otherwise, and for the most part worse, than else they would have expressed them.

But greater purists might apply this logic to all the rest of the metrical devices. We turn to Milton's own unrhymed verse, and find:

> Thus, while he spake, each passion dimm'd his face
> Thrice chang'd with pale, ire, envy and despair,
> Which marr'd his borrow'd visage, and betray'd
> Him counterfeit, if any eye beheld.

The argument of this narrative passage would explain how Uriel, deceived once by Satan in his "stripling cherub's" disguise, perceives now his identity through the satanic passions registered in his face, and initiates the next cycle of action by informing the angels guarding Paradise. But the language, as is not uncommon with Milton, from the point of view of logic is almost like a telegraphic code in its condensation, and omission of connectives; it is expansible to two or three times its length in prose, and readable only with difficulty by unaccustomed readers. Yet it also lapses from strict logic in precisely the opposite direction, by the importation of superfluous detail.

The three successive increments of pallor and their respective causes would seem beyond the observation of Uriel, in the sun, and in fact we learn presently that what Uriel actually marked was Satan's "gestures fierce" and "mad demeanor." Milton is aware of this, and gives himself a technical alibi in our passage by being careful to say that the pallor stages betrayed the fraud not necessarily to Uriel but to any good eye that might be close enough to see them. Still, if Uriel did not see them they do not matter.

It would have been hard to persuade Milton out of this passage, with its deficiencies and superfluities; but suppose we might have proposed an alternative version, which would seem safely eclectic and within the traditional proficiencies of poetry and I shall not mind appearing ridiculous for the sake of the argument:

> Speaking, rank passion swelled within his breast
> Till all the organism felt its power
> And such a pallor in his face was wrought
> That it belied the angelic visage fair
> He had assumed. Uriel, unsleeping guard,
> With supernatural vision saw it plain.

But Milton in his turn would instantly have gibed at it, and on our terms; at the dangling participle and the poetic inversion as violations of good syntax; and then at the constant tendency, perhaps proceeding from our nervous desire to come with some spirit out of an embarrassing situation, to exceed the proper logical content, as shown in all four first lines by the verbs, *swelled, felt, was wrought,* and *belied.* They are ambitious, and start our minds upon little actions that would take us out of the plane of the argument.

Returning to rhymed verse, there is this passage from a poem which deserves its great fame, but whose fabulous "perfections" consist with indeterminacies that would be condemned in the prose of scientists, and also of college freshmen; though I think in the prose of college seniors they might have a different consideration:

Had we but world enough, and time,
This coyness, lady, were no crime.
We would sit down, and think which way
To walk, and pass our long love's day.
Thou by the Indian Ganges' side
Should'st rubies find: I by the tide
Of Humber would complain. I would
Love you ten years before the flood,
And you should, if you please, refuse
Till the conversion of the Jews;
My vegetable love should grow
Vaster than empires and more slow.

I will use the pedagogical red pencil, though I am loath. World, as distinguished from time, is not space, for the lovers already have all the space in the world, and long tenure would not increase it. It is a violent condensation meaning, I think, "the whole history of the world before us," and combining with the supposal of their having time to live through it; it supports the historical references which follow. *We would, thou should'st, my love should:* the use of the auxiliaries is precise, varying according to rule from person to person, and uniformly denoting determination or command: "we would arrange it so." But it is remarkable that in so firm a set of locutions, which attests the poet's logical delicacy, the *thou should'st* is interchangeable with *you should;* the meter is responsible for the latter version, since otherwise we should have the line, *And thou should'st, if* thou *pleased'st, refuse;* or, taking the same liberty with tenses which we find actually taken (again for metrical reasons), *And thou should'st, if thou pleas'st, refuse;* but either line clogs the meter. *Which way* is one phrase, but language is an ambiguous thing, and it has two meanings: *in which direction* as applied to *walk,* and *in what manner* as applied to *pass our day.* The parallel series in lines 5–7 is in three respects not uniform: *Ganges* has little need of a defining adjective, except the metrical one, but when once it has become *Indian Ganges* there is every right on the part of its analogue to be styled *English Humber;* and *Ganges' side* calls for *Humber's side,* or for merely *Humber's,* with *side* understood, but rhyme produces for Humber a *tide;* and the possessive case in the first member would call for the same in the second member, but is replaced there actually by an *of*-phrase. *Refuse* brings out of the rhyming dictionary the *Jews,* which it will tax the poet's invention to supply with a context; but for our present purposes the poet has too much invention, for it gives him the historical period from the Flood to the conversion of the Jews, which is a handsome way of saying ten thousand years, or some other length of time, and seems disproportionate to the mere ten years of the same context, the only other period mentioned. *Vegetable* is a grotesque qualification of love, and on the whole decidedly more unsuitable than suitable, though there are features in which it is suitable. *Vaster* would correlate with *slower,* but not with *more slow;* but they would not be correlatives at all after *grow,* for *vaster* is its factitive complement and *slower* can only be for *more slowly,* its adverb. Finally, there is the question of how the vastness of the poet's love can resemble the vastness of empires; the elegance of the terms seems to go along with the logic of a child.

7

But the important stage of indeterminacy comes, in the experiment of composition, when the imagination of the poet, and not only his verbal mechanics, is engaged. An "irrelevance" may feel forced at first, and its overplus of meaning unwanted, because it means the importation of a little foreign or extraneous content into what should be determinate, and limited; but soon the poet comes upon a kind of irrelevance that seems desirable, and he begins to indulge it voluntarily, as a new and positive to the meaning. And this is the principle: the importations which the imagination introduces into discourse have the value of developing the freedom which lurks in the "body," under the surface, of apparently determinate situations. Even Marvell is persuaded by the rhyme consideration to instill the Humber with a tide, or to furnish his abstract calendar with specifications about the Flood, and the conversion of the Jews, he does not make these additions reluctantly. On the contrary, he knows that the brilliance of the poetry depends on the shock, accompanied at once by the realism or the naturalness, of its powerful individuality. But the mere syllabic measure, and not only the rhyme, can induce this effect. When the poet investigates the suitability of a rhyme word for his discourse, he tries the imaginative contexts in which it could figure; but the process is the same when he tries many new phrases in the interest of the rhythm, for their suitability, though his imagination has to do without the sharp stimuli of the rhyme words. And by suitability I mean the propriety which consists in their denoting the proper effect which really belongs to the object. In this way what is irrelevant for one kind of discourse becomes the content for another kind, and presently the new kind stands up firmly if we have the courage to stand by it.

The passages cited above were in support of the negative and corrupt IM, but they illustrate also the positive IM, which is poetic texture, for the critic, and ontological freedom for the philosopher. Wordsworth has the most abstract argument, but instead of pursuing it closely and producing a distinguished logical structure—it might have come to a really superior version of the argument we are here trying to build up, something about the meaning of poetry—he wavers toward some interesting concrete objects, producing a mansion, a veil, a light, and a set of intricate turnings; but here too he is stopped, as if by some puritan inhibition, from looking steadily at his objects to obtain a clear image; so that his discourse is not distinguished either for its argument or for its texture. Pope unquestionably has the narrative gift, which means that he has access to the actual stream of events covered by the abstract argument; he is perhaps one of many poets prefiguring our modern prose fiction, and knows that he may suspend his argument whenever he pleases, provided he may substitute another equally positive content, namely, a subnarrative account of the independent character and history of its items. Milton looks principally like a man out of a more heroic age than Pope, in the casualness and roughness of his indeterminacy, but he is bolder also in the positive detail: nothing in Pope's passage compares with his stopping to name the three specific passions in the mind of Satan, and to imagine each one as turning Satan's visage paler than the one before had left it. As for Marvell, we are unwilling to praise or to condemn the peccadilloes of his logic, and here is a case where we take no account of the indeterminacy of the bad sort that results from the metering process, and distresses so many hardheaded readers. This is all overshadowed, and we are absorbed, by the power of his positive details.

Indeterminacy of this positive or valuable sort is introduced when the images make their entry. It looks as if there might be something very wise in the social, anonymous, and universal provision of metrical technique for poetry. The meter seems only to harm the discourse, till presently it works a radical innovation: it induces the provision of individual icons among the hard-and-fast logical symbols. This launches poetry upon its career.

8

The development of metrical content parallels that of meaning. As the resonant meter undetermines the meaning and introduces IM, so in turn the likely meaning undetermines the meter and introduces the variations of IS.

The usual minimum of a meter, in English practice, is a succession of lines having a determinate number of determinate feet, and a foot is some syllabic combination having one accented syllable. The most general consequence is that a unit of phonetic structure—a few lines of blank verse, a stanza of rhymed verse, a sonnet or whole poem sometimes—is superimposed upon a unit of meaning-structure; within it the foot may not coincide with the word or small logical unit, but the two structures use precisely the same constituent language in the long run, and come out at the end together; and this is a summary feat of remarkable coordination, when we approach it with the prejudice of a person used to working in pure structures, that is, in one structure at a time. In reading the poem we have our ear all the time immediately upon the progress of the meter, just as we have our discursive mind all the time on the course of the argument; so that the two structures advance simultaneously if not by the same steps, and every moment or so two steps finish together, and two new steps start together. And what we call a "phrase" is at once a period in the argument and a definable element in the metrical structure, and "phrasing" means to the poet the act of grouping the words to serve the two purposes as simultaneously as possible.

We may suppose that the phonetic effect and the meaning effect are, in theory, perfectly equal and coordinate. But probably we all have much more interest in the meaning than in the sound. Therefore it is convenient to say that the phonetic effect serves as a sort of texture to the meaning. This is to assign to the meaning an ontological addition.

But within the phonetic effect considered for itself alone we find the poet developing for his meter, which is the regular phonetic structure, its own kind of texture, which consists in the metrical variations. He is driven into this course by considerations exactly the same, except in reverse, as those we have seen compelling him to develop within the meaning a texture of meaning. The latter was forced upon him by the necessity of adapting his meaning to the meter; and this is forced upon him by the necessity of adapting his meter to the meaning when he cannot further reduce his meaning to language more accurately metrical, he accepts a "last version" and allows the variations to stand. These variations of course present the contingency and unpredictability, or in one word the "actuality," of the world of sound. Many phonetic effects are possible really; and here and there a foot or a phrase holds stubbornly to its alien character and is not quite assimilated to the poet's purpose.

But the texture that is realized within a meter is under conventional restrictions, the like of which have not been formulated for the texture within the meaning. Variations from the meter are permissive, but they must be of certain kinds. I suppose experience has shown, or else there is a strange consent of feeling, that the phrasing of the determinate meaning can always be roughly accomplished if allowed a few permissive variations; that the metrical effects, plus the effects allowed in the variations, make language sufficiently flexible to carry any meaning. Take iambic verse, for example, which is the staple for English. Elizabethan dramatic verse became somewhat loosened up or "Websterized" before it finished; and later Coleridge very nearly got the anapestic foot adopted as a legitimate variation for the iambic within short rhymed lines. But with such exceptions the poets have confined their metrical departures from iambic verse to the permissive variations with remarkable unanimity. So at least until our own period. There have been many poets recently, including the lettered as well as the unlettered, who have cast off the "bondage" of the meters, and employ them only as they find it convenient, or else make it their rule on principle not to cultivate anything approaching metrical determinateness. But I am talking here about the traditional practice. The critic must take it into account if he cares to discuss the traditional poets; there can be no dispute about that.

Shakespeare wrote,

```
    /              /                   /    /          /
When to | the ses | sions of | sweet si | lent thought
   /            /         /                 /     /
I sum | mon up | remem | brance of | things past,
```

but we may safely suppose that he was aware of the possibility of many other versions, as for example,

```
          /        /          /          /         /
When sits | my par | liament | of si | lent thought
    /      /            /         /           /
To try | afresh | the sweet | remem | bered past.
```

The assumption that this version entered his mind is of course improbable for more reasons than one, but at least it represents a common situation: the option between a fairly determinate meaning consisting with a variant or indeterminate meter, and a revised and less determinate meaning leading to a more determinate meter. Decision is in favor of the former alternative, but it is in the light of the fact that the metrical variations are all permissive and conventional. Here they consist in the following substitutions: a trochaic for the first iambic of the first line; a double foot or ionic for the third and fourth iambics of that line and a double foot or ionic for the fourth and fifth iambics of the second line. But the meaning is slightly more severe than the alternative meaning, and Shakespeare does not care to tinker with it. In the alternative version the boldness of the figure may be too odd; and even in that version the third foot of the first line would have in *párliamént* an extra syllable, unless we take advantage again of the permissions and say it is "accounted for by elision."[3]

In Donne, unless it is in Wyatt, whose meters are very difficult to construe, we have the feeling that we should find indeterminacy of metric carried furthest, sometimes almost to the point of unseating the iambic principle:

> /　　/　　/
> Two graves | must hide | thine and | my corse;
> /　　/　　/　/
> If one | might, death | were no | divorce.

The difficulty of the first line is that every one of the monosyllables, except possibly *and,* is capable of taking a strong logical accent. We do not in fact know how to read it; we do know that the line from which it is in variation is iambic tetrameter; see the following line, completing the couplet, which is dutifully regular. We assign therefore some reading, almost arbitrary, which perhaps metrifies the line sufficiently and respects its structural logic, and we think of that perverseness in Donne which led him so often to mock the law without technically breaking it. Perverseness, that is, as Ben Jonson construed it; and by any account an insubordinacy, or an individualism, which was reluctant to conform, and seemed to offer the pretense that a meaning was involved which was too urgent to tamper with in the interest of meter. But we can defend the substantive orthodoxy of this poet's metrical technique if we should hear complaint against the following line; it has ten syllables, and is shown by its context to be intended for an iambic pentameter:

> /　　/　　/　/　　/
> Blasted | with sighs, | and sur | rounded | with tears.

The parallelism of *with sighs* and *with tears* suggests that the participles on which they depend are also closely coupled; if we are blasted by the sighs, as by winds, we ought to be fairly drowned by the tears, as by floods. But this last is precisely what *surrounded* means. It is from the French *suronder* (Lat. *superundare*), to overflow. The verb in its weak modern sense could hardly find room for two logical accents, and the iambic structure might collapse; but then the logical structure would be impaired too, because it would come in this word to a foolish anticlimax. The only proper reader of the line is the one who trusts the integrity of Donne's metrical intention and looks to see how it can propose to conform here. To this reader the metric is informative. It is strictly the meaning of the line which has determined the variations in the meter, but we have found a meaning which does not destroy the meter, and it is decisive.

Milton is bold in his metric, but his conscience is exacting, and his irregularities come under the conventions. He writes:

> / / / / /
> Weep no | more, woe | ful Shep | herd, weep | no more.

The brilliance of this line consists in its falling eventually, and after we have tried other readings in vain, into the entire regularity which was the last thing we expected of it. We are used to receiving the impression, which he likes to give, and which represents a part of the truth, that his determinate meaning produces an indeterminateness in the local meters of nearly every line, even if we understand that this indeterminateness stops at the limits of the permissive convention. Under that impression we were inclined to scan the line this way

> / / / / /
> Weep no | more, woe | ful Shep | herd, weep | no more,

which is a metrical line found many times in Milton; but we were troubled over what happened to the logic of the accentless *woeful*. We said to ourselves, however, that the first *weep no more* had precisely the same logical values as the second one. All the same, the *woeful* is really not up to Milton's level as a workman, and we are not content with it. We finally try the normal meter, and we see that Milton intended us to come to it, and thought we must come to it if we believed in his technical competence. In the phrase *weep no more* it is difficult to say that one word has a heavier logical accent than another; yet we cannot accent them all, as we should like to do, and would do in prose. Or can we? The fact is that, reading the line as we finally do, we not only accent all three words but are obliged to: first *no,* then *weep,* then *more;* for the phrase occurs twice. Again the meter is informative. It could not be so if there were not the most minute give-and-take between the meaning and the meter as principles trying to determine each other, and arriving every moment or so at peace with honor, which means careful adjustments by means of reciprocal concessions.

And now I must make an admission that my readers will surely have anticipated. It is not telling the whole truth to say that Shakespeare and other accomplished poets resort to their variations, which are metrical imperfections, because a determinate meaning has forced them into it. The poet likes the variations regardless of the meanings, finding them essential in the capacity of a sound-texture to go with the sound-structure. It is in no very late stage of a poet's advancement that his taste rejects a sustained phonetic regularity as something restricted and barren, perhaps ontologically defective. Accordingly he is capable of writing smooth meters and then roughening them on purpose. And it must be added, while we are about it, that he is capable of writing a clean logical argument, and then of roughening that too, by introducing logical violence into it, and perhaps willful obscurity. We have therefore this unusual degree of complexity in the total structure: the indeterminate sound or the indeterminate meaning, IS or IM, may have been really come to independently, by a poet who senses the aesthetic value of indeterminateness and is veteran enough to go straight after it. But nothing can be introduced into the meaning without affecting the meter, and vice versa; so that IM, and not only DM as was represented in the beginning, undetermines the meter again and produces IS; and, conversely, IS, and not only DS, may undetermine the meaning again and produce IM. It will sound very complicated, but good poets will attest it if we ask them, and I think they will also offer the objective evidences in their poetry if we are skillful enough to read them.

It is necessary to offer some sort of formal disposition of one very large and vague character in the poetic effect: the euphony of the language. Under that head will come the liquidity of the consonantal sequences, which is much more marked in poetry than in prose; the elimination or reduction of harsh consonantal combinations, such as arise naturally in the juxtaposition of words selected on any pure meaning-principle; and the fixing up of the succession of vowel sounds, by way of ensuring variation, or at least avoiding sequences of flat or light vowels. These are working principles of composition also, and naturally they are of effect in undetermining the meaning. To that extent they are structural principles. Doubtless we think of euphony ordinarily as a principle striving for pure luxury of sound; it pleases the musical ear, and we may be sure it pleases also the articulatory sense, even when we read the poem silently. But that is not our kind of argument. Euphony is a sort of last textural refinement within the phonetic dimension of poetry. I believe that in evaluating it we must give "refinement" precedence over "textural." To refine the texture is to make it less perceptible, to make it smoother, to subtract from its private character, and that is to make it consist better with the structure. I incline therefore to think of euphony as a determinate phonetic principle, like meter, though much less binding and interfering in relation to the meaning. Theoretical complications present themselves when we think of it as coming into conflict with meter as a rival structural principle. But I believe we have seen complications enough in this section.

9

And finally we must take account of a belief that is all but universal among unphilosophical critics, and flourishes at its rankest with the least philosophical. It is this: the phonetic effect in a poem not only is (a) metrical and (b) euphonious, but preferably, and very often actually, is (c) "expressive"; that is, offers a sort of sound which "resembles" or partly "is" or at least "suggests" the object that it describes. It is necessary to say rather flatly that the belief is almost completely fallacious; both theoretically on the whole, and specifically in detail, for most of the cases that are cited to prove it. The single word does not in fact resemble appreciably the thing it denotes. The notion that it does is fully disposed of by Mr. I. A. Richards in Chapter III of his *Philosophy of Rhetoric,* assisted by Mr. Leonard Bloomfield's *Language* and Aristotle's *Poetics,* on which Mr. Richard draws for authoritative support. Furthermore, the phrase, or sustained passage, does not in its "movement" resemble the denoted situation at all closely. I do not know any authoritative analysis to cite against this latter form of the fallacy, and I shall not try to improvise one here. I am content—though not all my readers may be—to say that the resemblance usually alleged turns out to be, for hardheaded judges, extremely slight and farfetched; and, to make up for default of argument about this, to offer a little ontological speculation which might make the popular error intelligible by showing what it is really trying to say. There is some sort of truth in even a misstatement.

A wonderful "fitness," harmony, or propriety, even an enduring stability, seems to obtain in the combination of the semantic property and the phonetic property into a fine poetic phrase. It is something we all feel, and I believe it is the fact we need to account for here. But what is the law of its corporate existence? The law is an ontological one: the two properties shall not be identical, or like, homogeneous; they shall be other, unlike, and heterogeneous. It is the law of the actual world everywhere; all sorts of actual things are composed on this principle. It is only the naive prejudice of our first way of thought, our Eleatic stage of thought, that makes us conceive that the properties must unite by virtue of their sameness. The passage from that stage into the riper stage of thought has its first and most famous description in the discourse of the Eleatic Stranger in Plato's *Sophist;* it has systematic exploitation in Hegel and many other logicians. Red and red will not cohere with each other to make anything but an aggregate of red, nor even do red and yellow make anything astonishing; but red and big, along with a multitude of other properties, heterogeneous properties, cohere into an apple, which is a One formed out of the Many. I suppose we do not understand in any rational sense a particular object, such as an apple, holding together not by mathematical composition but by its own heterogeneity. But we recognize it perceptually. The World of Appearance (or opinion) seemed to Plato inferior to the World of Pure Being (or reason), but he acknowledged that the former was the world which our perceptions took hold of, and indeed was the world of nature.[4]

The poetic phrase is not very much like an apple, and we must concentrate upon that. In what world of discourse does it have its existence? As a thing of sounds it exists in the words; as a thing of meanings it exists in a world beyond the words. The heterogeneity is rather extreme. We recall the old puzzle; the debate on whether the poem resides in the physical words uttered or in the interpretation that is given them. But it exists in both at once; and for fear we forget about the words, they are metered, so that they may be forced upon our attention. One of the "touchstones" used by Matthew Arnold, and fancied by Mr. Eliot and many others, is Dante's line,

> In la sua volontade è nostra pace.

But the English translation is only,

> In His will is our peace,

which is not a poetic touchstone at all. The meaning is not combined now with the sounds; the words have become mere symbols, used but not incorporated into the object. The line in its English version has suffered ontological annihilation, it has lost one of its worlds. But it seems rather irresponsible to claim that Dante's own version has its superior virtue in the fact that its sound seems to "express" or "suggest" its meaning; though I think I know critics who might be prepared after a little time argue it, with much circumstance.

The triumphant citations from poetry, the "proofs" that we offer of its power, the touchstones, are always phrases, not single words nor little groups of words; they may be lines, passages of some lines each. I find more significance in this respect than, merely, that a distinguished piece of logical discourse, to have extension in order to have complexity. It is even true that a compelling phonetic character cannot be imposed upon the words unless there are enough of them to organize into a recognizable meter. Furthermore, and beyond that, the meaning employs the words, but the meter employs the syllables. There is no point-to-point coordination between the development of the semantic structure and that of the phonetic structure. The relation between the two in a poetic phrase seems nothing like the relation between two melodies in counterpoint, except that our two structures originally look much more heterogeneous than the melodies. Perhaps the aesthetic import of the semantic-phonetic combination is also like that of counterpoint. But I am not sure what profit there is in saying is. It is not obvious that musical aesthetic is much more articulate than literary aesthetic, even allowing for the genius of Schopenhauer. I should think it true of the counterpoint, but at any rate I should judge of the double structure of the poetic phrase, that its force is in its speculative or ontological intimations. The semantic structure alone, like the melody in the treble, may be an aesthetic structure, for it is a logical structure which at the same time admits body, or texture, as pure logical structures do not; yet the phonetic structure, which would seem perfectly unrelated to it, is made to combine with it. It seems a tighter job, stronger, and more wonderful, than the counterpoint can be, for the melodies are two, though they are simultaneous, while the poetic phrase is a single event. Ontologically, it is a case of bringing into experience both a denser and a more contingent world, and commanding a discourse in more dimensions.

10

This has probably gone far enough as an ontological brief in the study of poetic discourse in English. I am aware of its insufficiencies. It is the ontological sense of the traditionalist poets, and their readers, that I have wished to discover. It feels congenial for me.

But what should the ontological critic say about the moderns? Much of our own poetry is conspicuously other than traditional. Not, I believe, the poetry of Robinson, Frost, Bridges, Yeats, perhaps even Hopkins; who have adhered, or almost adhered, or intended to adhere, to the tradition. The poetry I am talking about is written by such poets as Pound, Eliot, Tate, Stevens, perhaps Auden, though I do not mean to list them formally, nor suggest that any of them is uniformly accountable to a critique. These poets are generally known to have high regard for traditionalism, but they make wide and deliberate departures from it for the sake of their own poetry.

The superficial marks of our modernist poetry are very well known. An excellent brief assemblage of them into a list is in "A Note on Poetry," by Mr. Randall Jarrell, prefacing his own verses in *Five Young American Poets.* He considers modernist poetry to be substantially "romantic," and lists its marks, as follows:

> I have no space for the enormous amount of evidence all these generalizations require; but consider some of the qualities of typical modernistic poetry: very interesting language, a great emphasis on connotation, "texture"; extreme intensity, forced emotion—violence; a good deal of obscurity; emphasis on sensation, perceptual nuances; emphasis on details, on the part rather than the whole; experimental or novel qualities of some sort; a tendency toward external formlessness and internal disorganization—these are justified, generally, as the disorganization required to express a disorganized age, or alternatively, as newly-discovered and more complex types of organization; an extremely personal style—*refine* your singularities; lack of restraint—all tendencies are forced to their limits; there is a good deal of emphasis on the unconscious, dream-structure, the thoroughly subjective; the poet's attitudes are usually anti-scientific, anti-commonsense, anti-public—he is, essentially, removed;

> poetry is primarily lyric, intensive—the few long poems are aggregations of lyric details; poems usually have, not a logical, but the more or less associational structure of dramatic monologue; and so on and so on.

My notes on this poetry are provisional and unsure, but I shall risk them in order to come down to date. The following account will be the merest sketch of a criticism, and will not even cite any of this poetry specifically.

The fundamental consideration is that the moderns are well instructed in the practice of the traditionalists. But this is what has happened: they find the old practice trite, and ontologically inadequate for them. Yet they lack any consistent conception of what a new practice might be—and a new practice that would be radical enough is probably not possible—and therefore they work by taking liberties with the old practice, and irregularize and desystematize it, without denying it.

They do not find sufficient profit in that traditional poetic labor which consists in the determinate metering of a determinate discourse. I have argued that some ontological triumph, something impossible for pure discourse, may be secured in this way. They are acquainted with the technique, and find it too easy. The well-metered discourse is impaired for them because it is transparently artful; they want a more direct and less formal knowledge.

They will not tolerate the experience of having the meaning brought by the meter into an indeterminateness of the compelled variety, with the only half-concealed irregularities such as those of Pope and Marvell above, or the resonances like those of the Romantic Wordsworth. Their disaffection is rather advanced. I suppose it is due fundamentally, though paradoxically, to their revulsion against scientific discourse. In seeking a discourse of greater ontological competence they do not propose to exhibit faults that are beneath the enemy standard of performance; and with the rapid and visible perfection of scientific discourse, occurring for the most part since the poetic achievements of the great traditionalists, indeterminateness of the ragged sort can be detected by the literate public everywhere, and is too disreputable. The age of prose, they might argue, has made obsolete the faltering logic of old-fashioned metered poetry. The disabilities of the procedure are too obvious; the advantages promised in it they propose to secure otherwise.

Being technically experienced, they have command of their own imagination, and when they seek indeterminateness of the positive sort, such as is denoted by the iconic signs, they do it directly. They have the power. They manage without the suggestion that comes in the verbal manipulations of metering. Perhaps their imagination, which might otherwise be confined by scientific discourse, has been in the long run released by precisely the kind of poetic exercise described above as elementary in the traditional technique, with meter working functionally in the composition. If so, the moderns might be called the products of a poetic tradition; but they are only its end products; or their status is even post-traditional: they are only the heirs of a tradition.

They have no enthusiasm for the meters, with the result that their poetry is far gone in its natural indeterminateness on that side. But they are committed on principle to an unprecedented degree of indeterminateness in the meaning, and their poetry is let down on that side too. This latter indeterminateness yields brilliant images; but it tends to logical inconsequence. The inconsequence does not come from haggling with the meter but from the intractable energy of the images. Evidence of this is that the mode of the inconsequence is chiefly ellipsis: the crowding of the images together without the terms for their logical relations; but also, as we think in view of the honesty of the work, the crowding together very largely without the logical relations themselves. The effect is an ontological density which proves itself by logical obscurity.

The dense and brilliant yet obscure world of the modern poets may reflect a certain initial ontological sense. Their most actual world, as they sense it, resists mastery, is more mysterious than intelligible, perhaps is more evil than good. It is a world of appearances, and suggests, for example, the world of Heraclitus; as if they had knocked the bottom out of history and language and become early Greeks again. They are antipathetic to the modern everyday world of business, science, and positivism, which ontologically disconcerts them. Their early Greek is pluralist, relativist, and irrational.

Their poetry is the manifest of such a skepticism, and virtual if tacit abjuration, as to seem to subject this generation to the category of decadence—if we know enough about the cycle of a culture to apply the term responsibly.

But, for that sense, it probably does not give quite the necessary impression of spent energies. And in that sense it is not quite thorough. A thing that is in startling exception occurs now and then in the practice of every one of the poets: the perfect poetic phrase. This phrase, which may well stand isolated in the context of indeterminacy, will lack nothing that is achievable of realizing the virtue intended by the traditional technique. It is a touchstone. The occasion of so sudden flight may be simple nostalgia, looking backward.

But also it may be a reluctant testimony to real ontologic efficacy, very much as it has been arrived at in the past experience of the race with its language; and to the impatience of spirited modern youth who will probably come eventually to sobriety and to power.

NOTES

1. It is true that in one context he talks about the icon as representing a "consummatory" or final value, as if constituting the image of a body so obviously meant for consumption, so ripe for immediate consumption, that nobody could resist knowing the value it meant to put forward. But even so I do not know what the body is for. The body is an impediment, and has to be waived, in order to attend to the value that interests the consumer, or even the strict discourser. But it is much easier to suppose that the body is there to be attended to as much as the value; and that attention to the body may not be characteristic of scientific discourse, but is the distinguishing characteristic of aesthetic discourse.

2. Mr. Cleanth Brooks reproves the sentimentality of simple poets, but puts himself rather off guard by his blanket counterendorsement of the wit

of university or sophisticated poets. If we had an aesthetician's version of Horace's fable of the town mouse and the country mouse, we would be sure to find the latter uttering countrified sentimental discourse, and scorned by the other; but the discourse of the town mouse not only would be smart, it would presently become oversmart, and silly; so that in the long run we should smile at her as at the country cousin, and for much the same reason: naïveté, as plain in personal vanity as in simplicity. Elizabethan comedy finds its butt in the smart town character as readily as in the country simpleton.

3. The three permissive variations in iambic verse have now all been named: trochaic for iambic, ionic for two iambics, and extra syllable accounted for by elision.

4. For the sake of accuracy I should say that the preference was that of Socrates, or of the Plato of the early dialogues.

KENNETH BURKE

FREUD—AND THE ANALYSIS OF POETRY

The reading of Freud I find suggestive almost to the point of bewilderment. Accordingly, what I should like most to do would be simply to take representative excerpts from his work, copy them out, and write glosses upon them. Very often these glosses would be straight extensions of his own thinking. At other times they would be attempts to characterize his strategy of presentation with reference to interpretative method in general. And, finally, the Freudian perspective was developed primarily to chart a psychiatric field rather than an aesthetic one; but since we are here considering the analogous features of these two fields rather than their important differences, there would be glosses attempting to suggest how far the literary critic should go along with Freud and what extra-Freudian material he would have to add. Such a desire to write an article on Freud in the margins of his books, must for practical reasons here remain a frustrated desire. An article such as this must condense by generalization, which requires me to slight the most stimulating factor of all—the detailed articulacy in which he embodies his extraordinary frankness.

Freud's frankness is no less remarkable by reason of the fact that he had perfected a method for being frank. He could say

---

Reprinted from Kenneth Burke, "Freud—and the Analysis of Poetry," in *The Philosophy of Literary Form: Studies in Symbolic Action,* 3d ed. (Berkeley: University of California Press, 1973), 258–92.

humble, even humiliating, things about himself and us because he had changed the rules somewhat and could make capital of observations that others, with vested interests of a different sort, would feel called upon to suppress by dictatorial decree. Or we might say that what for him could fall within the benign category of observation could for them fall only within its malign counterpart, spying.

Yet though honesty is, in Freud, methodologically made easier, it is by no means honesty made easy. And Freud's own accounts of his own dreams show how poignantly he felt at times the "disgrace" of his occupation. There are doubtless many thinkers whose strange device might be *ecclesia super cloacam*. What more fitting place to erect one's church than above a sewer! One might even say that sewers are what churches are for. But usually this is done by laying all the stress upon the ecclesia and its beauty. So that, even when the man's work fails to be completed for him as a social act, by the approval of his group, he has the conviction of its intrinsic beauty to give him courage and solace.

But to think of Freud, during the formative years of his doctrines, confronting something like repugnance among his colleagues, and even, as his dreams show, in his own eyes, is to think of such heroism as Unamuno found in Don Quixote; and if Don Quixote risked the social judgment of ridicule, he still had the consolatory thought that his imaginings were beautiful, stressing the ecclesia aspect, whereas Freud's theories bound him to a more drastic self-ostracizing act—the charting of the relations between ecclesia and cloaca that forced him to analyze the cloaca itself. Hence, his work was with the confessional as cathartic, as purgative; this haruspicy required an inspection of the entrails; it was, bluntly, an interpretative sculpting of excrement, with beauty replaced by a science of the grotesque.

Confronting this, Freud does nonetheless advance to erect a structure which, if it lacks beauty, has astounding ingeniousness and fancy. It is full of paradoxes, of leaps across gaps, of vistas—much more so than the work of many a modern poet who sought for nothing else but these and had no search for accuracy to motivate his work. These qualities alone would make it unlikely that readers literarily inclined could fail to be attracted, even while repelled. Nor can one miss in it the profound charitableness that is missing in so many modern writers who, likewise concerned with the cloaca, become efficiently concerned with nothing else, and make of their work pure indictment, pure oath, pure striking-down, pure spitting-upon, pure kill. True, this man, who taught us so much about father-rejection and who ironically became himself so frequently the rejected father in the works of his schismatic disciples, does finally descend to quarrelsomeness, despite himself, when recounting the history of the psychoanalytic movement. But, over the great course of his work, it is the matter of human rescue that he is concerned with—not the matter of vengeance. On a few occasions, let us say, he is surprised into vengefulness. But the very essence of his studies, even at their most forbidding moments (in fact, precisely at those moments), is its charitableness, its concern with salvation. To borrow an excellent meaningful pun from Trigant Burrow, this salvation is approached not in terms of religious hospitality but rather in terms of secular hospitalization. Yet it is the spirit of Freud; it is what Freud's courage is for.

Perhaps, therefore, the most fitting thing for a writer to do, particularly in view of the fact that Freud is now among the highly honored class—the exiles from Nazi Germany (how accurate those fellows are! how they seem, with almost 100 per cent efficiency, to have weeded out their greatest citizens!) — perhaps the most fitting thing to do would be simply to attempt an article of the "homage to Freud" sort and call it a day.

However, my job here cannot be confined to that. I have been commissioned to consider the bearing of Freud's theories upon literary criticism. And these theories were not designed primarily for literary criticism at all but were rather a perspective that, developed for the charting of a nonaesthetic field, was able (by reason of its scope) to migrate into the aesthetic field. The margin of overlap was this: The acts of the neurotic are symbolic acts. Hence in so far as both the neurotic act and the poetic act share this property in common, they may share a terminological chart in common. But in so far as they deviate, terminology likewise must deviate. And this deviation is a fact that literary criticism must explicitly consider.

As for the glosses on the interpretative strategy in general, they would be of this sort: For one thing, they would concern a distinction between what I should call an essentializing mode of interpretation and a mode that stresses proportion of ingredients. The tendency in Freud is toward the first of these. That is, if one found a complex of, let us say, seven ingredients in a man's motivation, the Freudian tendency would be to take one of these as the essence of the motivation and to consider the other six as sublimated variants. We could imagine, for instance, manifestations of sexual impotence accompanying a conflict in one's relations with his familiars and one's relations at the office. The proportional strategy would involve the study of these three as a cluster. The motivation would be synonymous with the interrelationships among them. But the essentializing ego would, in Freud's case, place the emphasis upon the sexual manifestation, as causal ancestor of the other two.

This essentializing strategy is linked with a normal ideal of science: to "explain the complex in terms of the simple." This ideal almost vows one to select one or another motive from a cluster and interpret the others in terms of it. The naive proponent of economic determinism, for instance, would select the quarrel at the office as the essential motive, and would treat the quarrel with familiars and the sexual impotence as mere results of this. Now, I don't see how you can possibly explain the complex in terms of the simple without having your very success used as a charge against you. When you get through, all that your opponent need say is: "But you have explained the complex in terms of the simple—and the simple is precisely what the complex is not."

Perhaps the faith philosophers, as against the reason philosophers, did not have to encounter a paradox at this point. Not that they avoided paradoxes, for I think they must always cheat when trying to explain how evil can exist in a world created by an all-powerful and wholly good Creator. But at least they did not have to confront the complexity simplicity difficulty, since their theological reductions referred to a ground in God, who was simultaneously the ultimately complex and the ultimately simple. Naturalistic strategies lack this convenient "out"—hence their explanations are simplifications, and every simplification is an oversimplification.[1]

It is possible that the literary critic, taking communication as his basic category, may avoid this particular paradox (communication thereby being a kind of attenuated God term). You can reduce everything to communication—yet communication is extremely complex. But, in any case, communication is by no means the basic category of Freud. The sexual wish, or libido, is the basic category; and the complex forms of communication that we see in a highly alembicated philosophy would be mere sublimations of this.

A writer deprived of Freud's clinical experience would be a fool to question the value of his category as a way of analyzing the motives of the class of neurotics Freud encountered. There is a pronouncedly individualistic element in any technique of salvation (my toothache being alas! my private property), and even those beset by a pandemic of sin or microbes will enter heaven or get discharged from the hospital one by one; and the especially elaborate process of diagnosis involved in Freudian analysis even to this day makes it more available to those suffering from the ills of preoccupation and leisure than to those suffering from the ills of occupation and unemployment (with people generally tending to be only as mentally sick as they can afford to be). This state of affairs makes it all the more likely that the typical psychoanalytic patient would have primarily private sexual motivations behind his difficulties. (Did not Henry James say that sex is something about which we think a great deal when we are not thinking about anything else?)[2] Furthermore, I believe that studies of artistic imagery, outside the strict pale of psychoanalytic emphasis, will bear out Freud's brilliant speculations as to the sexual puns, the *double-entendres,* lurking behind the most unlikely facades. If a man acquires a method of thinking about everything else, for instance, during the sexual deprivations and rigors of adolescence, this cure may well take on the qualities of the disease; and in so far as he continues with this same method in adult years, though his life has since become sexually less exacting, such modes as incipient homosexuality or masturbation may very well be informatively interwoven in the strands of his thought and be discoverable by inspection of the underlying imagery or patterns in this thought.

Indeed, there are only a few fundamental bodily idioms—and why should it not be likely that an attitude, no matter how complex its ideational expression, could only be completed by a channelization within its corresponding gestures? That is, the details of experience behind A's dejection may be vastly different from the details of experience behind B's dejection, yet both A and B may fall into the same bodily posture in expressing their dejection. And in an era like ours, coming at the end of a long individualistic emphasis, where we frequently find expressed an attitude of complete independence, of total, uncompromising self-reliance, this expression would not reach its fulfillment in choreography except in the act of "practical narcissism" (that is, the only wholly independent person would be the one who practiced self-abuse and really meant it).

But it may be noticed that we have here tended to consider mind-body relations from an interactive point of view rather than a materialistic one (which would take the body as the essence of the act and the mentation as the sublimation).

Freud himself, interestingly enough, was originally nearer to this view (necessary, as I hope to show later, for specifically literary purposes) than he later became. Freud explicitly resisted the study of motivation by way of symbols. He distinguished his own mode of analysis from the symbolic by laying the stress upon free association. That is, he would begin the analysis of a neurosis without any preconceived notion as to the absolute meaning of any image that the patient might reveal in the account of a dream. His procedure involved the breaking-down of the dream into a set of fragments, with the analyst then inducing the patient to improvise associations on each of these fragments in turn. And afterward, by charting recurrent themes, he would arrive at the crux of the patient's conflict.

Others (particularly Stekel), however, proposed a great short cut here. They offered an absolute content for various items of imagery. For instance, in Stekel's dictionary of symbols, which has the absoluteness of an old-fashioned dreambook, the right-hand path equals the road to righteousness, the left-hand path equals the road to crime, in anybody's dreams (in Lenin's presumably, as well as the Pope's). Sisters are breasts and brothers are buttocks. "The luggage of a traveller is the burden of sin by which one is oppressed," etc. Freud criticizes these on the basis of his own clinical experiences —and whereas he had reservations against specific equations, and rightly treats the method as antithetical to his own contribution, he decides that a high percentage of Stekel's purely intuitive hunches were corroborated. And after warning that such a gift as Stekel's is often evidence of paranoia, he decides that normal persons may also occasionally be capable of it.

Its lure as efficiency is understandable. And, indeed, if we revert to the matter of luggage, for instance, does it not immediately give us insight into a remark of Andre Gide, who is a specialist in the portrayal of scrupulous criminals, who has developed a stylistic trick for calling to seduction in the accents of evangelism, and who advises that one should learn to "travel light"?

But the trouble with short cuts is that they deny us a chance to take longer routes. With them, the essentializing strategy takes a momentous step forward. You have next but to essentialize your short cuts in turn (a short cut atop a short cut), and you get the sexual emphasis of Freud, the all-embracing ego compensation of Adler, or Rank's master-emphasis upon the birth trauma, etc.

Freud himself fluctuates in his search for essence. At some places you find him proclaiming the all-importance of the sexual, at other places you find him indignantly denying that his psychology is a pansexual one at all, and at still other places you get something halfway between the two, via the concept of the libido, which embraces a spectrum from phallus to philanthropy.

The important matter for our purposes is to suggest that the examination of a poetic work's internal organization would bring us nearer to a variant of the typically Freudian free-association method than to the purely symbolic method toward which he subsequently gravitated.[3]

The critic should adopt a variant of the free-association method. One obviously cannot invite an author, especially a dead author, to oblige him by telling what the author thinks of when the critic isolates some detail or other for improvisation. But what he can do is to note the context of imagery and ideas in which an image takes its place. He can also note, by such analysis, the kinds of evaluations surrounding the image of a crossing; for instance, is it an escape from or a return to an evil or a good, etc.? Until finally, by noting the ways in which this crossing behaves, what subsidiary imagery accompanies it, what kind of event it grows out of, what kind of event grows out of it, what altered rhythmic and tonal effects characterize it, etc., one grasps its significance as motivation. And there is no essential motive offered here. The motive of the work is equated with the structure of interrelationships within the work itself.

"But there is more to a work of art than that." I hear this objection being raised. And I agree with it. And I wonder whether we could properly consider the matter in this wise:

For convenience using the word "poem" to cover any complete made artistic product, let us divide this artifact (the invention, creation, formation, poetic construct) in accordance with three modes of analysis: dream, prayer, chart.

The psychoanalysis of Freud and of the schools stemming from Freud has brought forward an astoundingly fertile range of observations that give us insight into the poem as dream. There is opened up before us a sometimes almost terrifying glimpse into the ways in which we may, while overtly doing one thing, be covertly doing another. Yet, there is nothing mystical or even unusual about this. I may, for instance, consciously place my elbow upon the table. Yet at the same time I am clearly unconscious of the exact distance between my elbow and my nose. Or, if that analogy seems like cheating, let us try another: I may be unconscious of the way in which a painter-friend, observant of my postures, would find the particular position of my arm characteristic of me.

Or let us similarly try to take the terror out of infantile regression. In so far as I speak the same language that I learned as a child, every time I speak there is, within my speech, an ingredient of regression to the infantile level. Regression, we might say, is a function of progression. Where the progression has been a development by evolution or continuity of growth (as were one to have learned to speak and think in English as a child, and still spoke and thought in English) rather than by revolution or discontinuity of growth (as were one to have learned German in childhood, to have moved elsewhere at an early age, and since become so at home in English that he could not even understand a mature conversation in the language of his childhood), the archaic and the now would be identical. You could say, indifferently, either that the speech is regression or that it is not regression. But were the man who had forgot the language of his childhood, to begin speaking nothing but this early language (under a sudden agitation or as the result of some steady pressure), we should have the kind of regression that goes formally by this name in psychoanalytic nomenclature.

The ideal growth, I suppose—the growth without elements of alienation, discontinuity, homelessness—is that wherein regression is natural. We might sloganize it as "the adult a child matured." Growth has here been simply a successive adding of cells—the growth of the chambered nautilus. But there is also the growth of the adult who, "when he became a man, put away childish things." This is the growth of the crab, that grows by abandoning one room and taking on another. It produces moments of crisis. It makes for philosophies of emancipation and enlightenment, where one gets a jolt and is "awakened from the sleep of dogma" (and alas! in leaving his profound "Asiatic slumber," he risks getting in exchange more than mere wakefulness, more than the eternal vigilance that is the price of liberty—he may get wakefulness plus, i.e., insomnia).

There are, in short, critical points (or, in the Hegel-Marx vocabulary, changes of quantity leading to changes of quality) where the process of growth or change converts a previous circle of protection into a circle of confinement. The first such revolution may well be, for the human individual, a purely biological one—the change at birth when the fetus, heretofore enjoying a larval existence in the womb, being fed on manna from the placenta, so outgrows this circle of protection that the benign protection becomes a malign circle of confinement, whereat it must burst forth into a different kind of world—a world of locomotion, aggression, competition, hunt. The mother, it is true, may have already been living in such a world; but the fetus was in a world within this world—in a monastery—a world such as is lived in by "coupon clippers," who get their dividends as the result of sharp economic combat but who may, so long as the payments are regular, devote themselves to thoughts and diseases far "above" these harsh material operations.

In the private life of the individual there may be many subsequent jolts of a less purely biological nature, as with the death of some one person who had become pivotal to this individual's mental economy. But whatever these unique variants may be, there is again a universal variant at adolescence, when radical changes in the glandular structure of the body make this body a correspondingly altered environment for the mind, requiring a corresponding change in our perspective, our structure of interpretations, meanings, values, purposes, and inhibitions, if we are to take it properly into account.

In the informative period of childhood our experiences are strongly personalized. Our attitudes take shape with respect to distinct people who have roles, even animals and objects being vessels of character. Increasingly, however, we begin to glimpse a world of abstract relationships, of functions understood solely through the medium of symbols in books. Even such real things as Tibet and Eskimos and Napoleon are for us, who have not been to Tibet, or lived with Eskimos, or fought under Napoleon, but a structure of signs. In a sense, it could be said that we learn these signs flat. We must start from scratch. There is no tradition in them; they are pure present. For though they have been handed down by tradition, we can read meaning into them only in so far as we can project or extend them out of our own experience. We may, through being burned a little, understand the signs for being burned a lot—it is in this sense that the coaching of interpretation could be called traditional. But we cannot understand the signs for being burned a lot until we have in our own flat experience, here and now, been burned a little.

Out of what can these extensions possibly be drawn? Only out of the informative years of childhood. Psychoanalysis talks of purposive forgetting. Yet purposive forgetting is the only way of remembering. One learns the meaning of "table," "book," "father," "mother," "mustn't," by forgetting the contexts in which these words were used. The Darwinian ancestry (locating the individual in his feudal line of descent from the ape) is matched in Freud by a still more striking causal ancestry that we might sloganize as "the child is father to the man."[4]

As we grow up new meanings must either be engrafted upon old meanings (being to that extent *double-entendres*) or they must be new starts (hence, involving problems of dissociation).

It is in the study of the poem as dream that we find revealed the ways in which the poetic organization takes shape under these necessities. Revise Freud's terms, if you will. But nothing is done by simply trying to refute them or to tie them into knots. One may complain at this procedure, for instance: Freud characterizes the dream as the fulfillment of a wish; an opponent shows him a dream of frustration, and he answers: "But the dreamer wishes to be frustrated." You may demur at that, pointing out that Freud has developed a "heads I win, tails you lose" mode of discourse here. But I maintain that, in doing so, you have contributed nothing. For there are people whose values are askew, for whom frustration itself is a kind of grotesque ambition. If you would, accordingly, propose to chart this field by offering better terms, by all means do so. But better terms are the only kind of refutation here that is worth the trouble. Similarly, one may be unhappy with the concept of ambivalence, which allows pretty much of an open season on explanations (though the specific filling-out may provide a better case for the explanation than appears in this key term itself). But, again, nothing but an alternative explanation is worth the effort of discussion here. Freud's terminology is a dictionary, a lexicon for charting a vastly complex and hitherto largely uncharted field. You can't refute a dictionary. The only profitable answer to a dictionary is another one.

A profitable answer to Freud's treatment of the Oedipus complex, for instance, was Malinowski's study of its variants in a matriarchal society.[5] Here we get at once a corroboration and a refutation of the Freudian doctrine. It is corroborated in that the same general patterns of enmity are revealed; it is refuted in that these patterns are shown not to be innate but to take shape with relation to the difference in family structure itself, with corresponding difference in roles.

Freud's overemphasis upon the patriarchal pattern (an assumption of its absoluteness that is responsible for the Freudian tendency to underrate greatly the economic factors influencing the relationships of persons or roles) is a prejudicial factor that must be discounted, in Freud, even when treating the poem as dream. Though totemistic religion, for instance, flourished with matriarchal patterns, Freud treats even this in patriarchal terms. And I submit that this emphasis will conceal from us, to a large degree, what is going on in art (still confining ourselves to the dream level—the level at which Freudian coordinates come closest to the charting of the logic of poetic structure). In the literature of transitional eras, for instance, we find an especial profusion of rebirth rituals, where the poet is making the symbolic passes that will endow him with a new identity. Now, imagine him trying to do a very thorough job of this reidentification. To be completely reborn, he would have to change his very lineage itself. He would have to revise not only his present but also his past. (Ancestry and cause are forever becoming intermingled—the thing is that from which it came—cause is *Ur-sache,* etc.) And could a personalized past be properly confined to a descent through the father, when it is the *mater* that is *semper certa?* Totemism, when not interpreted with Freud's patriarchal bias, may possibly provide us with the necessary cue here. Totemism, as Freud himself reminds us, was a magical device whereby the members of a group were identified with one another by the sharing of the same substance (a process often completed by the ritualistic eating of this substance, though it might, for this very reason, be prohibited on less festive occasions). And it is to the mother that the basic informative experiences of eating are related.

So, all told, even in strongly patriarchal societies (and much more so in a society like ours, where theories of sexual equality, with a corresponding confusion in sexual differentiation along occupational lines, have radically broken the symmetry of pure patriarchalism), would there not be a tendency for rebirth rituals to be completed by symbolizations of matricide and without derivation from competitive, monopolistic ingredients at all?[6]

To consider explicitly a bit of political dreaming, is not Hitler's doctrine of Aryanism something analogous to the adoption of a new totemic line? Has he not voted himself a new identity and, in keeping with a bastardized variant of the strategy of materialistic science, rounded this out by laying claim to a distinct blood stream? What the Pope is saying, benignly, in proclaiming the Hebrew prophets as the spiritual ancestors of Catholicism, Hitler is saying malignly in proclaiming for himself a lineage totally distinct.

Freud, working within the patriarchal perspective, has explained how such thinking becomes tied up with persecution. The paranoid, he says, assigns his imagined persecutor the role of rejected father. This persecutor is all-powerful, as the father seems to the child. He is responsible for every imagined machination (as the Jews, in Hitler's scheme, become the universal devil-function, the leading brains behind every "plot").

Advancing from this brilliant insight, it is not hard to understand why, once Hitler's fantasies are implemented by the vast resources of a nation, the "persecutor" becomes the persecuted.

The point I am trying to bring out is that this assigning of a new lineage to one's self (as would be necessary, in assigning one's self a new identity) could not be complete were it confined to symbolic patricide. There must also be ingredients of symbolic matricide intermingled here (with the phenomena of totemism giving cause to believe that the ritualistic slaying of the maternal relationship may draw upon an even deeper level than the ritualistic slaying of the paternal relationship). Lineage itself is charted after the metaphor of the family tree, which is, to be sure, patriarchalized in Western heraldry, though we get a different quality in the tree of life. MacLeish, in his period of aesthetic negativism, likens the sound of good verse to the ring of the ax in the tree, and if I may mention an early story of my own, *In Quest of Olympus,* a rebirth fantasy, it begins by the felling of a tree, followed by the quick change from child to adult, or, within the conventions of the fiction, the change from tiny "Treep" to gigantic "Arjk"; and though, for a long time, under the influence of the Freudian patriarchal emphasis, I tended to consider such trees as fathers, I later felt compelled to make them ambiguously parents. The symbolic structure of Peter Blume's painting, "The Eternal City," almost forces me to assign the tree, in that instance, to a purely maternal category, since the rejected father is pictured in the repellent phallus-like figure of Mussolini, leaving only the feminine role for the luxuriant tree that, by my interpretation of the picture, rounds out the lineage (with the dishonored Christ and the beggarwoman as vessels of the past lineage, and the lewd Mussolini and the impersonal tree as vessels of the new lineage, which I should interpret on the nonpolitical level as saying that sexuality is welcomed, but as a problem, while home is relegated to the world of the impersonal, abstract, observed).

From another point of view we may consider the sacrifice of gods, or of kings, as stylistic modes for dignifying human concerns (a kind of neo-euhemerism). In his stimulating study of the ritual drama, *The Hero,* Lord Raglan overstresses, it seems to me, the notion that these dramas appealed purely as spectacles. Would it not be more likely that the fate of the sacrificial king was also the fate of the audience, in stylized form, dignified, "writ large"? Thus, their engrossment in the drama would not be merely that of watching a parade, or the utilitarian belief that the ritual would insure rainfall, crops, fertility, a good year, etc.; but, also, the stages of the hero's journey would chart the stages of their journey (as an Elizabethan play about royalty was not merely an opportunity for the pit to get a glimpse of high life, a living newspaper on the doings of society, but a dignification or memorializing of their own concerns, translated into the idiom then currently accepted as the proper language of magnification).[7]

But though we may want to introduce minor revisions in the Freudian perspective here, I submit that we should take Freud's key terms, "condensation" and "displacement," as the over-all categories for the analysis of the poem as dream. The terms are really two different approaches to the same phenomenon. Condensation, we might say, deals with the respects in which house in a dream may be more than house, or house plus. And displacement deals with the way in which house may be other than house, or house minus. (Perhaps we should say, more accurately, minus house.)

One can understand the resistance to both of these emphases. It leaves no opportunity for a house to be purely and simply a house—and whatever we may feel about it as regards dreams, it is a very disturbing state of affairs when transferred to the realm of art. We must acknowledge, however, that the house in a poem is, when judged purely and simply as a house, a very flimsy structure for protection against wind and rain. So there seems to be some justice in retaining the Freudian terms when trying to decide what is going on in poetry. As Freud fills them out, the justification becomes stronger. The ways in which grammatical rules are violated, for instance; the dream's ways of enacting conjunctions, of solving arguments by club offers of mutually contradictory assertions; the importance of both concomitances and discontinuities for interpretative purposes (the phenomena of either association or dissociation, as you prefer, revealed with greatest clarity in the *lapsus linguae*); the conversion of an expression into its corresponding act (as were one, at a time when "over the fence is out" was an expression in vogue, to apply this comment upon some act by following the dream of this act by a dreamed incident of a ball going over a fence); and, above all, the notion that the optative is in dreams, as often in poetry and essay, presented in the indicative (a Freudian observation fertile to the neopositivists' critique of language)—the pliancy and ingenuity of Freud's researches here make entrancing reading, and continually provide insights that can be carried over, *mutatis mutandis,* to the operations of poetry. Perhaps we might sloganize the point thus: In so far as art contains a surrealist ingredient (and all art contains some of this ingredient), psychoanalytic coordinates are required to explain the logic of its structure.

Perhaps we might take some of the pain from the notions of condensation and displacement (with the tendency of one event to become the synecdochic representative of some other event in the same cluster) by imagining a hypothetical case of authorship. A novelist, let us say, is trying to build up for us a sense of secrecy. He is picturing a conspiracy, yet he was never himself quite this kind of conspirator. Might not this novelist draw upon whatever kinds of conspiracy he himself had experientially known (as for instance were he to draft for this purpose memories of his participation in some childhood *Bund*)? If this were so, an objective breakdown of the imagery with which he surrounded the conspiratorial events in his novel would reveal this contributory ingredient. You would not have to read your interpretation into it. It would be objectively, structurally, there, and could be pointed to by scissor work. For instance, the novelist might explicitly state that, when joining the conspiracy, the hero recalled some incident of his childhood. Or the adult conspirators would, at strategic points, be explicitly likened by the novelist to children, etc. A statement about the ingredients of the work's motivation would thus be identical with a statement about the work's structure—a statement as to what goes with what in the work itself. Thus, in Coleridge's "The Eolian Harp," you do not have to interpret the poet's communion with the universe as an affront to his wife; the poet himself explicitly apologizes to her for it. Also, it is an objectively citable fact that imagery of noon goes with this apology. If, then, we look at other poems by Coleridge, noting the part played by the Sun at noon in the punishments of the guilt-laden Ancient Mariner, along with the fact that the situation of the narrator's confession involves the detention of a wedding guest from the marriage feast, plus the fact that a preference for church as against marriage is explicitly stated at the end of the poem, we begin to see a motivational cluster emerging. It is obvious that such structural interrelationships cannot be wholly conscious, since they are generalizations about acts that can only be made inductively and statistically after the acts have been accumulated. (This applies as much to the acts of a single poem as to the acts of many poems. We may find a theme emerging in one work that attains fruition in that same work—the ambiguities of its implications where it first emerges attaining explication in the same integer. Or its full character may not be developed until a later work. In its ambiguous emergent form it is a synecdochic representative of the form it later assumes when it comes to fruition in either the same work or in another one.)

However, though the synecdochic process (whereby something does service for the other members of its same cluster or as the foreshadowing of itself in a later development) cannot be wholly conscious, the dream is not all dream. We might say, in fact, that the Freudian analysis of art was handicapped by the aesthetic of the period—an aesthetic shared even by those who would have considered themselves greatly at odds with Freud and who were, in contrast with his delving into the unbeautiful, concerned with beauty only. This was the aesthetic that placed the emphasis wholly upon the function of self-expression. The artist had a number—some unique character or identity—

and his art was the externalizing of this inwardness. The general Schopenhauerian trend contributed to this. Von Hartmann's *Philosophy of the Unconscious* has reinforced the same pattern. This version of voluntaristic processes, as connected with current theories of emancipation, resulted in a picture of the dark, unconscious drive calling for the artist to "out with it." The necessary function of the Freudian secular confessional, as a preparatory step to redemption, gave further strength to the same picture. Add the "complex in terms of the simple" strategy (with its variants—higher in terms of lower, normal as a mere attenuation of the abnormal, civilized as the primitive sublimated); add the war of the generations (which was considered as a kind of absolute rather than as a by-product of other factors, as those who hated the idea of class war took in its stead either the war of the generations or the war of the sexes)—and you get a picture that almost automatically places the emphasis upon art as utterance, as the naming of one's number, as blurting-out, as catharsis by secretion.

I suggested two other broad categories for the analysis of poetic organization: prayer and chart.

Prayer would enter the Freudian picture in so far as it concerns the optative. But prayer does not stop at that. Prayer is also an act of communion. Hence, the concept of prayer, as extended to cover also secular forms of petition, moves us into the corresponding area of communication in general. We might say that, whereas the expressionistic emphasis reveals the ways in which the poet, with an attitude, embodies it in appropriate gesture, communication deals with the choice of gesture for the inducement of corresponding attitudes. Sensory imagery has this same communicative function, inviting the reader, within the limits of the fiction at least, to make himself over in the image of the imagery.

Considering the poem from this point of view, we begin with the incantatory elements in art, the ways of leading in or leading on the hypothetical audience X to which the poem, as a medium, is addressed (though this hypothetical audience X be nothing more concrete, as regards social relations, than a critical aspect of the poet's own personality). Even Freud's dream had a censor; but the poet's censor is still more exacting, as his shapings and revisions are made for the purpose of forestalling resistances (be those an essay reader's resistances to arguments and evidence or the novel reader's resistance to developments of narrative or character). We move here into the sphere of rhetoric (reader-writer relationships, an aspect of art that Freud explicitly impinges upon only to a degree in his analysis of wit), with the notion of address being most evident in oration and letter, less so in drama, and least in the lyric. Roughly, I should say that the slightest presence of revision is per se indication of a poet's feeling that his work is addressed (if only, as Mead might say, the address of an "I" to its "me").

Here would enter consideration of formal devices, ways of pointing up and fulfilling expectations, of living up to a contract with the reader (as Wordsworth and Coleridge might put it), of easing by transition or sharpening by ellipsis; in short, all that falls within the sphere of incantation, imprecation, exhortation, inducement, weaving and releasing of spells; matters of style and form, of meter and rhythm, as contributing to these results; and thence to the conventions and social values that the poet draws upon in forming the appropriate recipes for the roles of protagonist and antagonist, into which the total agon is analytically broken down, with subsidiary roles polarized about one or the other of the two agonists tapering off to form a region of overlap between the two principles—the ground of the agon. Here, as the reverse of prayer, would come also invective, indictment, oath. And the gestures might well be tracked down eventually to choices far closer to bodily pantomime than is revealed on the level of social evaluation alone (as were a poet, seeking the gestures appropriate for the conveying of a social negativeness, to draw finally upon imagery of disgust, and perhaps even, at felicitous moments, to select his speech by playing up the very consonants that come nearest to the enacting of repulsion).

As to the poem as chart: the Freudian emphasis upon the pun brings it about that something can only be in so far as it is something else. But, aside from these ambiguities, there is also a statement's value as being exactly what it is. Perhaps we could best indicate what we mean by speaking of the poem as chart if we called it the poet's contribution to an informal dictionary. As with proverbs, he finds experience or relationship typical, or recurrent, or significant enough for him to need a word for it. Except that his way of defining the word is not to use purely conceptual terms, as in a formal dictionary, but to show how his vision behaves, with appropriate attitudes. In this, again, it is like the proverb that does not merely name but names vindictively, or plaintively, or promisingly, or consolingly, etc. His namings need not be new ones. Often they are but memorializings of an experience long recognized.

But, essentially, they are enactments, with every form of expression being capable of treatment as the efficient extension of one aspect or another of ritual drama (so that even the scientific essay would have its measure of choreography, its pedestrian pace itself being analyzed as gesture or incantation, its polysyllables being as style the mimetics of a distinct monasticism, etc.). And this observation, whereby we have willy-nilly slipped back into the former subject, the symbolic act as prayer, leads us to observe that the three aspects of the poem, here proposed, are not elements that can be isolated in the poem itself, with one line revealing the "dream," another the "prayer," and a third the "chart." They merely suggest three convenient modes in which to approach the task of analysis.[8]

The primary category, for the explicit purposes of literary criticism, would thus seem to me to be that of communication rather than that of wish, with its disguises, frustrations, and fulfillments. Wishes themselves, in fact, become from this point of view analyzable as purposes that get their shape from the poet's perspective in general (while this perspective is in turn shaped by the collective medium of communication). The choice of communication also has the advantage, from the sociological point of view, that it resists the Freudian tendency to overplay the psychological factor (as the total medium of communication is not merely that of words, colors, forms, etc., or of the values and conventions with which these are endowed, but also the productive materials, cooperative resources, property rights, authorities, and their various bottlenecks, which figure in the total act of human conversation).

Hence, to sum up: I should say that, for the explicit purposes of literary criticism, we should require more emphasis than the Freudian structure gives, (1) to the proportional strategy as against the essentializing one, (2) to matriarchal symbolizations as against the Freudian patriarchal bias, (3) to poem as prayer and chart, as against simply the poem as dream.

But I fully recognize that, once the ingenious and complex structure has been erected, nearly anyone can turn up with proposals that it be given a little more of this, a little less of that, a pinch of so-and-so, etc. And I recognize that, above all, we owe an enormous debt of gratitude to the man who, by his insight, his energy, and his remarkably keen powers of articulation, made such tinkering possible. It is almost fabulous to think that, after so many centuries of the family, it is only now that this central factor in our social organization has attained its counterpart in an organized critique of the family and of the ways in which the informative experience with familiar roles may be carried over, or "metaphored," into the experience with extra-familiar roles, giving these latter, in so far as they are, or are felt to be, analogous with the former, a structure of interpretations and attitudes borrowed from the former. And in so far as poets, like everyone else, are regularly involved in such informative familiar relationships, long before any but a few rudimentary bodily gestures are available for communicative use (with their first use unquestionably being the purely self-expressive one), the child is indeed the adult poet's father, as he is the father of us all (if not so in essence, then at least as regards an important predisposing factor "to look out for"). Thence we get to "like father like son." And thence we get to Freud's brilliant documentation of this ancestry, as it affects the maintenance of a continuity in the growing personality.

Only if we eliminate biography entirely as a relevant fact about poetic organization can we eliminate the importance of the psychoanalyst's search for universal patterns of biography (as revealed in the search for basic myths which recur in new guises as a theme with variations); and we can eliminate biography as a relevant fact about poetic organization only if we consider the work of art as if it were written neither by people nor for people, involving neither inducements nor resistances.[9] Such can be done, but the cost is tremendous in so far as the critic considers it his task to disclose the poem's eventfulness.

However, this is decidedly not the same thing as saying that "we cannot appreciate the poem without knowing about its relation to the poet's life as an individual." Rather, it is equivalent to saying: "We cannot understand a poem's structure without understanding the function of that structure. And to understand its function we must understand its purpose." To be sure, there are respects in which the poem, as purpose, is doing things for the poet that it is doing for no one else. For instance, I think it can be shown by analysis of the imagery in Coleridge's "Mystery Poems" that one of the battles being fought there is an attempt to get self-redemption by the poet's striving for the vicarious or ritualistic redemption of his drug. It is obvious that this aspect of the equational structure is private and would best merit discussion when one is discussing the strategy of one man in its particularities. Readers in general will respond only to the sense of guilt, which was sharpened for Coleridge by his particular burden of addiction, but which may be sharpened for each reader by totally different particularities of experience. But if you do not discuss the poem's structure as a function of symbolic redemption at all (as a kind of private-enterprise Mass, with important ingredients of a black Mass), the observations you make about its structure are much more likely to be gratuitous and arbitrary (quite as only the most felicitous of observers could relevantly describe the distribution of men and postures in a football game if he had no knowledge of the game's purpose and did not discuss its formations as oppositional tactics for the carrying-out of this purpose, but treated the spectacle simply as the manifestation of a desire to instruct and amuse).

Thus, in the case of "The Ancient Mariner," knowledge of Coleridge's personal problems may enlighten us as to the particular burdens that the Pilot's boy ("who now doth crazy go") took upon himself as scapegoat for the poet alone. But his appearance in the poem cannot be understood at all, except in superficial terms of the interesting or the picturesque, if we do not grasp his function as a scapegoat of some sort—a victimized vessel for drawing off the most malign aspects of the curse that afflicts the "graybeard loon" whose cure had been effected under the dubious aegis of moonlight. And I believe that such a functional approach is the only one that can lead into a profitable analysis of a poem's structure even on the purely technical level. I remember how, for instance, I had pondered for years the reference to the "silly buckets" filled with curative rain. I noted the epithet as surprising, picturesque, and interesting. I knew that it was doing something, but I wasn't quite sure what. But as soon as I looked upon the Pilot's boy as a scapegoat, I saw that the word *silly* was a technical foreshadowing of the fate that befell this figure in the poem. The structure itself became more apparent: the "loon"-atic Mariner begins his cure from drought under the aegis of a moon that causes a silly rain, thence by synecdoche to silly buckets, and the most malignant features of this problematic cure are transferred to the Pilot's boy who now doth crazy go. Now, if you want to confine your observations to the one poem, you have a structural-functional-technical analysis of some important relationships within the poem itself. If you wish to trail the matter farther afield, into the equational structure of other work by Coleridge, you can back your interpretation of the moon by such reference as that to "moon-blasted madness," which gives you increased authority to discern lunatic ingredients in the lunar. His letters, where he talks of his addiction in imagery like that of the "Mystery Poems" and contemplates entering an insane asylum for a cure, entitle you to begin looking for traces of the drug as an ingredient in the redemptive problem. His letters also explicitly place the drug in the same cluster with the serpent; hence, we begin to discern what is going on when the Mariner transubstantiates the water snakes, in removing them from the category of the loathsome and accursed to the category of the blessed and beautiful. So much should be enough for the moment. Since the poem is constructed about an opposition between punishments under the aegis of the sun and cure under the aegis of the moon, one could proceed in other works to disclose the two sets of equations clustered about these two principles. Indeed, even in "The Ancient Mariner" itself we get a momentous cue, as the sun is explicitly said to be "like God's own head." But, for the moment, all I would maintain is that, if we had but this one poem by Coleridge, and knew not one other thing about him, we could not get an insight into its structure until we began with an awareness of its function as a symbolic redemptive process.

I can imagine a time when the psychological picture will be so well known and taken into account—when we shall have gone so far beyond Freud's initial concerns—that a reference to the polymorphous perverse of the infantile, for instance, will seem far too general—a mere first approximation. Everyone provides an instance of the polymorphous perverse, in attenuated form, at a moment of hesitancy; caught in the trackless maze of an unresolved, and even undefined, conflict, he regresses along this channel and that, in a formless experimentation that "tries anything and everything, somewhat." And in so far as his puzzle is resolved into pace, and steady rhythms of a progressive way out are established, there is always the likelihood that this solution will maintain continuity with the past of the poet's personality by a covert drawing upon analogies with this past. Hence the poet or speculator, no matter how new the characters with which he is now concerned, will give them somewhat the roles of past characters; whereat I see nothing unusual about the thought that a mature and highly complex philosophy might be so organized as to be surrogate for, let us say, a kind of adult breast-feeding—or, in those more concerned with alienation, a kind of adult weaning. Such categories do not by any means encompass the totality of a communicative structure; but they are part of it, and the imagery and transitions of the poem itself cannot disclose their full logic until such factors are taken into account.

However, I have spoken of pace. And perhaps I might conclude with some words on the bearing that the Freudian technique has upon the matter of pace. The Freudian procedure is primarily designed to break down a rhythm grown obsessive, to confront the systematic pieties of the patient's misery with systematic impieties of the clinic.[10] But the emphasis here is more upon the breaking of a malign rhythm than upon the upbuilding of a benign one. There is no place in this technique for examining the available resources whereby the adoption of total dramatic enactment may lead to correspondingly proper attitude. There is no talk of games, of dance, of manual and physical actions, of historical role, as a "way in" to this new upbuilding. The sedentary patient is given a sedentary cure. The theory of rhythms—work rhythms, dance rhythms, march rhythms—is no explicit part of this scheme, which is primarily designed to break old rhythms rather than to establish new ones.

The establishing of a new pace, beyond the smashing of the old puzzle, would involve in the end a rounded philosophy of the drama. Freud, since his subject is conflict, hovers continually about the edges of such a philosophy; yet it is not dialectical enough. For this reason Marxists properly resent his theories, even though one could, by culling incidental sentences from his works, fit him comfortably into the Marxist perspective. But the Marxists are wrong, I think, in resenting him as an irrationalist, for there is nothing more rational than the systematic recognition of irrational and nonrational factors. And I should say that both Freudians and Marxists are wrong in so far as they cannot put their theories together, by an overall theory of drama itself (as they should be able to do, since Freud gives us the material of the closet drama, and Marx the material of the problem play, the one worked out in terms of personal conflicts, the other in terms of public conflicts).

The approach would require explicitly the analysis of role: salvation via change or purification of identity (purification in either the moral or chemical sense); different typical relationships between individual and group (as charted attitudinally in proverbs, and in complex works treated as sophisticated variants); modes of acceptance, rejection, self-acceptance, rejection of rejection[11] ("the enemies of my enemies are my friends"); transitional disembodiment as intermediate step between old self and new self (the spirituality of Shelley and of the Freudian cure itself); monasticism in the development of methods that fix a transitional or other-worldly stage, thereby making the evanescent itself into a kind of permanency—with all these modes of enactment finally employing, as part of the gesture idiom, the responses of the body itself as actor. (If one sought to employ Freud, as is, for the analysis of the poem, one would find almost nothing on poetic posture or pantomime, tonality, the significance of different styles and rhythmic patterns, nothing of this behaviorism.) Such, it seems to me, would be necessary, and much more in that direction, before we could so extend Freud's perspective that it revealed the major events going on in art.

But such revisions would by no means be anti-Freudian. They would be the kind of extensions required by reason of the fact that the symbolic act of art, whatever its analogies with the symbolic act of neurosis, also has important divergences from the symbolic act of neurosis. They would be extensions designed to take into account the full play of communicative and realistic ingredients that comprise so large an aspect of poetic structure.

NOTES

1. The essentializing strategy has its function when dealing with classes of items; the proportional one is for dealing with an item in its uniqueness. By isolating the matter of voluntarism, we put Freud in a line or class with Augustine. By isolating the matter of his concern with a distinction between unconscious and conscious, we may put him in a line with Leibniz's distinction between perception and apperception. Or we could link him with Spinozistic *conatus* and the Schopenhauerian will. Or, as a rationalist, he falls into the bin with Aquinas (who is himself most conveniently isolated as a rationalist if you employ the essentializing as against the proportional strategy, stressing what he added rather than what he retained). Many arguments seem

to hinge about the fact that there is an unverbalized disagreement as to the choice between these strategies. The same man, for instance, who might employ the essentializing strategy in proclaiming Aquinas as a rationalist, taking as the significant factor in Aquinas' philosophy his additions to rationalism rather than considering this as an ingredient in a faith philosophy, might object to the bracketing of Aquinas and Freud (here shifting to the proportional strategy, as he pointed out the totally different materials with which Aquinas surrounded his rational principle).

2. We may distinguish between a public and universal motive. In so far as one acts in a certain way because of his connections with a business or party, he would act from a public motive. His need of response to a new glandular stimulation at adolescence, on the other hand, would arise regardless of social values, and in that sense would be at once private and universal. The particular forms in which he expressed this need would, of course, be channelized in accordance with public or social factors.

3. Perhaps, to avoid confusion, I should call attention to the fact that symbolic in this context is being used differently by me from its use in the expression "symbolic action." If a man crosses a street, it is a practical act. If he writes a book about crossings—crossing streets, bridges, oceans, etc.—that is a symbolic act. Symbolic, as used in the restricted sense (in contrast with free association), would refer to the imputation of an absolute meaning to a crossing, a meaning that I might impute even before reading the book in question. Against this, I should maintain: one can never know what a crossing means, in a specific book, until he has studied his tie-up with other imagery in that particular book.

4. Maybe the kind of forgetting that is revealed by psychoanalysis could, within this frame, be better characterized as an incomplete forgetting. That is, whereas table, for instance, acquires an absolute and emotionally neutral meaning, as a name merely for a class of objects, by a merging of all the contexts involving the presence of a table, a table becomes symbolic, or a *double entendre,* or more than table, when some particular informative context is more important than the others. That is, when table, as used by the poet, has overtones of, let us say, *one* table at which his mother worked when he was a child. In this way the table, its food, and the cloth may become surrogates for the mother, her breasts, and her apron. And incest awe may become merged with "mustn't touch" injunctions, stemming from attempts to keep the child from meddling with the objects on the table. In a dream play by Edmund Wilson, *The Crime in the Whistler Room,* there are two worlds of plot, with the characters belonging in the one world looking upon those in the other as dead, and the hero of this living world taking a dream shape as werewolf. The worlds switch back and forth, depending upon the presence or removal of a gateleg table. In this instance I think we should not be far wrong in attributing some such content as the above to the table when considering it as a fulcrum upon which the structure of the plot is swung.

5. It is wrong, I think, to consider Freud's general picture as that of an individual psychology. Adler's start from the concept of ego compensation fits

this description par excellence. But Freud's is a family psychology. He has offered a critique of the family, though it is the family of neo-patriarch. It is interesting to watch Freud, in his *Group Psychology and the Analysis of the Ego,* frankly shifting between the primacy of group psychology, changing his mind as he debates with himself in public and leaves in his pages the record of his fluctuations, frankly stated as such. Finally, he compromises by leaving both, drawing individual psychology from the role of the monopolistic father, and group psychology from the roles of the sons, deprived of sexual gratification by the monopolistic father, and banded together for their mutual benefit. But note that the whole picture is that of a family albeit of a family in which the woman is a mere passive object of male wealth.

6. Or you might put it this way: Rebirth would require a killing of the old self. Such symbolic suicide, to be complete, would require a snapping of the total ancestral line (as being an integral aspect of one's identity). Hence, a tendency for the emancipatory crime to become sexually ambivalent. Freud's patriarchal emphasis leads to an overstress upon father-rejection as a basic cause rather than as a by-product of conversion (the Kierkegaard earthquake, that was accompanied by a changed attitude toward his father). Suicide, to be thorough, would have to go farther, and the phenomena of identity revealed in totemism might require the introduction of matricidal ingredients also. Freud himself, toward the end of *Totem and Taboo,* gives us an opening wedge by stating frankly, "In this evolution I am at a loss to indicate the place of the great maternal deities who perhaps everywhere preceded the paternal deities . . . ." This same patriarchal emphasis also reinforces the Freudian tendency to treat social love as a mere sublimation of balked male sexual appetite, whereas a more matriarchal concern, with the Madonna and Child relationship, would suggest a place for affection as a primary biological motivation. Not even a naturalistic account of motivation would necessarily require reinforcement from the debunking strategy (in accordance with which the real motives would be incipient perversions, and social motives as we know them would be but their appearance, or censored disguise).

7. Might not the sacrificial figure (as parent, king, or god) also at times derive from no resistance or vindictiveness whatsoever, but be the recipient of the burden simply through "having stronger shoulders, better able to bear it"? And might the choice of guilty scapegoats (such as a bad father) be but a secondary development for accommodating this socialization of a loss to the patterns of legality?

8. Dream has its opposite, nightmare; prayer has its opposite, oath. Charts merely vary—in scope and relevance. In "Kubla Khan," automatically composed during an opium dream, the dream ingredient is uppermost. In "The Ancient Mariner," the prayer ingredient is uppermost. In "Dejection" and "The Pains of Sleep," the chart ingredient is uppermost: here Coleridge is explicitly discussing his situation.

9. Those who stress form of this sort, as against content, usually feel that they are concerned with judgments of excellence as against judgments of the merely representative. Yet, just as a content category such as the Oedipus

complex is neutral, i.e., includes both good and bad examples of its kind, so does a form category, such as sonnet or iambic pentameter, include both good and bad examples if its kind. In fact, though categories or classifications may be employed for evaluative purposes, they should be themselves nonevaluative, Apples is a neutral, nonevaluative class, including firm apples and rotten ones. Categories that are in themselves evaluative are merely circular arguments—disguised ways of saying "this is good because it is good." The orthodox strategy of disguise is to break the statement into two parts, such as: "This is good because it has form; and form is good." The lure behind the feeling that the miracle of evaluation can be replaced by a codified scientific routing of evaluation seems to get its backing from the hope that a concept of quality can be matched by a number. The terms missing may be revealed by a diagram, thus:

Quantity . . . . Number
  Weight . . . . Pound
  Length . . . . Foot
  Duration . . . . Hour
Quality . . . . (   )
  Excellence . . . . (   )
  Inferiority . . . . (   )

Often the strategy of concealment is accomplished by an ambiguity, as the critic sometimes uses the "poetry" to designate good poetry, and sometimes uses it to designate "poetry, any poetry, good, bad, or indifferent." I do, however, strongly sympathize with the formalists, as against the sociologists, when the sociologist treats poetry simply as a kind of haphazard sociological survey—a report about world-conditions that often shows commendable intuitive insight but is handicapped by a poor methodology of research and controls.

10. There are styles of cure, shifting from age to age, because each novelty becomes a commonplace, so that the patient integrates his conflict with the ingredients of the old cure itself, thus making them part of his obsession. Hence, the need for a new method of jolting. Thus, I should imagine that a patient who had got into difficulties after mastering the Freudian technique would present the most obstinate problems for a Freudian cure. He would require some step beyond Freud. The same observation would apply to shifting styles in a poetry and philosophy, when considered as cures, as the filling of a need.

11. I am indebted to Norbert Gutermann for the term "selfacceptance" and to William S. Knickerbocker for the term "rejection of rejection."

Louise Bogan

SOME NOTES ON POPULAR AND UNPOPULAR ART

Will folk art save us from creative and moral aridity if we can find and use it? The reiterated insinuation that formal art is fraudulent because it is difficult to understand and makes no effort to appeal to the majority—that it is, in fact, somehow treasonable to mankind's higher purposes and aims—is a typical bourgeois notion that has been around for a long time. That formal art cannot be put to any immediate use also lays it open to materialist denigration. The conviction that the simple is straight and pure and true, while the complex is concocted and double-dealing, is a partially moral one. It is a conviction which shares room, in the minds and emotions of many people, with an unconscious yearning for a lost rural world. In America, just enough time has elapsed since real urbanization set in for this yearning to roll up to its present proportions and to have acquired its present rationalizations. In spite of these desires and beliefs of the middle-class subconscious, the fact remains that no civilization has ever produced a literature out of folk (either current or revived) alone. The formal artist cannot be outlawed. The whole question is muddled in the extreme. Let us examine it with as much detachment as possible.

It is true that the formal artist, at least twice within living

Reprinted from Louise Bogan, "Some Notes on Popular and Unpopular Art" in *Selected Criticism: Prose, Poetry* (New York: Noonday, 1955), 238–51.

memory, has succeeded in getting past modern barriers to a real folk tradition, and that remarkable literature has resulted in both cases from the intersection of the formal with the folk line. Lorca's genius was ignited in the most brilliant way by Flamenco tradition, and Yeats was fortified and refreshed from the beginning by his close knowledge of the Irish peasant. Both these poets received the experience of poetry still attached to music, at the improvisatory stage; and of an audience creatively involved (actually listeners, as distinguished from mere readers) in what they as poets produced.

But the fact is that only the most abnormal situations, political or otherwise, kept these two folk traditions alive so late in an industrial and urbanized Europe. The turning toward the folk, at the end of the eighteenth century, was not only preindustrial but prerevolutionary; and the same sort of ferments were present in Yeats' Ireland and Lorca's Spain. The current attempts in America to get back to primitive material are natural enough, but they are different. They are the desire of a far from revolutionary population to get back to some earlier fun, as well as some earlier integrity. Certainly the material is there. We can trace the line of the American folk song through the ballads of English, Irish, and Scotch origin (broken away from their original scene and transformed) through the work songs of all kinds (sea chanteys, songs of the plantation and the cattlerange), the hymns and spirituals, up to the beginning of town life. Then the culmination of the American folk song appears. Stephen Foster, the untrained and greatly gifted writer of "popular songs," managed to express fully the emotions common during this period of transition. On the one hand, through him the loneliness as well as the rough gaiety of a primitive society found its voice. On the other, Foster gave expression to something quite new: an emotion which was to become increasingly persistent in the American spirit—the sense of profound nostalgia for an already disappearing nonurban way of life. The strong sentimentalization of Foster by his modern audience proceeds from the holdover of this crucial though hidden nostalgia into our own time. Clearly, he was the end of one kind of American folk, the point beyond which no unadulterated development of his kind of material was possible.

We begin to get the production of the urbanized folk after the hymns and marching songs of the Civil War. The railroads building and having been built, we get the railroad songs. The cities once made, we get the hybrid genteel, and the barbershop ballads, and, what is more vivid and interesting, the songs of the "underworld": brothel, saloon, dope-joint, and prison. The earlier tradition fell into neglect as the way back to the farm became more and more closed. It was rediscovered and refurbished, along with hooked rugs and pine blanket chests, when the 1914 War broke up American Victorian and aroused, in some not quite understandable fashion, the middle-class enthusiasm for the American antique. The folk tradition, as a result, has become thoroughly "bourgeoizified." At present there is no way for the artist to get at it, for it has been dragged into a region where nothing living or nutritious for his purposes exists. It can be looked at and listened to, admired and imitated; but it cannot at the present time be called upon to do any truly important task. Only a writer thoroughly immersed in middle-class values, and soaked through and through with the sentimentality of the middle, could for a moment believe that this mummified and genteelized folk could contribute any spark of life to his purposes.

The English and French tradition of town-folk (with a head start of some forty or fifty years of true industrialism over the United States) channeled itself into the music hall. "The supreme embodiment of the surviving character of the English working people," writes one chronicler of the English nineteenth-century scene, "was the music hall. . . . Springing spontaneously out of the sing-song of the upper tavern room and the old out-of-door gardens of the artisans of the pastoral past, it became for a space of time a British institution. Its morality was to make the best of a bad job; its purpose to make everyone free and easy. . . ." The authenticity of this institution, created by the first articulate development of urban folk for its own enjoyment, soon impressed itself on the artists and writers of the time. Through it, they were able to skirt the middle, find excitement and restorative energy, and make a point of contact with "life." But the music hall decayed. It was based on that period of "proletarian" existence when the workers were stiffly encased in the tradition of knowing their place and imitating their betters. This tradition exploded in 1918; and we hear Eliot making a final tribute to Marie Lloyd, with added gloomy prognostications for the future:

> . . . It was her capacity for expressing the soul of a people that made her unique. . . . It was her understanding of the people and sympathy with them, and the people's recognition of the fact that she embodied the virtues that they most genuinely respected in private life, that raised her to the position she occupied at her death. I have called her the expressive figure of the lower classes. There is no such expressive figure for any other classes. The middle classes have no such idol: the middle classes are morally corrupt . . .

Eliot then goes on to express his fear that, with the disappearance of the music hall, and "the encroachment of the cheap and rapid-breeding cinema, the lower classes will drop to the same state of protoplasm as the bourgeoisie," and, moreover, when this state has overcome them, that they may die off from sheer boredom! This essay, written in 1923, closes with words of deep dismay as to the possibility of the hastening of this general disintegration by the development of another mechanical device for transmitting entertainment—the radio.

Eliot underestimated his "lower classes." The music hall disappeared only after it had reached a high point of breadth and elegance. Folk expression continually runs toward this elegance, contrary to the *idée reçue* of its being by necessity clumsy and "vulgar." (And this elegance is not to be confused with the empty slickness of the *revue* kind.) But as a rather stuffy set of prewar conventions broke, the urban crowd shifted toward a freer, less imitative and reverent habit of mind and manner. Something new began immediately; persistent energy released itself into new forms and new media.

The energy is now at a more primitive level than formerly; these shifts go back and forth, as this current of urban life or that is released and breaks; many reasons requiring specialized attention are here involved. But the fact remains that American folk has never been more vigorous than at this moment. In "hot jazz," words are attached to music, as in all primitive states of poetry and music. Improvisation (the "lick") is in every talented performer's power. The rhythm is the important matter; the music has all the harmonic tricks under control with which to surround and embellish the beat. The various mechanical devices which Eliot feared and deplored have served, as a matter of fact, to aid the development and dissemination of this folk art. The folk now gets exactly what it wants to listen to. If the radio does not give it what it needs in sufficient quantity, people have their records and juke boxes, and, of course, the live performers. The vigor of folk at present is shown by its tendency to raid over into "classical" and bring back whatever tunes please it. The juke-box repertoire is a thing in itself: there the hymn tune (disguised) shares popularity with the crooned ballad and with certain holdovers from the open spaces of the past. Compared to the songs of the upright piano and sheet music era, even the most naive songs are less awkward and saccharine, more vitalized. And the imitation "folk song," such as the really remarkable "Blues in the Night," has taken on a finish which always characterizes folk in a good creative period *of its own*.

It is interesting to note that at this particular stage, "popular" interest in accident, sudden death, and the morbid in general (unlike American songs of an earlier day) has very nearly disappeared, along with the "topical song," that sister to the broadsheet.

A proposition could be drawn up:

Folk crosses formal art:

1. When folk has reached a moment of comparative breadth and elegance (when it can express anything, from the grotesque through emotion and satire, well).

2. When formal art has become easy and secular enough to recognize just where folk lies; and having located folk, understands what is happening there.

A long period of time must elapse before, in America, the demands of this proposition can be fulfilled. But Eliot's fears were unjustified; just as the present middle-class hope that L. Stokowski can be crossed with Disney, or some genteel poet with the songs of pioneering backwoodsmen, is at once previous and misplaced.

Let us now take a brief glance at the American intellectual. The intellectual is a middle-class product; if he is not born into the class he must soon insert himself into it, in order to exist. He is the fine nervous flower of the bourgeoisie. His task, ideally, would be the close critical observation of the field in which he stands, while keeping his attention alert for new movement in the landscape as a whole. That the intellectual fails in this job is one reason for the wholesale mixture of genres, the unrebuked mistakes of prize committees, publishers, etc., the general insolence of entrepreneurs—in fact the general failure to understand what is going on which marks the small remaining section of American life still interested in literature.

The intellectual, being nervous, is subject to all the floating airs of modern religion (present in quantity, no matter how fogged and misted into the semblance of something else). One must not forget that religious enthusiasm (and intolerance) has always been inextricably mixed with every materialist idea; has been a concomitant of all material push since Calvin. Intellectuals range through the finest gradations of kind and quality: from those who are merely educated neurotics, usually with strong hidden reactionary tendencies, through mediocrities of all kinds, to men of real brains and sensibility, more or less stiffened into various respectabilities or substitutes for respectability. The number of Ignorant Specialists is large. The number of hysterics and compulsives is also large. It is natural that the truly sensitive intellectual should have spiritual needs;

for such a person the necessity for those moments in life when one is forced to see reality without wraps and unrationalized is strong. This necessity leads to a real breakthrough into maturity on the part of some individuals. For the less sensitive, the spiritual necessity hardly exists; they require not steadying insight but emotional outlet. It is in this class that we find the hot-gospellers, the morally pretentious, the reformers, and the seekers of closed systems of salvation. These men and women are not entirely the products of an imperfect culture (for the type appeared in quantity in France in the nineteenth century) but of a culture somehow blocked and mixed; and of the impact of this curious situation upon natures more simply constituted than they themselves suppose. Flaubert wrote down an approximation of the type in *Bouvard et Pécuchet*. He gave the two simple-minded copyists a set of manias which is still complete for the dislocated middle-class mind of our time; manias ranging from the collecting of antiques to an absorption in various forms of science and politics. These two prototypes of the middle-class yearner with a few retouches could represent not only the modern lecture-listening audience, but many of "the experts who tend the complicated machinery of modern civilization."

One characteristic of the Bouvard-Pécuchet sort of enthusiasm is the violent repudiation after violent interest of one craze after another when the satiation point is reached. The revulsion shown by the intellectual toward the artist, during recent years, resembles this sort of compensating tendency. The too-great emphasis of emotion and hope placed upon the artist in the preceding period is lifted and placed at an opposite point. The D. H. Lawrence, Proust, Hart Crane kind of semiworship went over, for a time, to Malraux; and then became transformed into something else. The very complexity of the artist's equipment became as much a target for the subsequent badgering and denigration as the nonmaterial quality of his aims. It is moral blame of the most childish kind that we find most frequently expressed; and real puzzlement, also at a childish level. The atmosphere of former religious paroxysms and squabblings returns; the old fights between established religion and the sects and between the sects themselves; the old tiresome yet dangerous extremes of the persecutory centuries.

Now, one would think that the unstable intellectual should stand out against all these moral acrobatics and tergiversations: if not as judge, at least as arbiter. If he cannot remain firm, he should at least be in another part of the field, out of the melee and ahead of it. But as things turn out, he is either squarely in the mix-up, name-calling with the best or making motions of advancing, the while he has managed rapidly to retreat into something truly comforting in the way of preCopernican scholasticism, or has made a full flight back to Aristotle. And if he is of no real use in reconciling embattled sects, perhaps he could do a little simple journeyman's work in keeping entrepreneurism in its place. But here he rather fails us, too.

At this point it is necessary to remember that the middle class has produced, at the expense of much time and effort, a whole literature of its own. Its own writers, bred out of its own bone and flesh, educated in its own schools and amenable to its own scheme of manners and custom, have fanned out into the middle region; adapted in every way to express the middle intellect, temperament, grasp of reality, powers of analysis and emotion. Some of these poets, novelists, critics, biographers, and belletrists were born middle; some either rose or sank to where they at length find themselves. The complicated but smoothly oiled machinery of the publishing business, the general run of reviewers, the committees giving out literary awards, the more benumbed mass of academics: all these agents function, for the most part (and changing the figure), inside the same structure. During certain short periods, certain wild individuals stay outside and throw rocks, but since these intransigents tend to disappear for long intervals, the easiest supposition is that they are absorbed. And the periods of almost complete absorption present a very amusing spectacle indeed. These are the times when the book sections produce, week after week, month after month, serious judgments on books, but when everything judged and the judges themselves are cut out of the same piece of medium material. The commodity books are being dealt with by the commodity critics—a spectacle which would be purely funny if there were not elements of rather tragic irony in it.

The intellectual should at least know the difference between kinds, and have the courage to speak up when matters get really out of hand. He should make some admonishing gesture when a particularly startling piece of mutual aid comes through. He should know how the literary mechanism works: the way blurb-writing and prize-giving, journalists and literary impresarios engage with each other. He should be able to sense, watching the open pulls and twitches given reputations, all the subterranean maneuvering which must go on so that certain effects are produced at eye-level. What about the distinguished specialists who write blurbs for dustjackets? Is this a harmless bit of fun, or a plan to get around the subsequent remarks of the book reviewer? What about the American prize committee (situated rather disadvantageously, one might suppose, for anyone not a journalist, in a school of journalism) which, having ignored brilliant talent, young and old, falls back ever again upon old standbys? What about the extra-literary influences which manage, from time to time, to bring to laudatory view a book of gibberish? What about certain anthologists who teeter on the verge of being members of the vanity press: are all their contributors paid? Who is to deal with these matters but the intellectual?

Meanwhile, the cry rises that poetry has disappeared. This plaint often comes from the dead center, say from the core of the Sunday book section. It rises with particular sharpness during times of cataclysm. The middle wishes poetry to throb, as it were, under the historic processes without a break; to light up ambiguous terrain with continual succeeding flashes of "inspiration." But poetry cannot be counted upon to act as a sort of combination faith-healing and artificial thunder and lightning. Poetry of the lyric order disappears for a century at a time. It shifts. And when the formal line has in some manner been exhausted, the vigor goes back to the base. The middle must put up with what it has: their flabby little songs, their attempts at reviving the "golden" American past; and their more ambitious flights: those attempts to combine autobiography with *post hoc ergo propter hoc* comment on the world situation.

"The function of the great individual is to take up and transform what has been communally produced." For this function one must wait, when the folk material is in a transitional phase—unmalleable and too full of its own rough vigor to be handled, and when "great individuals" seem to be lacking. Even the artist may misjudge the time. In Eliot's "Sweeney Agonistes" and "Fragment of an Agon" the two lines—of formal treatment and "rough" material—are somehow artificially combined; the result cannot really move us. But there are times when the poet can deal with whatever comes to hand. And folk will not always remain ungraspable.

A few notes on the future direction of the poet:

The true hierarchic attitude as exemplified by some "inheritors of Symbolism" (Stefan George and to a lesser degree Valéry and Yeats) seems to be exhausted. George's "willed rationalism toward the antique, his aesthetic and individualist humanism . . . which seeks in the universe the exaltation of man"—this line we have seen warped and corrupted; it now leads nowhere. The lesser task of the poet at present is satire. But satire cannot be asked to bear all of the weight of the diversified and subtle modern spirit. There is another development of this century's early period of aesthetic experiment and moral explanation. This proceeds from Rilke. "In Rilke (as opposed to George)," writes Genevieve Bianquis, already quoted above, "exists the most absolute abandonment to the laws of the inanimate; the need to unknot, to detach the bonds of the individual; the need to love everything, to absorb everything into himself and to absorb himself in all; to channel toward God or toward things all happiness, all sorrow and all emotion." This is the contrast between the will which builds Ages of Faith and the act of faith itself; between compulsion and serenity; arrogance and humility; between the raw act of force and the more complex refusal of force but openness to spiritual power.

The foundation-material is ready for this tendency. The only really usable and incontrovertible modern discoveries are in the spiritual field; and these have their everyday diagnostic and therapeutic uses. Truth has been told, experience undergone, and movement undertaken—"forward" as Eliot says; but this forward has not its old "progressive" connotation. The number of individuals engaged in writing poetry of this order will not be large, and, as is so often the case, may be unseen by their generation. The forms will be kept clear and the tone uninflated. No more rhetoric; no more verbalizing; no more exhortations or elegies or eulogies. No more conscious and affected investigations of dark corridors and deserted strands; no more use of the universe as a backdrop against which one acts out hope or despair. No more dejected sitting about. No more searching nature for an answering mood. . . .

This exploration and movement can go on without having to search out the folk for refreshment. The more complex tasks have been neglected for a long time; attention to them is overdue. Compared to these at once subtle and difficult necessities the reiterated standardized demands of the bourgeois yearner sound incredibly stupid and outdated.

> Is it possible that despite our discoveries and progress, despite our culture, religion and world-wisdom, we still remain on the surface of life? Is it possible that we have even covered this surface which might still have been something, with an incredibly uninteresting stuff which makes it look like drawing-room furniture during the summer holidays?
>
> Yes, it is possible . . .
>
> But if all this is possible . . . then surely, for all the world's sake, something must be done. The first comer, he who has had these disturbing thoughts, must begin to do some of the neglected things; even if he be just anybody, by no means the most suitable person: there is no one else at hand. This young insignificant foreigner, Brigge, will have to sit down in his room five flights up, and write, day and night. Yes, he will have to write; that will be the end of it.

This was written at the beginning of the century; but nothing much seems to have been accomplished. Now that a good deal of the drawing-room furniture lies in ruins, there may be another beginning.

Allen Tate

TENSION IN POETRY

I

Many poems that we ordinarily think of as good poetry—and some, besides, that we neglect—have certain common features that will allow us to invent, for their sharper apprehension, the name of a single quality. I shall call that quality tension. In abstract language, a poetic work has distinct quality as the ultimate effect of the whole, and that whole is the "result" of a configuration of meaning which it is the duty of the critic to examine and evaluate. In setting forth this duty as my present procedure I am trying to amplify a critical approach that I have used on other occasions, without wholly giving up the earlier method, which I should describe as the isolation of the general ideas implicit in the poetic work.

Towards the end of this essay I shall cite examples of "tension," but I shall not say that they exemplify tension only, or that other qualities must be ignored. There are all kinds of poetry, as many as there are good poets, as many even as there are good poems, for poets may be expected to write more than one kind of poetry; and no single critical insight may impute an exclusive validity to any one kind. In all ages there are schools

Reprinted from Allen Tate, "Tension in Poetry," in *Essays of Four Decades* (Chicago: Swallow, 1968), 56–71.

demanding that one sort only be written—their sort: political poetry for the sake of the cause; picturesque poetry for the sake of the home town; didactic poetry for the sake of the parish; even a generalized personal poetry for the sake of the reassurance and safety of numbers. This last I suppose is the most common variety, the anonymous lyricism in which the common personality exhibits its commonness, its obscure yet standard eccentricity, in a language that seems always to be deteriorating; so that today many poets are driven to inventing private languages, or very narrow ones, because public speech has become heavily tainted with mass feeling.

Mass language is the medium of "communication," and its users are less interested in bringing to formal order what is sometimes called the "affective state" than in arousing that state.

> Once you have said that everything is One it is obvious that literature is the same as propaganda; once you have said that no truth can be known apart from the immediate dialectical process of history it is obvious that all contemporary artists must prepare the same fashionplate. It is clear too that the One is limited in space as well as time, and the no less Hegelian Fascists are right in saying that all art is patriotic.

What Mr. William Empson calls patriotic poetry sings not merely in behalf of the State; you will find it equally in a ladylike lyric and in much of the political poetry of our time. It is the poetry of the mass language, very different from the "language of the people" which interested the late W. B. Yeats. For example:

> What from the splendid dead
> We have inherited—
> Furrows sweet to the grain, and the weed subdued—
> See now the slug and the mildew plunder.
> Evil does overwhelm
> The larkspur and the corn;
> We have seen them go under.

From this stanza by Miss Millay we infer that her splendid ancestors made the earth a good place that has somehow gone bad—and you get the reason from the title: "Justice Denied in Massachusetts." How Massachusetts could cause a general desiccation, why (as we are told in a footnote to the poem) the execution of Sacco and Vanzetti should have anything to do with the rotting of the crops, it is never made clear. These lines are mass language: they arouse an affective state in one set of terms, and suddenly an object quite unrelated to those terms gets the benefit of it; and this effect, which is usually achieved, as I think it is here, without conscious effort, is sentimentality. Miss Millay's poem was admired when it first appeared about ten years ago, and is no doubt still admired, by persons to whom it communicates certain feelings about social justice, by persons for whom the lines are the occasion of feelings shared by them and the poet. But if you do not share those feelings, as I happen not to share them in the images of desiccated nature, the lines and even the entire poem are impenetrably obscure.

I am attacking here the fallacy of communication in poetry. (I am not attacking social justice.) It is no less a fallacy in the writing of poetry than of critical theory. The critical doctrine fares ill the further back you apply it; I suppose one may say—if one wants a landmark—that it began to prosper after 1798; for on the whole nineteenth-century English verse is a poetry of communication. The poets were trying to use verse to convey ideas and feelings that they secretly thought could be better conveyed by science (consult Shelley's *Defence*), or by what today we call, in a significantly bad poetic phrase, the Social Sciences. Yet possibly because the poets believed the scientists to be tough, and the poets joined the scientists in thinking the poets tender, the poets stuck to verse. It may scarcely be said that we change this tradition of poetic futility by giving it a new name, Social Poetry. May a poet hope to deal more adequately with sociology than with physics? If he seizes upon either at the level of scientific procedure, has he not abdicated his position as poet?

At a level of lower historical awareness than that exhibited by Mr. Edmund Wilson's later heroes of the Symbolist school, we find the kind of verse that I have been quoting, verse long ago intimidated by the pseudo-rationalism of the Social Sciences. This sentimental intimidation has been so complete that, however easy the verse looked on the page, it gave up all claim to sense. (I assume here what I cannot now demonstrate, that Miss Millay's poem is obscure but that Donne's "Second Anniversarie" is not.) As another example of this brand of obscurity I have selected at random a nineteenth-century lyric, "The Vine," by James Thomson:

> The wine of love is music,
>   And the feast of love is song:
> When love sits down to banquet,
>   Love sits long:
>
> Sits long and rises drunken,
>   But not with the feast and the wine;
> He reeleth with his own heart,
>   That great rich Vine.

The language here appeals to an existing affective state; it has no coherent meaning either literally or in terms of ambiguity or implication; it may be wholly replaced by any of its several paraphrases, which are already latent in our minds. One of these is the confused image of a self-intoxicating man-about-town. Now good poetry can bear the closest literal examination of every phrase, and is its own safeguard against our irony. But the more closely we examine this lyric, the more obscure it becomes; the more we trace the implications of the imagery, the denser the confusion. The imagery adds nothing to the general idea that it tries to sustain; it even deprives that idea of the dignity it has won at the hands of a long succession of better poets going back, I suppose, to Guinizelli:

> *Al cor gentil ripara sempre Amore*
> *Come alla selva augello in la verdura . . .*

What I want to make clear is the particular kind of failure, not the degree, in a certain kind of poetry. Were we interested in degrees we might give comfort to the nineteenth century by citing lines from John Cleveland or Abraham Cowley, bad lyric verse no better than "The Vine," written in an age that produced some of the greatest English poetry. Here are some lines from Cowley's "Hymn: to Light," a hundred-line inventory of some of the offices performed by the subject in a universe that still seems to be on the whole Ptolemaic; I should not care to guess the length the poem might have reached under the Copernican system. Here is one of the interesting duties of light:

> Nor amidst all these Triumphs does thou scorn
> The humble glow-worn to adorn,
> And with those living spangles gild,
> (O Greatness without Pride) the Bushes of the Field.

Again:

> The Violet, springs little Infant, stands,
> Girt in thy purple Swadling-bands:
> On the fair Tulip thou dost dote;
> Thou cloath'st it in a gay and party-colour'd Coat.

This, doubtless, is metaphysical poetry; however bad the lines may be—they are pretty bad—they have no qualities, bad or good, in common with "The Vine." Mr. Ransom has given us, in a remarkable essay, "Shakespeare at Sonnets,"[1] (*The World's Body,* 1938), an excellent description of this kind of poetry: "The impulse to metaphysical poetry . . . consists in committing the feelings in the case . . . to their determination within the elected figure." That is to say, in metaphysical poetry the logical order is explicit; it must be coherent; the imagery by which it is sensuously embodied must have at least the appearance of logical determinism: perhaps the appearance only, because the varieties of ambiguity and contradiction possible beneath the logical surface are endless, as Mr. Empson has demonstrated in his elucidation of Marvell's "The Garden." Here it is enough to say that the development of imagery by extension, its logical determinants being an Ariadne's thread that the poet will not permit us to lose, is the leading feature of the poetry called metaphysical.

But to recognize it is not to evaluate it; and I take it that Mr. Ransom was giving us a true Aristotelian definition of a *genus,* in which the identification of a type does not compel us to discern the implied values. Logical extension of imagery is no doubt the key to the meaning of Donne's "A Valediction: Forbidding Mourning"; it may equally initiate inquiry into the ludicrous failure of "Hymn: to Light," to which I now return.

Although "The Vine" and "Hymn: to Light" seem to me equally bad poetry, Cowley's failure is somewhat to be preferred; its negative superiority lies in a firmer use of the language. There is no appeal to an affective state; the leading statement can be made perfectly explicit: God is light, and light is life. The poem is an analytical proposition exhibiting the properties inherent in the major term; that is, exhibiting as much of the universe as Cowley could get around to before he wearied of logical extension. But I think it is possible to infer that good poetry could have been written in Cowley's language; and we know that it was. Every term, even the verbs converted into nouns, denotes an object, and in the hands of a good poet would be amenable to controlled distortions of literal representation. But here the distortions are uncontrolled. Everything is in this language that a poet needs except the poetry, or the imagination, or what I shall presently illustrate under the idea of tension.

I have called "Hymn: to Light" an analytical proposition. That is the form in which the theme must have appeared to Cowley's mind; that is to say, simple analysis of the term God gave him, as it gave everybody else in Christendom, the proposition: God is light. (Perhaps, under Neo-Platonic influence, the prime Christian symbol, as Professor Fletcher and others have shown in reducing to their sources the powers of the Three Blessed Ladies of *The Divine Comedy.*) But in order to write his poem Cowley had to develop the symbol by synthetic accretion, by adding to light properties not inherent in its simple analysis:

The Violet, springs little Infant, stands,
    Girt in thy purple Swadling-bands . . .

The image, such as it is, is an addition to the central figure of light, an assertion of a hitherto undetected relation among the objects, light, diapers, and violets—a miscellany that I recommend to the consideration of Mr. E. E. Cummings, who could get something out of it that Cowley did not intend us to get. If you will think again of "The Vine," you will observe that Thomson permits, in the opposite direction, an equal license with the objects *de*noted by his imagery, with the unhappy results that we have already seen.

"The Vine" is a failure in denotation. "Hymn: to Light" is a failure in connotation. The language of "The Vine" lacks objective content. Take "music" and "song" in the first two lines; the context does not allow us to apprehend the terms in extension; that is, there is no reference to objects that we may distinguish as "music" and "song"; the wine of love could have as well been song, its feast music. In "Hymn: to Light," a reduction to their connotations of the terms *violet, swadling-bands,* and *light* (the last being represented by the pronoun thou) yields a clutter of images that may be unified only if we forget the firm denotations of the terms. If we are going to receive as valid the infancy of the violet, we must ignore the metaphor that conveys it, for the metaphor renders the violet absurd; by ignoring the diaper, and the two terms associated with it, we cease to read the passage, and begin for ourselves the building up of acceptable denotations for the terms of the metaphor.

Absurd: but on what final ground I call these poems absurd I cannot state as a principle. I appeal to the reader's experience, and invite him to form a judgment of my own. It is easy enough to say, as I shall say in detail in a moment, that good poetry is a unity of all the meanings from the furthest extremes of intension and extension. Yet our recognition of the action of this unified meaning is the gift of experience, of culture, of, if you will, our humanism. Our powers of discrimination are not deductive powers, though they may be aided by them; they wait rather upon the cultivation of our total human powers, and they represent special application of those powers to a single medium of experience—poetry.

I have referred to a certain kind of poetry as the embodiment of the fallacy of communication: it is a poetry that communicates the affective state, which (in terms of language) results from the irresponsible denotations of words. There is a vague grasp of the "real" world. The history of this fallacy, which is as old as poetry but which towards the end of the eighteenth century began to dominate not only poetry, but other arts as well—its history would probably show that the poets gave up the language of denotation to the scientists, and kept for themselves a continually thinning flux of peripheral connotations. The companion fallacy, to which I can give only the literal name, the fallacy of mere denotation, I have also illustrated from Cowley: this is the poetry which contradicts our most developed human insights insofar as it fails to use and direct the rich connotation with which language has been informed by experience.

II

We return to the inquiry set for this discussion: to find out whether there is not a more central achievement in poetry than that represented by either of the extreme examples that we have been considering. I proposed as descriptive of that achievement, the term *tension*. I am using the term not as a general metaphor, but as a special one, derived from lopping the prefixes off the logical terms *ex*tension and *in*tension. What I am saying, of course, is that the meaning of poetry is its "tension," the full organized body of all the extension and intension that we can find in it. The remotest figurative significance that we can derive does not invalidate the extensions of the literal statement. Or we may begin with the literal statement and by stages develop the complications of metaphor: at every stage we may pause to state the meaning so far apprehended, and at every stage the meaning will be coherent.

The meanings that we select at different points along the infinite line between extreme intension and extreme extension will vary with our personal "drive" or "interest" or "approach":

the Platonist will tend to stay pretty close to the end of the line where extension, and simple abstraction of the object into a universal, is easiest, for he will be a fanatic in morals or some kind of works, and will insist upon the shortest way with what will ever appear to him the dissenting ambiguities at the intensive end of the scale. The Platonist (I do not say that his opponent is the Aristotelian) might decide that Marvell's "To His Coy Mistress" recommends immoral behavior to young men, in whose behalf he would try to suppress the poem. That, of course, would be one "true" meaning of "To His Coy Mistress," but it is a meaning that the full tension of the poem will not allow us to entertain exclusively. For we are compelled, since it is there, to give equal weight to an intensive meaning so rich that, without contradicting the literal statement of the lover-mistress convention, it lifts that convention into an insight into one phase of the human predicament—the conflict of sensuality and asceticism.

I should like to quote now, not from Marvell, but a stanza from Donne that I hope will reinforce a little what I have just said and connect it with some earlier remarks.

> Our two soules therefore, which are one,
>   Though I must goe, endure not yet
> A breach, but an expansion,
>   Like gold to aiery thinnesse beate.

Here Donne brings together the developing imagery of twenty lines under the implicit proposition: the unity of two lovers' souls is a nonspatial entity, and is therefore indivisible. That, I believe, is what Mr. John Crowe Ransom would call the logic of the passage, it is the abstract form of its extensive meaning. Now the interesting feature here is the logical contradiction of embodying the unitary, nonspatial soul in a spatial image: the malleable gold is a plane whose surface can always be extended mathematically by one half towards infinity; the souls are this infinity. The finite image of the gold, in extension, logically contradicts the intensive meaning (infinity) which it conveys; but it does not invalidate that meaning. We have seen that Cowley compelled us to ignore the denoted diaper in order that we might take seriously the violet which it pretended to swathe. But in Donne's "A Valediction: Forbidding Mourning" the clear denotation of the gold contains, by intension, the full meaning of the passage. If we reject the gold, we reject the meaning, for the meaning is wholly absorbed into the image of the gold. Intension and extension are here one, and they enrich each other.

Before I leave this beautiful object, I should like to notice two incidental features in further proof of Donne's mastery. "Expansion"—a term denoting an abstract property common to many objects, perhaps here one property of a gas: it expands visibly the quality of the beaten gold.

> . . . endure not yet
> A breach . . .

But if the lovers' souls are the formidable, inhuman entity that we have seen, are they not superior to the contingency of a breach? Yes and no: both answers are true answers; for by means of the sly "yet" Donne subtly guards himself against our irony, which would otherwise be quick to scrutinize the extreme metaphor. The lovers have not endured a breach, but they are simple, miserable human beings, and they may quarrel tomorrow.[2]

Now all this meaning and more, and it is all one meaning, is embedded in that stanza: I say more because I have not exhausted the small fraction of significance that my limited powers have permitted me to see. For example, I have not discussed the rhythm, which is of the essential meaning; I have violently isolated four lines from the meaning of the whole poem. Yet, fine as it is, I do not think the poem the greatest poetry; perhaps only very little of Donne makes that grade, or of anybody else. Donne offers many examples of tension in imagery, easier for the expositor than greater passages in Shakespeare.

But convenience of elucidation is not a canon of criticism. I wish now to introduce other kinds of instance, and to let them stand for us as sorts of Arnoldish touchstones to the perfection that poetic statement has occasionally reached. I do not know what bearing my comment has had, or my touchstones may have, upon the larger effects of poetry or upon long poems. The long poem is partly a different problem. I have of necessity confined both commentary and illustration to the slighter effects that seemed to me commensurate with certain immediate qualities of language. For, in the long run, whatever the poet's "philosophy," however wide may be the extension of his meaning—like Milton's Ptolemaic universe in which he didn't believe—by his language shall you know him; the quality of his language is the valid limit of what he has to say.

I have not searched out the quotations that follow: they at once form the documentation and imply the personal bias from which this inquiry has grown. Only a few of the lines will be identified with the metaphysical technique, or, in Mr. Ransom's fine phrase, the metaphysical strategy. Strategy would here indicate the point on the intensive-extensive scale at which the poet deploys his resources of meaning. The metaphysical poet as a rationalist begins at or near the extensive or denoting end of the line; the romantic or Symbolist poet at the other, intensive end; and each by a straining feat of the imagination tries to push his meanings as far as he can towards the opposite end, so as to occupy the entire scale. I have offered one good and one bad example of the metaphysical strategy, but only defective examples of the Symbolist, which I cited as fallacies of mass language: Thomson was using language at its mass level, unhappily ignorant of the need to embody his connotations in a rational order of thought. (I allude here also, and in a quite literal sense, to Thomson's personal unhappiness, as well as to the excessive pessimism and excessive optimism of other poets of his time.) The great Symbolist poets, from Rimbaud to Yeats, have heeded this necessity of reason. It would be a hard task to choose between the two strategies, the Symbolist and the metaphysical; both at their best are great, and both are incomplete.

These touchstones, I believe, are not poetry of the extremes, but poetry of the center: poetry of tension, in which the "strategy" is diffused into the unitary effect.

Ask me no more whither doth hast
The Nightingale when *May* is past:
For in your sweet dividing throat
She winters, and keeps warm her note.

O thou Steeled Cognizance whose leap commits
The agile precincts of the lark's return . . .

That time of year thou mayst in me behold
When yellow leaves, or none, or few do hang
Upon those boughs which shake against the cold,
Bare ruined choirs where late the sweet birds sang.

Beauty is but a flower
Which wrinkles will devour;
Brightness falls from the air,
Queens have died young and fair,
Dust hath closed Helen's eye.
I am sick, I must die.
    Lord, have mercy upon us!

And then may chance thee to repent
The time that thou hast lost and spent
    To cause thy lovers sigh and swoon;
Then shalt thou know beauty but lent,
And wish and want as I have done.

We have lingered in the chambers of the sea
By seagirls wreathed with seaweed red and brown
Till human voices wake us and we drown.

I am of Ireland
And the Holy Land of Ireland
And time runs on, cried she.
Come out of charity
And dance with me in Ireland.

And my poor fool is hanged! No, no, no life!
Why should a dog, a horse, a rat, have life
And thou no breath at all? Thou'lt come no more,
Never, never, never, never, never!—
Pray you undo this button; thank you, sir.—
Do you see this? Look on her,—look,—her lips,—
Look there, look there!

'Tis madness to resist or blame
The force of angry heavens flame:
    And, if we would speak true,
    Much to the Man is due,
Who, from his private Gardens, where
He liv'd reserved and austere,
    As if his highest plot
    To plant the Bergamot,
Could by industrious Valour climbe
To ruin the great Work of Time,
    And cast the Kingdome old
    Into another Mold.

Cover her face; mine eyes dazzle; she died young.

III

There are three more lines that I wish to look at: a terzina from *The Divine Comedy.* I know little of either Dante or his language; yet I have chosen as my final instance of tension—the instance itself will relieve me of the responsibility of the term—not a great and difficult passage, but only a slight and perfect one. It is from a scene that has always been the delight of the amateur reader of Dante; we can know more about it with less knowledge than about any other, perhaps, in the poem. The damned of the Second Circle are equivocally damned: Paolo and Francesca were illicit lovers but their crime was incontinence, neither adultery nor pandering, the two crimes of sex for which Dante seems to find any real theological reprobation, for they are committed with the intent of injury.

You will remember that when Dante first sees the lovers they are whirling in a high wind, the symbol here of lust. When Francesca's conversation with the poet begins, the wind dies down, and she tells him where she was born, in these lines:

Siede la terra dove nata fui
Sulla marina dove il Po discende
Per aver pace co' seguaci sui.

Courtney Landon renders the tercet:

The town where I was born sits on the shore,
Whither the Po descends to be at peace
Together with the streams that follow him.

But it misses a good deal; it misses the force of *seguaci* by rendering it as a verb. Professor Grandgent translates the third line: "To have peace with its pursuers," and comments: "The tributaries are conceived as chasing the Po down to the sea." Precisely; for if the *seguaci* are merely followers, and not pursuers also, the wonderfully ordered density of this simple passage is sacrificed. For although Francesca has told Dante where she lives, in the most directly descriptive language possible, she has told him more than that. Without the least imposition of strain upon the firmly denoted natural setting, she fuses herself with the river Po near which she was born. By a subtle shift of focus we see the pursued river as Francesca in Hell: the pursuing tributaries are a new visual image for the pursuing winds of lust. A further glance yields even more: as the winds, so the tributaries at once pursue and become one with the pursued; that is to say, Francesca has completely absorbed the substance of her sin—she is the sin; as, I believe it is said, the damned of the *Inferno* are plenary incarnations of the sin that has put them there. The tributaries of the Po are not only the winds of lust by analogy to visual images; they become identified by means of sound:

. . . discende
Per aver pace co' seguaci sui.

The sibilants dominate the line; they are the hissing of the wind.

But in the last line of the preceding tercet Francesca has been grateful that the wind has subsided so that she can be heard—

> *Mentre che il vento, come fa, si tace.*

After the wind has abated, then, we hear in the silence, for the first time, its hiss, in the susurration to the descending Po. The river is thus both a visual and an auditory image, and since Francesca is her sin and her sin is embodied in this image, we are entitled to say that it is a sin that we can both hear and see.

NOTES

1. His rejection of Shakespeare's sonnets seems to be a result of deductive necessity in his premises, or of the courage of mere logic; but the essay contains valuable insights into the operation of the metaphysical "conceit."

2. Mr. F. O. Matthiessen informs me that my interpretation here, which detaches the "yet" from the developing figure, is not the usual one. Mr. Matthiessen refers the phrase to the gold, for which in his view it prepares the way.

Yvor Winters

THE AUDIBLE READING OF POETRY

My title may seem to have in it something of the jargon of the modern Educationist; if so, I am sorry, but I mean to indicate something more than the reading of poetry aloud. I mean to indicate the reading of poetry not merely for the sensual ear, but for the mind's ear as well; yet the mind's ear can be trained only by way of the other, and the matter, practically considered, comes inescapably back to the reading of poetry aloud.

It is also important to learn to read prose aloud, and to hear the prose when one reads it silently. Melville, Gibbon, or Samuel Johnson about equally will be lost on us if we do not so hear it. Yet the readers are numerous who hear nothing when they read silently and who are helpless in their efforts to read aloud: some of them have defective sensibilities; some have merely never been trained; some have been trained by one or another of our psychological educationalists to read in this fashion in order that they may read more rapidly. That they can read more rapidly without hearing, I believe there is no doubt, especially if the matter with which they are dealing is trivial. The trouble is that the activity cannot properly be called reading. Such "readers" are barbarians; literature is closed to them, in spite of the fact that they may think otherwise. The

Reprinted from Yvor Winters, "The Audible Reading of Poetry" in *The Function of Criticism: Problems and Exercises* (Denver: Swallow, 1957), 79–100.

scholar who appears to have read everything has commonly understood very little, and his failure to hear is one of the reasons.

My subject may seem a bit precious and tenuous, but it is neither; it is a matter of the utmost importance to the proper understanding of poetry, a matter fully as important as the philosophical speculation and learned paraphrasing of the New Critics, of whom I am sometimes reputed to be one. It is a matter of which there is almost no understanding at the present time.

Poetry, as nearly as I can understand it, is a statement in words about a human experience, whether the experience be real or hypothetical, major or minor; but it is a statement of a particular kind. Words are symbols for concepts, and the philosopher or scientist endeavors as far as may be to use them with reference to nothing save their conceptual content. Most words, however, connote feelings and perceptions, and the poet, like the writer of imaginative prose, endeavors to use them with reference not only to their denotations but to their connotations as well. Such writers endeavor to communicate not only concepts, arranged, presumably, either in rational order or in an order apprehensible by the rational mind, but the feeling or emotion which the rational content ought properly to arouse. The poet differs from the writer of any kind of prose in that he writes in metrical language. Any good prose is rhythmical up to a certain point: even purely expository prose should be rhythmical to the point that audible obstructions are minimized and meanings are emphasized; the prose of such a writer as Melville is far more elaborately rhythmical than this. But a rhythm which is not controlled by a definite measure will be relatively loose and lacking in subtlety. Poetry and music are based upon definite measure; in this they differ from all other forms of composition.

Rhythm and meter, it should be observed, are quite distinct from each other, in spite of the fact that many critics (myself among them) sometimes use the two words as if they meant the same thing. Meter is the arithmetical norm, the purely theoretic structure of the line; rhythm is controlled departure from that norm. The iambic pentameter norm, for example, proceeds as follows:

> One *two,* one *two,* one *two,* one *two,* one *two.*

Yet no other line in the language corresponds exactly to the line just given; and to achieve another as regular one will have to resort to the same repetitive structure with a new pair of syllables. Every other line will depart from this one for these reasons: no two syllables ever have the same degree of accent—that is, so far as versification is concerned there is no such thing as an inherently accented or unaccented syllable, but syllables which count technically as accented can be recognized as such only with reference to the other syllable or syllables within the same foot; secondly, although quantity or syllable-length has no part in the measure, it is, like accent, infinitely variable and it affects the rhythm; and thirdly, feet of other types may be substituted for iambic feet, at least within reason. As I have said, rhythm results from the proper control and manipulation of these sources of variation.

Now rhythm is in a measure expressive of emotion. If the poet, then, is endeavoring to make a statement in which rational understanding and emotion are properly related to each other, metrical language will be of the greatest advantage to him, for it will provide him with a means of qualifying his emotion more precisely than he could otherwise do, of adjusting it more finely to the rational understanding which gives rise to it. The rational and emotional contents of the poem thus exist simultaneously, from moment to moment, in the poem; they are not distinct, but are separable only by analysis; the poet is not writing in language which was first conceptual and then emotionalized, nor in prose which has been metered; he is writing in poetical language. And the rhythm of the poem permeates the entire poem as pervasively as blood permeates the human body: remove it and you have a corpse. It is for this reason that the audible reading of poetry is quite as important as the philosophical understanding of poetry; without audible reading, and adequate audible reading, you simply do not have poetry.

We are thus confronted with the question of what constitutes adequate audible reading. From what I have just said, it should be obvious that adequate audible reading will be reading in which the rhythm of the poem is rendered intact, without the sacrifice of any other element. But what variety of reading will best achieve this end, and what are some of the problems which arise in connection with it?

Since I am defending an unpopular cause, I shall not scruple to avail myself of eminent support. In looking over the *Selected Writings* of Paul Valéry recently issued by New Directions, I found Valéry writing as follows:

> . . . in studying a piece of poetry one intends to recite. One should not take as source or point of departure ordinary conversation and common parlance, in order to rise from this level of prose to the desired poetic tone: but, on the contrary, I thought one should take song as a base, and should put oneself in the state of a singer; adjust one's voice to the plenitude of musical sound, and from there descend to the somewhat less resonant state suitable to verse. This, it seemed to me, was the only way to preserve the musical essence of poems. Above all, the voice must be placed quite away from prose, and the text studied from the point of view of necessary attack, modulation, sustained tone, little by little, lowering this musical disposition, which in the beginning one has exaggerated, to bring it down to the proportions of poetry. . . . above all do not be in a hurry to arrive at the meaning. Approach it without effort and, as it were, insensibly. And only in or by means of the music attain to tenderness or to violence. . . . Remain in this pure musical state until such time as the meaning, appearing little by little, can no longer mar the musical form. You will introduce it at the end as the supreme nuance that will transfigure the passage without altering it.[1]

This appears to be a plea for a restrained but formal chant, in which a sustained tone and movement will serve as an impersonal but definite base for subtle variation. It is only by such a reading, for example, that *Le Cimetière Marin* can be rendered; it is only by a man who so read that such a poem could have been written.

A poem in the very nature of the case is a formal statement; and the reading of a poem is thus a formal occasion. A poem is not conversation; neither is it drama. Conversation is in general the least premeditated and least rhythmical of human utterance; and it depends very heavily upon intonations and even gestures and facial expressions which are not at the disposal of the poet. Dramatic speech is merely more or less formalized conversation. Dramatic poetry, of course, presents a special problem, and one with which I shall not at present concern myself, though it is closer to the kind of poetry with which I am dealing than it is to dramatic prose, and I agree with Valéry that it is commonly botched by the actors. I have never witnessed a performance of Shakespeare without more of pain than of profit or of pleasure. I have been repeatedly reminded of a story told by W. B. Yeats of the great Shakespearian actor of whom it was said that he read Shakespeare so beautifully that no one could tell it was poetry. In general I think the world would be well enough off without actors: they appear to be capable of any of three feats—of making the grossly vulgar appear acceptably mediocre; of making the acceptably mediocre appear what it is; and of making the distinguished appear acceptably mediocre. In any event, they cannot read poetry, for they try to make it appear to be something else, something, in brief, which they themselves can understand.

A poem calls for a formal reading, partly because the poem itself is of its own nature a formal statement, and partly because only such a reading will render the rhythm with precision. Furthermore, it is only with a formal tone as a basis that variations of tone within the poem can be rendered with precision: without such a formal tone to unify the poem, the poem becomes merely a loose assortment of details. The situation here is precisely analogous to that which I have described elsewhere[2] with regard to rhythm and meter: the firmer the metric structure, the more precise can be the rhythmic variations, and the greater the effect obtainable with a very slight variation; whereas if the structure is loose the variations lack significance.

A formal reading which avoids dramatic declamation will necessarily take on something of the nature of a chant. This kind of reading itself has dangers, however, for the reader may carry the procedure so far as to appear precious, and worse, he may deform syllables in the interests of what he considers musical intonation, much as a musical composer will draw syllables out or hurry over them in setting a poem to music. I never heard the late W. B. Yeats read aloud, but I have been told that he was guilty of both of these vices: if it is true that he was guilty of them, one has some reason to suspect that he never properly heard his own poems, a fact which may have been responsible for a number of curious rhythmical mishaps which are scattered through his works. A poem should, on the contrary, be conceived as having a movement of its own, an autonomous movement, which should be rendered as purely and as impersonally as possible. The reader has no more right to revise the rhythms in the interest of what he considers an effective presentation than he has a right to revise any other aspects of the language. The poem, once set in motion, should appear to move of its own momentum.

A more or less recent poet who went farther than any other has gone in deforming the inherent rhythmic elements in our language and so rendering the structure of his poems indecipherable is Gerard Manley Hopkins. Hopkins held a theory of dramatic or declamatory reading, and I suspect from a few passages in his prose that he combined this with a theory of musical intonation. Hopkins was an eccentric and extremely egoistic man, and he worked in isolation. He apparently failed to realize that his own dramatic and musical deformations of language were not based on universal principles but were purely private. As a result one can often be only dumfounded when he indicates his intentions by metrical signs, and one can often be only baffled when he fails to do so. In "Spelt from Sibyl's Leaves," for example, Hopkins uses an extremely long line, which, if it is read with normal accentuation, produces the effect of a loosely irregular but still readable verse. He does not provide us with many accent marks until he is about halfway through the poem; from there on he provides marks in abundance, frequently with strange results. The last two lines will serve as illustration:

> /   /   /   /   /
> But these two; ware of a world where but these / two
>   tell, each off the other; of a rack
> Where, selfwrung, selfstrung, sheathe- and shelterless,
>   /   /   /   /
>   / thoughts against thoughts in groans grind.

We have here a kind of bad writing which is purely the result of bad reading; and even the best reading, if superimposed upon what the poet offers, can salvage the poem but very imperfectly.

In T. S. Eliot's reading of *The Waste Land,* as we have it on the recordings issued by The Library of Congress, we have another kind of dramatic reading, and conceivably a relationship between the way of reading and the way of writing. In those portions which exhibit a more or less definite rhythmic structure—for example, in "Death by Water"—Eliot reads more or less in the fashion which I am recommending, with a minimum of dramatic improvement on the text, and with a maximum of attention to movement. But in those portions of the poem—and they are the greater part of it—in which the rhythm does not cohere, in which the poem tends to fall apart in sandy fragments, Eliot reads dramatically; he does this with a good deal of skill, but most of what he puts into his voice is not in the poem—he descends to the practice of the actor who is salvaging a weak text. It would be interesting to know whether Eliot devised this mode of reading in order to rescue a weak poem, or whether the weak poem resulted in part from his having come gradually to employ such a mode of reading, so that he tended to see in his text as he was composing it something which he was not actually getting down on paper. This latter procedure in any event probably accounts for a good deal of the unrealized poetry of our time. For example, Randall Jarrell's reading of his poem "Lady Bates," in The Library of

Congress series, is very dramatic, very emotional, and very bad: I am unable to hear it without the conviction that Jarrell felt his emotions about his subject so readily and so uncritically that he did not trouble himself to write the poem. The poem itself is formless and dull.

The dependence upon superimposed rhythms or other effects which we get in a grotesque form in some of Hopkins and in a more skillful form in Eliot's reading of *The Waste Land* can lead to an astonishing degree of imperception on the part of critics (which is merely an impressive way of saying on the part of readers). In the volume entitled *Gerard Manley Hopkins,* by the Kenyon Critics, Mr. Harold Whitehall informs us that from about the year 1300 English poetry has become less and less amenable to being read aloud, because less and less rhythmical. And in another volume on Hopkins, edited by Norman Weyand, S. J., and written by a group of Jesuits, a volume entitled *Immortal Diamond,* Walter J. Ong arrives at similar conclusions. Both of these writers believe that there is no real rhythm without heavy stress; both believe that meter is based on declamatory rather than mechanical stress. Ong gives us no clue as to how we are to recognize our stressed syllables, and he fails to explain how Hopkins arrived at any of the stresses which he marked. Whitehall gives us his own system of stressing Hopkins, but it is quite as arbitrary as that of Hopkins, and when Whitehall's marked passages are finished we are left with no means of proceeding. Ong, convinced that there is no fine rhythm without heavy and obvious stress, is oblivious of the sensitivity of Sidney and the post-Sidneyan metrists, and equally of the structural principles of their verse; and his concept of reading aloud is indicated by the following passage: "If the poem calls for shouting, the shouting need not be kept imaginary for fear the beat of the rhythm will go. Shout, declaim, and you will only have thrust this rhythm home. So, too, if the shout should need to die to a whisper..." This clerical type of rendition strikes me as about equally impractical, insensitive, and indecorous.

Nevertheless, rhetorical stress has a certain relationship to the structure of meter, but it is not the relationship sought by

Hopkins. As I have already said, the language does not divide itself evenly into accented and unaccented syllables, but there is almost infinite variation in degrees of accent. For this reason, the basic rule of English scansion is this: that the accented syllable can be determined only in relationship to the other syllable or syllables within the same foot. The accented syllable of a given foot, as we shall eventually see, may be one of the lightest syllables in its line. But with this rule as a reservation, we may go on to say that poetic meter must be constructed out of the inherent (or mechanical) accentual materials of the language, so that the accented syllable of a foot will be naturally heavier than the unaccented; and if the poet desires to indicate a rhetorical stress he should do it by a metrical stress, or if he is using two syllables either of which might receive heavier stress than the other, then the rhetorical stress should fall where the reader as a result of the previously established pattern will expect the metrical stress.

Keats neglects these considerations in the first line of his last sonnet. The inexpert reader who endeavors to render this line conversationally or dramatically will read it as if he were a sociable lady addressing another sociable lady at a party:

> Bright star,   would *I* were steadfast   as *thou* art,

and the rhythm is destroyed along with the possibility of a proper rhyme. The fault, however, lies largely with Keats. It is natural to stress the two contrasting pronouns somewhat, although one need not carry the stress all the way to the ridiculous. Furthermore, on the first pronoun the metrical stress indicates the rhetorical, so that the two are not in conflict. If we consider the words *Would I* in isolation, we shall see that so far as their mechanical properties are concerned, either can be stressed at the expense of the other; however, in this line the stressing of *would* would result in an inverted foot in the second position, and although inversion is possible in this position, it is difficult and generally unlikely, so that we naturally expect the stress to fall on *I,* which likewise is the natural recipient of the rhetorical stress. If we employ the four words *Would I were steadfast* in isolation, the stress may fall variously according to our meaning. If we are implying a contrast between steadfastness and our lack of it, the heaviest stress falls on *would;* if we are implying a contrast between steadfastness and another particular quality, a light stress falls on *would* and a heavy on *stead;* if we are implying a contrast between our own lack of steadfastness and the steadfastness of another, the heavy stress falls on *I,* as in the actual line, but if, as in this line, the comparison is completed, an equal stress should fall on the second pronoun; but since this pronoun also is coupled with a verb which is mechanically its equal and on the basis of its inherent nature could as well take the accent, and since the foot ends the line, and a rhymed line at that, the accent must fall on *art*. This blunder by Keats could scarcely have occurred as a result of his reading poetry in a dramatic fashion, for he understood the structure of English poetry very well, and had he read the line dramatically he would have noticed the error. It probably occurred as a result of his reading with a somewhat mechanical scansion, so that he failed to observe that the meaning was struggling with the meter. One can read it, of course, by means of a more or less evasive glide, but it constitutes an unhappy moment.

One can observe a related difficulty in the sixth line of Wordsworth's sonnet "Upon Westminster Bridge":

> Ships, towers, domes, theatres, and temples lie.

The first four words of this line are coördinate in grammatical function and in importance, and in ordinary prose the first four syllables would be indistinguishable to the ear in the matter of accent. The average reader, if asked to mark the scansion of this poem, will indicate two spondees at the beginning of the line, but the first two feet are not spondaic—in spite of everything they are iambic. The truly spondaic foot is extremely rare in English; presently I shall have occasion to illustrate it, but for the present I shall merely describe it. It can occur as a variant in iambic verse, only if the accented syllables in the iambic feet are heavily accented and the unaccented are very light, and only if the cesural pause is heavily marked; and these conditions must prevail not merely in the line in question, but throughout much of the poem. The true spondee is a violent aberration—it is a form of what Hopkins calls sprung rhythm—and it is possible only where the rhythm is heavy and obvious. It can be found at least as early as Barnabe Googe and as late as the songbooks of John Dowland, and within these limits it may conceivably be found in as many as thirty poems, but I think it will be difficult to find it elsewhere except in the work of Gerard Hopkins, although something approaching it occurs occasionally in Henry Vaughan. In this sonnet by Wordsworth an extremely smooth iambic movement has been established in the first five lines, so effectively established that it dominates the sixth line, and almost any reader who is aware of rhythm at all will be forced to impose a very light iambic emphasis on the first two feet of the sixth line; to do otherwise will bring the poem apart in ruins. This can be done; but the difficulty indicates a defect in the poem, and a defect again which probably stems from faulty reading on the part of the poet. The difficulty is enhanced by the length of the syllables (a length increased by the commas) and by the all but insufferable series of dentals.

The relationship of rhetorical stress to metrical stress, and hence to reading, would appear, then, to be real, although the relationship can obviously be abused. Perhaps I should conclude the matter by offering these rules for poet and reader alike: (1) There should be no conflict between rhetorical stress and metrical stress, but insofar as it is possible the metrical stress should point the meaning; (2) where the mechanical potentialities of the language indicate the possibility of a stress in either of two directions, the grammatical structure should be so definite that a certain rhetorical stress will be unmistakable and will force the metrical interpretation in the right direction; and (3) the reader should deal with rhetorical stresses with the utmost restraint—he should indicate them as far as the occasion requires, but he should not become enthusiastic, undignified, or unmetrical about them. They are not to be superimposed upon the basic rhythm, nor can the basic rhythm be constructed from them.

I would like next to illustrate the importance of reading, by illustrating certain very marked differences in rhythm which may occur within the limits of the iambic pentameter line. English verse is predominantly iambic in structure, and although this fact has irritated certain poets and stirred them to curious experiments, the fact that so vast a number of eminent poets have found the iambic movement more useful than any other must have some kind of explanation. In the anapestic or dactylic foot the accented syllable must be definitely heavy or the identity of the foot and of the line will disappear, and this necessity makes for monotony and a jingling obviousness:

> I sprang to the stirrup, and Joris, and he;
> I galloped, Dirck galloped, we galloped all three. . . .

The unequivocally trochaic line tends to exhibit some of the same heaviness (as in *Hiawatha,* for example) although the reason for this is less clear. The seven-syllable tetrameter line may be described as trochaic, with a monosyllabic foot in the last position, or as iambic with a monosyllabic foot in the first position; since it is frequently used as a variant on iambic tetrameter, the second classification would seem the better. When this line is used throughout a poem, the poem will be short, or else will become monotonous: the accents again are usually heavy most of the time, and although the meter may be used in a short poem for the purpose of obtaining a didactic or semi-songlike effect, it appears to have few other uses. The iambic movement, however, appears to be natural to the language; it asserts itself easily, and the poet does not have to hammer his accents out to maintain it. This situation allows the poet to vary the degrees of his accents widely, to vary his cesuras, and to employ substitution with a certain freedom. Contrary to the views of Mr. Whitehall and of Father Ong, this type of meter lends itself very well to audible reading, but one must first know how to read. And when well written and well read it is far more flexible and perceptive than any other kind of English verse thus far devised.

My first example is by Barnabe Googe and was written

early in the reign of Elizabeth, before the advent of Spenser and Sidney:

> Give money me, take friendship who so list,
> For friends are gone, come once adversity,
> When money yet remaineth safe in chest
> That quickly can thee bring from misery;
> Fair face show friends, when riches do abound,
> Come time of proof, farewell they must away;
> Believe me well, they are not to be found,
> If God but send thee once a lowering day.
> Gold never starts aside, but in distress,
> Finds ways enough to ease thine heaviness.

This poem has certain characteristics which one would expect to find in a period in which the pentameter line was new, when the misunderstandings of Wyatt had been only recently overcome: first of all there are no inverted feet and no trisyllabic feet; secondly the accented syllables are almost all heavy and of nearly the same weight—there are only two feet in the poem in which the accented syllables are noticeably light; thirdly the cesuras are all heavily marked, and in six of the ten lines they fall at the end of the second foot. The poem shows only one type of metrical variation; that is, the use of spondaic feet (or what I have elsewhere called syllabic sprung meter). The introduction of this variation into the newly acquired iambic pentameter line is Googe's principle contribution to the technique of English verse, and it is a contribution of no mean importance. There are two spondees at the beginning of line five; there is one at the beginning of six; there is one at the beginning of nine; and the first foot of the last line may be read with equal success as a spondee or as an iamb. All of these spondees can be forced into the iambic pattern, but they will have to be forced, and the poem will suffer. It is only in a poem such as this one, in which the rhythm is strongly and obviously marked by a great and regular distinction between accented and unaccented syllables that the true spondee can occur; in a smoother and subtler type of structure, such as my next example, two syllables of nearly the same degree of accent will be absorbed into the iambic pattern and will not stand out as approximately equal to each other; furthermore, any attempt to read them as spondees will destroy the movement of the poem.

My next example is from Shakespeare. Before this sonnet was written, Sidney and other early experimenters had rendered the line smoother, more varied, and more subtle:

> When to the sessions of sweet silent thought
> I summon up remembrance of things past,
> I sigh the lack of many a thing I sought,
> And with old woes new wail my dear time's waste:
> Then can I drown an eye unused to flow,
> For precious friends, hid in death's dateless night,
> And weep afresh love's long-since-cancelled woe,
> And moan th'expense of many a vanish'd sight:
> Then can I grieve at grievances foregone,
> And heavily from woe to woe tell o'er
> The sad account of fore-bemoaned moan
> Which I new pay as if not paid before.
> But if the while I think on thee, dear friend,
> All losses are restored and sorrows end.

The position of the cesura in this sonnet is less varied than in the poem by Googe; it falls after the second foot in eleven out of fourteen lines; but the cesura is much less noticeable, partly because it is not emphasized by heavy grammatical breaks, and partly because of other qualities of the rhythm. Aside from this difference in cesural value, the most considerable rhythmic difference between this poem and the poem by Googe resides in the fact that there are great differences in the degrees of accent to be found *among the syllables which count metrically as accented*. It will be remembered that I remarked earlier that the accented syllable can be recognized as such only with reference to the other syllable or syllables within the same foot, for no two syllables bear exactly the same degree of accent: it is this fact which gives the rhythm of the best English verse its extreme sensitivity. But rhythm, in poetry as in music, is controlled variation from an arithmetical norm; and the rhythm ceases to be rhythm, and becomes merely movement, whenever the norm itself is no longer discernible.

I will illustrate what I have been saying by two lines from the sonnet. The scansion of the first line gives us a trochee followed by four iambs. The third foot, however, which is composed of the second syllable of *sessions* followed by the preposition *of* (the accented syllable), is very lightly accented. In the following foot, which is composed of *sweet,* followed by the first syllable of *silent, sweet,* the unaccented syllable, is more heavily stressed than the accented syllable of the preceding foot, so that we have in effect a series of four degrees of accent within two successive feet. Furthermore, if the reader should suffer from the delusion (a common one) that the second of these feet is really a spondee, let him read it the way he is forced to read the true spondees in the poem by Googe, and he will discover that spondaic rhythm is a very different matter from what he has here, and that the attempt to introduce it into this poem will be disastrous. The same thing occurs in the fourth and fifth feet of line nine:

> Then can I grieve at grievances foregone.

It occurs in the first two feet of Bryant's line:

> Where thy pale form was laid with many tears.

It occurs in the last two feet of Ben Jonson's line:

> Drink to me only with thine eyes.

It is, in fact, one of the commonest phenomena in English verse, yet I have seen a good many distinguished scholars and eminent poets interpret it wrongly.

I shall now quote a well-known song from John Dowland's *Second Book of Aires:*

> Fine knacks for ladies, cheap, choice, brave and new!
>   Good pennyworths! but money cannot move.
> I keep a fair but for the fair to view;
>   A beggar may be liberal of love.
> Though all my wares be trash, the heart is true.

Great gifts are guiles and look for gifts again;
    My trifles come as treasures from my mind.
It is a precious jewel to be plain;
    Sometimes in shell the Orient's pearls we find.
Of others take a sheaf, of me a grain.

Within this pack, pins, points, laces, and gloves,
    And divers toys, fitting a country fair.
But my heart lives where duty serves and loves,
    Turtles and twins, court's brood, a heavenly pair.
Happy the heart that thinks of no removes.

There are sprung, or spondaic, feet in the first, second, sixth, seventh, eleventh, thirteenth, and fourteenth lines of this poem. These feet represent the same kind of variant which we found in Googe, and for the most part we have the same strongly marked difference between accented and unaccented syllables and similarly strong cesural pauses, even in lines in which no spondees occur. Yet whereas the rhythm of Googe is hard, fast, and didactic, the rhythm of this poem is slower, more complicated, and very songlike. The result is partly due to more spondaic variants than we found in Googe, and to spondaic variants in other positions than the initial ones; it is partly due to the introduction at certain points of the type of line which we found in Shakespeare, such as the following:

It is a precious jewel to be plain.

a line in which the iambic fourth foot, composed of the second syllable of *jewel* and the preposition *to,* is extremely light and short and is followed by a final foot (*be plain*) in which the unaccented syllable is heavier than the accented syllable *to* before it; yet in this last foot the difference between *be* and *plain* is so marked that no one would be tempted to call the foot a spondee.

The author likewise does certain strange and ingenious things with his spondees. The first line, for example, goes as follows:

Fine knacks for ladies, cheap, choice, brave and new!

The first foot is spondaic, the second iambic; the third foot, consisting of the second syllable of *ladies* and of *cheap,* is likewise iambic, but the cesura, reinforced by the comma, in mid-foot, throws the accent onto *cheap* with unusual force, and cheap is then followed by the spondaic foot consisting of two syllables which are almost exactly equal to it, and which are likewise set off by commas, so that we have the illusion of a foot consisting of three accented syllables, or an English molossus. The author does something similar but almost more adventurous in the eleventh line, where the heavily iambic foot *this pack* is followed by the heavy spondee *pins, points,* which in turn is followed by the heavily inverted foot, *laces,* with the result that we get four strong accents in sequence, though only one spondee. Technically, this is one of the most brilliant poems in the language. Dowland (or his unknown poet) learned what he could from Googe and improved upon it; and he complicated the method (without destroying it—a difficult feat) by rhythms acquired from the refiners of the intervening period.

I shall now show the use of different types of iambic pentameter rhythm employed in a regular pattern. To do this, I shall employ a song by Campion. The song rhymes in couplets. The metric pattern begins with two lines of what one might call the primitive type, with heavy stresses and heavy cesuras, but with no spondees: in these two lines the first and third feet are inverted, the rest iambic, and the cesura falls after the second foot. The third and fifth lines are evenly iambic and are less heavily stressed, and the cesuras in these lines occur in different positions and are so light as to be all but imperceptible. The fourth and sixth lines are of the same type of iambic movement as the last lines mentioned, but contain seven feet instead of five. There are two stanzas, and the pattern in the two is as nearly identical as the inescapable variations of language permit:

> Follow your saint, follow with accents sweet!
> Haste you, sad notes, fall at her flying feet!
> There, wrapt in cloud of sorrow, pity move,
> And tell the ravisher of my soul I perish for her love:

But if she scorns my never ceasing pain,
Then burst with sighing in her sight, and ne'er return again.

All that I sung still to her praise did tend;
Still she was first, still she my songs did end;
Yet she my love and music both doth fly,
The music that her echo is and beauty's sympathy:
Then let my notes pursue her scornful flight!
It shall suffice that they were breathed and died for her delight.

I shall now quote a sonnet by Gerard Hopkins, which is basically iambic pentameter, but which employs every conceivable variant. I have marked and described the scansion of this sonnet in my essay on Hopkins, and at this time I shall make only a few general remarks about the structure. The poem contains iambic feet, trochees, spondees, one molossus (a foot of three accented syllables), monosyllabic feet, trisyllabic feet of one accent each, and one or two feet which must be considered either as containing more than three syllables or else as containing syllables which are extrametrical or elided. The poem is successful as regards structure and rhythm, and it offers a rhythmic departure from the norm about as extreme as anyone is likely to achieve:

No worst, there is none. Pitched past pitch of grief,
More pangs will, schooled at forepangs, wilder wring.
Comforter, where, where is your comforting?
Mary, mother of us, where is your relief?
My cries heave, herds-long; huddle in a main, a chief
Woe, world sorrow; on an age-old anvil wince and sing—
Then lull, then leave off. Fury had shrieked
'No lingering! Let me be fell: force I must be brief.'

O the mind, mind has mountains; cliffs of fall
Frightful, sheer, no-man-fathomed. Hold them cheap
May who ne'er hung there. Nor does long our small
Durance deal with that steep or deep. Here! creep,
Wretch under a comfort serves in a whirlwind: all
Life death does end and each day dies with sleep.

By the use of five short poems I have indicated a number

of widely varying rhythms all of which are measured by iambic pentameter. So far as meter and rhythm are concerned all five are masterpieces; and in spite of any faults which may be found in them with regard to other matters, all five are brilliant poems and should be part of the literary experience of any man using the English language. Yet not one of these poems amounts to anything if its rhythm is not rendered with great precision; to read the poem so that its rhythm does not emerge in its totality and in every detail is to reduce the poem to lifeless fragments. You cannot buy expert readings of these poems on disks, as you can buy expert renderings of Bach and Mozart; nor can you go to a concert and hear them—every man is his own performer. It is important, therefore, that one read properly. But to read properly one must understand the principles both of English meter and of English rhythm, and not in a haphazard manner, but precisely; and one must understand the use of one's own voice; and after that one must practice.

I am at a disadvantage in dealing with a subject of this kind before an audience whom I cannot reach with my voice, for I cannot demonstrate, but am forced to try to describe. The nearest thing to a demonstration that I can offer is my reading of my own poems in The Library of Congress series. I do not consider myself a finished performer, nor, I think, are these readings the best of which I am capable. But they are all I can offer, and they will serve to indicate the method in a general way.

I have been told that this method of reading makes all poems sound alike, but this can be true only for those persons to whom all poems sound alike in any event, or for whom essential differences are meaningless. The virtue of the method, on the contrary, is that it gives each poem its precise identity, and no other method will do this. If this precise identity does not interest you, then you are not interested in poetry and you will in all likelihood never discover poetry. Some time ago, when I was defending this method of reading in public, a well-known scholar objected to my theories with a good deal of indignation, and he objected especially to my reading of the Dowland poem which I have quoted in these pages. He said that it was a street song, or peddler's song, and should be rendered as such. I do not know exactly how Elizabethan street songs were rendered, and I do not believe that he knew; but any attempt so to render it would be, I am sure, unfortunate, even if one had the necessary information. The poem is not a street song; it is a poem on love and on the art of poetry and on a relationship between the two, and it is one of the most deeply serious and deeply moving short poems in the Elizabethan period—the peddler is purely metaphorical, and his part in the poem is both indicated and formalized by the metrical structure and it should remain formal and no more than indicated in the reading. If the poet refers by way of metaphor to a cow, the reader is not, I trust, expected to moo. I refer the reader back to my quotations from Valéry, especially the last sentence. Of the "meaning" of the poem he says: "You will introduce it at the end as the supreme nuance that will transfigure the poem without altering it." By "the end," he means the end of the process of studying the poem and arriving at the proper rendering.

Bad reading and bad (or no) training in metrical theory are largely to blame, I believe, for the insensitive literary judgments by many critics who in other matters are very brilliant, and they are to blame also for a fair amount of bad academic work in literature. At Stanford University, at this writing, we have over one hundred graduate students in English, and about half of these are candidates for the doctorate. We are in a position to select our graduate students very carefully. We accept none who have not made excellent records here or elsewhere, and although some come to us from the smaller institutions (and incidentally some of our best), many come from places like Yale, Harvard, Chicago, Columbia, Princeton, and the better state universities. These people have made excellent records in the past, and most of them make excellent records here; yet almost none can read a line of poetry aloud so that one can discern the structure, and very few can mark the scansion from a line of Shakespeare's sonnets. These people are in these respects the products of their teaching, and the teaching should be improved. Most of our best critics and many of our best-known poets are not much better off. We have sunk into amateurism; and as a result we have in our time the meters of Eliot and of his imitators at the fifth remove, instead of meters comparable to those of the Elizabethans. And we have, worse still, a coherent (and fairly vocal) body of readers so ignorant that they prefer the incompetent to the expert.

If you answer that there are different kinds of poetry and hence we have different kinds of reading (this, of course, is the genteel answer which points to my lack of gentility), I am bound to reply that you are right: there are inferior kinds of poetry. By "inferior," I mean inferior in quality, not smaller in scope. The kind of reading which I defend is equally appropriate to a song by Campion or to an epic by Milton. Any poem which cannot endure the impersonal illumination of such a reading or which requires the assistance, whether expert or clumsy, of shouting, whispering, or other dramatic improvement, is to that extent bad poetry, though it may or may not be a good scenario for a vaudeville performance.

There will never be a first-rate poet or a first-rate critic who lacks a first-rate ear; and no one will ever acquire a first-rate ear without working for it and in the proper manner. Poetry, alas, like painting and music, is an art—it is not a form of happy selfindulgence; and to master an art or even understand it, one has to labor with all of one's mind and with at least a part of one's body.

NOTES

1. Extracts from "A Discourse on the Declamation of Verse," by Paul Valéry, translated by Louise Varese, in *Paul Valéry, Selected Writings,* New Directions, 1950.

2. "The Influence of Meter on Poetic Convention," in *Primitivism and Decadence,* and the essay on John Crowe Ransom, Section IX, in *The Anatomy of Nonsense,* both reprinted in *In Defense of Reason.*

R. P. BLACKMUR

LORD TENNYSON'S SCISSORS: 1912–1950

I

I hope these reflections on the mother tongue of poetry during the last forty years may be, like their subject, inescapably frivolous and indestructibly serious. Poetry is a game we play with reality; and it is the game and the play—the game by history and training, the play by instinct and need—which make it possible to catch hold of the reality at all. Thus there is intimacy and irresponsibility, menace and caress, escape and aspiration, indigestion and sudden death: all this is in the play. I suppose Eliot meant something like this when he called poetry a superior form of amusement; Yeats something like this when he hoped his poems would wither into the truth; and I am sure that Falstaff had no less a message in mind when, in his dying, he babbled of green fields. Poetry is as near as words can get us to our behavior: near enough so that the words sing, for it is when words sing that they give that absolute moving attention which is beyond their prose powers. It is behavior, getting into our words, that sings. It may be only barely song as in Eliot's lines in "The Dry Salvages":

> The salt is on the briar rose,
> The fog is in the fir trees.

Reprinted from R. P. Blackmur, "Lord Tennyson's Scissors: 1912–1950," in *Form and Value in Modern Poetry* (Garden City, NY: Doubleday, 1952), 369–88.

Here is the salt of death and of truth and of savor, the salt in our souls of that which is not ours, moving there. The salt is on the wild and thorny rose grappling in the granite at sea's edge, grappling and in bloom, almost everblooming; and it is the rose which was before, and may yet be after, the rose of the Court of Love, or the rose of the Virgin. It is the rose out of the garden which includes the rose in the garden. There is in Eliot's line (alien but known to our line that we read) also all the roses that have been in his life, as in the next line is all the fog. The fog is another salt as the fir trees are another rose. It is all there is in fog that lowers, covers, silences, imperils, menaces and caresses; but in it, as it is in them; there is the slowed apparition, coming up under an island, of evergreen struggling, tenacious life. The two together make an image, and in their pairing reveal, by self-symbol declare, by verse and position unite, two halves of a tragic gesture.

> The salt is on the briar rose,
> The fog is in the fir trees.

I do not see that any other illustration is needed of how behavior gets into the words of the full mind, and how, a little beyond the time that it is there, it sings. It may have only a brusque lilt:

> I sing because I like to sing
> And not to hurt a living thing.

So the old song says, and it is enough till memory brings another song which shows that nothing is ever quite enough, either to say or sing. It may sing music not its own.

> Sweetheart, do not love too long:
> I loved long and long,
> And grew to be out of fashion
> Like an old song.

The author of those lines thought half the time that the poet had to choose between life and work, but when he looked at verse itself the occasion and the need for *that* choice had evaporated—true but gone—like a water-stain on stone; or had disappeared—true but changed—a snowflake in the river. This author—it was of course Yeats—sometimes resumed that self which is beyond choice by quoting lines made by a friend from the Irish: in song of a lifetime.

> When I was young,
> Who now am young no more,
> I did not eat things picked up from the shore:
> The periwinkle, and the tough dog-fish
> At even-tide have got into my dish.

At other times he found that unchoosable self as near at hand as the nearest door, or the clock's tick: in the song of the gathered moment.

> My fiftieth year had come and gone,
> I sat, a solitary man,
> In a crowded London shop,
> An open book and empty cup
> On the marble table-top.
>
> While on the shop and street I gazed
> My body of a sudden blazed;
> And twenty minutes more or less
> It seemed, so great my happiness,
> That I was blessed and could bless.

The truth of such a man—he is dead; and we may say it—is that neither his vices nor his poetry ever quitted him[1] and when we say that I think we have touched the quick and very membrane of style; or at any rate we have the gasp and thrill with which we respond to such penetrations: that is, with added song.

> Shakespearean fish swam the sea far away from land;
> Romantic fish swam in nets coming to the hand;
> What are all those fish that lie gasping on the strand?

Style is the quality of the act of perception but it is mere play and cannot move us much unless married in rhythm to the urgency of the thing perceived: or until—to say it again—behavior gets into the words and sings. Style, if you like, is how that kind of song is read; and it is sometimes, as a shudder may become a blush and a blush may drift into vertigo, by this sort of reading that the urgency of substance is found. There is a zero quality in style by which it seems to project, as it contains, the infinity of numbers. For example: Pound's "Medallion": a song of syllables.

> Luini im porcelain!
> The grand piano
> Utters a profane
> Protest with her clear soprano.
>
> The sleek head emerges
> From the gold-yellow frock
> As Anadyomene in the opening
> Pages of Reinach.

The name of Reinach's book was Apollo, and Apollo was Lord of the Lyre and Lord of the Light's Edge; in fact, Leader of the Muses, Apollo Musagete. Pound was not worried by all this; he grew up with Reinach, and by that and other hard training got to play a very complicated stylistic game by ear. Whatever words themselves can woo into being is wooed in his words. So to speak, he settled for what came from the conjugation of the spontaneous and the arbitrary through the mind's last mode of beautiful sound. I suppose this was one of the reasons why Eliot made Pound *il miglior fabbro.* "O brother," the lines go in Dante, "this one whom I distinguish to you with my finger, was a better craftsman of the mother tongue." This is too much to say of Pound (as it was not of Arnaut Daniel)—too much to say of anyone except in those moods when the mere movement of words in pattern turns the shudder of recognition into a blush and the blush into vertigo. Vertigo is one of the conditions in which we recognize our behavior. This is what Baudelaire only reminds us of when he says he was forever haunted by vertigo. Let it be, then; there is a true vertigo to be found through the exercise of the craft of the mother tongue. It is the naked voice that sings:

> *What are all those fish that lie gasping on the strand?*

II

Forty years of poetry took their rise in Eliot, Yeats, and Pound. Each of them in his own way understands what T. Tennyson meant when he said he knew the quantity of every English vowel except those in the word scissors—where each vowel is enclosed and made of uncertain quantity by two consonants. Most of their successors do not understand what Tennyson meant and many of them would repudiate the statement not for its arrogance but for its irrelevant nonsense. W. H. Auden would be an exception, and the knowledge is patent in some of his verse. There are other exceptions but they do not seem to me able to get their knowledge into their verse as a regular thing. This is the chief indictment against that aspect of our poetry which we call verse. Syllable and stress are not enough to make a metric into a style, although they are quite enough to make a doggerel. It only strengthens the indictment when we remember that between 1912 and 1922 Yeats, Pound, and Eliot won their own battle against doggerel and deliquescence and reached their heights of style and idiom. 1922 seems the great year of our time—especially if you let the months run a little both ways—for it holds a good many of Yeats's Tower poems, Pound's first eight Cantos, and Eliot's *The Waste Land,* not to mention *Ulysses,* the finishing of *The Magic Mountain,* and the beginning of *The Counterfeiters.* The year 1922 is almost inexhaustible in all the arts. But here we are concerned directly only with the triumphant style and idiom in our three poets: with their victory, finally achieved, in the revolution of 1912. In their different ways, "Prufrock," "The Second Coming," and *Hugh Selwyn Mauberley* released the expressive burden of sensibility into forms which were suddenly available for everybody for the whole period between the wars of 1914 and 1939. These poems are now the commonplace of our meeting and are known like afterthoughts in the blood-stream. At the time they were thought "new" and were mistaken, like any instinct in the process of formation; they assaulted the sensibility, either investing it or sacking it. As a result there came into print and gradually into reading and meaning many other poets new, and difficult, and damned, and denied who are now blessed and used, if they have not been forgotten. This is what is meant by the triumph of style and idiom; and it is almost as useful to say that this is what is meant by the defeat—temporary and precarious—of doggerel.

The history of any period of poetry seen from the point of view of its verse is the history of its struggle to prevent Language from becoming a new form of doggerel or—equally a hard job—to prevent an older form of language from relapsing into the basic doggerel of the mother tongue; just as, from a social point of view, it is the history of readers catching on to new rhythms or new relations between rhythm and meter. This is not a superficial but a primary interest. The business of rhythm is to move perception into meaning, and so to move meaning into words. The business of meter (the quantitative or numerical measure of words prescribed by laws only partly known) is to keep meaning in motion by giving the rhythm foot and hand holds on the up and down (the up *or* down) of the rock-face to be climbed or descended to reach the theoretic form of life we call poetry. Prosody—the precise and loving care of the motion of meaning in language—is of first but not necessarily conscious importance.

The general prosody of the 'teens and 'twenties had equally little to do with the practice of Yeats, Pound, and Eliot (which as I say understood Tennyson on scissors) and with the practice of the old conservatives. The general prosody was perhaps the weakest and least conscious in English since the dead poetry of the mid-sixteenth century. It ran, under various guises and doctrines, toward a combination of absolute doggerel and absolute expressionism. Ezra Pound was as responsible as anyone for this condition, not by the progress of his own work but by the procession of manifestoes which he promulgated by letter and print. His doctrine, however it may have promoted the incentive of writing, only got in the way of full work and when it got stronger, deeply damaged, though it never destroyed, his expressive powers. We see this if we trace the connection (it would be worth somebody's study in detail) between the Imagism of 1912, which was a mere lively heresy of the visual in the verbal, and the full doctrine of the Ideograph which seems to have undermined the structure of the later Cantos. The ideograph is actual picture-writing in verbal signs and although it has an attractive rationale in languages built upon it, it becomes an irrational agent in the languages of the West. In English, unless taken only as analogy like any other material of poetry, the ideograph destroys the composing power of the rational imagination because it can neither grasp nor replace the rational needs of the language. The procedure is very tempting, always, to get rid of what is behind one and what is ahead of one, neither by capitulation nor by mastery, but by declaring an arbitrary substitute. Then expression becomes immediate, which is good, and spontaneous, which is not; for spontaneity is the curse of poetry to at least the same degree that neologism is the curse of language. But the temptation is very deep; Art, as Maritain says, Art bitten by poetry longs to be freed from reason, but so long as nothing is substituted for reason the longing is not fatal and may indeed promote a fresh and rejoicing sense of disorder, as *The Waste Land* did, or a new underground for reason, as the work of Valéry and Mallarmé did.

Nor should Pound be blamed too much; the heresiarchs were everywhere; all that is known as semantics, semasiology, and semiotics was in the air, and it did no good but worse harm to replace these with Basic English, as Ogden and Richards did, for Basic English makes reading as well as writing an unbearable bore. What, should we get rid of our ignorance, of the very substance of our lives, merely in order to understand one another?

The poets did not think so either. They took both the ideograph and the semiotics (in the guise of free verse and the vade mecum of deliberate ambiguity, which is sometimes called irony or paradox) and made out of them a defense of absolute self-expressionism. The idea was that of absolute style (identity or abolition of form and content), which is all very well in a sacred book, after it has been made sacred, but which otherwise runs the risk of becoming absolute doggerel. *What are all those fish that lie gasping on the strand?*

What they did was to make just enough of a prosody to heroize the sensibility and not quite enough to make a heroic statement. Just enough meter to make a patter, just enough rhyme to make a noise, just enough reason to make an argument; never enough of anything to bind together what came out of the reservoir of their extraordinary sensibility into possible poetry. I refer, of course, to the bad poetry of the time and to the bad poetry which is called modern: to what Yeats meant when he said that the bad poet does with no trouble at all what the good poet does with great difficulty: that is to say, by prosody, by expertness, conscious or not. This bad poetry is not worth reference in itself - it is here only to represent the condition of the language and the state of ambition in which an unusually large amount of good—or partly good—poetry got written. It is here because, outside Yeats who had other wounds, hardly a good poet or a good poem but shows the permanent and somewhat crippling scars of these diseases. To heroize the sensibility is to heroize the very spontaneity which is the enemy of poetry.

Pound (out of Ford Madox Ford) had the cure for this heroism: in his notion of the Prose Tradition in Verse, where the edict was that verse ought to be at least as well-written as prose. But the cure was either unacceptable because of ignorant superstitions about inspiration or because, being by nature allergic to it, the patient would die of the cure. For the most part the bottle was bought but never used after the first gagging dose. Besides, it was seldom taken as it should always have been, along with another of Pound's prescriptions, and without which it could never do anything but harm. Verse should be written, said Pound, not to the metronome but in the sequence of the musical phrase. The prose tradition alone produces flatness, inhibits song, and excludes behavior; and I see no sense in welcoming these disorders, as Eliot has done in parts of the Quartets and as Schwartz has done in all but his earliest work, as other and desirable forms of order. I do not refer to careless writing but to deliberate flatness: which is only the contemporary form of Georgian deliquescence. Pound was right; never mind the metronome, which is the measure of doggerel; the necessity is absolute to compose in the sequence of the musical phrase. That is the difference between writing verse with only the care that goes with prose and writing verse better than prose. What is better is that words written in the prose tradition *and* composed in the sequence of the musical phrase become their own meaning: the meaning which, as Eliot says in prose, persists after the words have stopped; that very meaning of which he says in the better writing of verse: "you are the music while the music lasts." What could be better than that?

Who knows? It is always interesting to consult the two geneses of poetry in prose and in doggerel. In the prose lies the sensibility, in the doggerel the hope, of poetry. The curious may consult Yeats's *Autobiographies* and the versions of "Sailing to Byzantium" printed since his death; both the doggerel and the prose for many poems are there. So with Pound, there is the *ABC of Economics* and the Canto on Usury; and with Eliot there are the deep parallels between the series of essays and the series of poems. In each case the poems are better than the prose because in each the doggerel whether of the verse or of the mind has been lifted into composition in the sequence of the musical phrase; and in each the sensibility has been freed from the heroism of the spontaneous—the merely self-expressed, or the merely argued—and become in some sense an incarnation of actual behavior: so that you are the music while the music lasts.

Of course we have been talking about the history of poetry, not about the history of sensibility except as it affects poetry. Perhaps only because it is our own age and we have a kind of disadvantageous intimacy with it, it seems to have been an age when the sensibility took over much of the task of poetry. That is why we have created so many private worlds each claiming ascendancy over the real world about which nothing, or nearly nothing got said. That is why, too, Yeats and Eliot (though not Pound, except rarely) were almost alone able to express a version—an actual form—of the real world. In each the sensibility had other grounds than itself; the ground of beseeching, history, faith or momentum and the other ground, no less important to poetry, of prosody. To combine words of each poet in a single question, in

> A woman drew her long black hair out tight
> And fiddled whisper music on those strings—
>
> O body swayed to music, O brightening glance,
> How can we know the dancer from the dance?

I submit that in these lines the sensibility has disappeared into the words and the words have disappeared into what is sung, and nothing forgot. *Nothing forgot* because the meter is so united with the rhythm that the quality of the act of perception is united with the urgency of the thing perceived.

III

I suppose that all these words so far make up to an odd way of following Arnold step by step on his touchstones, but I hope the pace is lighter and comes out in another world than his, though I do not know what world because I trust it is the world in which we live. They are meant to give us, these stepping stones, points of perilous vantage from which to estimate the work of other poets *as poets,* and not only the poets who worked under their influence but also those who worked under the influence of other and as some say older parts of the traditions of poetry in English. If we think of Yeats, Pound, and Eliot—each with his pair of Lord Tennyson's scissors—it becomes easy to cut our way through the whole field. We see at once, for a rather lumped-up example, that only at a relatively low level did meter and rhythm unite in Housman, De la Mare, and Masefield; only at rough and uneven levels in Frost and Robinson; only at difficult and precarious levels in Empson and Auden; at faltering and ragged levels in Graves and Marianne Moore; at a chastened level in H. D. Similarly, in the metric of Sturge Moore there is a kind of woolly desperation, in Herbert Read, a brittle desperation, and a mechanical, relaxed desperation, striking idly on under-water objects, in Hardy. Desperation is the quality of action at some critical point unsuccessful because the right equipment is lacking. None of these poets in the bulk of their verse—though all of them by exception—took enough stock in the music of the muse. Hence there is not often enough the steady pressure of cohesion, speed, and exigence. But all of them are better than the flannel-mouthed inflation in the metric of Robinson Jeffers with his rugged rock-garden violence.

None of these men are bad poets; all of them require reading. I only say that what impedes full reading is a faulty relation between language and sensibility, between meter and rhythm. Their engines are inefficient; and they should have been either Keatsed or Vergilianized; where to Keats means to blush at language found and not to blush until it is found, and where Vergilianize means so to see things bound together in words that they build into permanent structures of the mind, that is, into statement: into reason that sings in the nerves because it's built into the body of the language.

But think—still with the scissors for hand-run reading—of the parallel Old-Timers' school, what we might call the school of Chaucer and the Ballad; think of Hardy, Housman, Robinson, and Frost: Frost with his close piety to experience; Robinson with his combination of Browning and New England; Housman with the movement of Herbert and the temperament of Hardy; Hardy with his country piety, emotional distrust, and Comtean positivism: each with his view and sense of nature, man, and God. The scissors tell us that the reputation of these men may improve, if not absolutely then relatively to Yeats and Eliot. Reading them, we see why Pound does not occupy a first position, but a position on one side. The superlative metric of Pound may be a clue to their weakness but it would never furnish an understanding of their imperfect strength. Their work stands ready to infect the work of young men who have not yet found a form for their ambition and who can no longer, since they apprehend what has happened to it, heroize their sensibility. At least I should suppose there might be a coming race of poets who would want to reverse Maritain's phrase and say Art, bitten by reason, longs to be freed from poetry: from the spontaneous and the private and the calculated public worlds. There might be a race of poets, that is, who would woo the excited miracles of absolute statement, not as a refuge, but to get their work done. For such a race, Hardy, Housman, Robinson, and Frost would be not masters but the nearest exemplars of the line of work into which the work, itself superior to theirs, of Yeats, Eliot, and Pound would disappear. It is with such an attitude in mind that the work of Lorca becomes important; it permits access without overestimation into the late school of Chaucer.

These young men—the next thing that happens, whatever it may be—would gain little but reaction from the works of the Apocalyptic or Violent school: a school that seemed so lively, so menacing to others, and so destructive of themselves, only twenty years ago—a school that now seems dead, with two exceptions. Here is where we find the remains of Vachel Lindsay, the evangel of enthusiastic rebirth; Robinson Jeffers, the classical Freudian; Roy Campbell, the animal, authoritarian evangel of anti-culture; Carl Sandburg, the bard of demagogic anti-culture; and of course others. Perhaps they have partial heirs in Kenneth Patchen who has a kind of *ex cathedra* automatism, Kenneth Fearing who envisages a city without a polity, and Kenneth Rexroth who sees anarchy as the form of culture. All of these stem poetically and emotionally from Whitman-Vates: and all are marked by ignorance, good will, solipsism, and evangelism. Lord Tennyson's scissors can find nothing but cloth in them to cut; nor should we think of them even so briefly as more than false alarms if it were not for the two extraordinary talents that must be grouped with them. With modifications because of their extreme eccentricity of vision or genius, their self-willed marvels of craft, and because of their absolute flair for meaning by rhythm, D. H. Lawrence and Hart Crane belong here. Each is a blow in the face but neither can hit you twice. Both left lasting poems naked as the sensibility itself, dark as their own rebirths in the darkness of blood. But it is Lord Tennyson's scissors, and not any other instruments of insight, that tell us sadly both Lawrence and Crane were outside the tradition they enriched. They stood at the edge of the precipice which yawns to those who lift too hard at their bootstraps.

Besides the Apocalyptic school, and related to it closely, there was another school of anti-intelligence (pro-culture and self-verbal varieties) who filled the little magazines of the 'twenties and early 'thirties, together with the attics and bars, with their random spontaneity and arbitrary rites on words. They got rid of too much of their reason, and as a result they effervesced rather than expressed, and what is left is flat. Nameless they shall be here; they belonged only to their principal journal *transition*. What was wrong with them is clear when you see how weak is their imitation of Apollinaire, Aragon, Cocteau, Soupault, and how great their misunderstanding of Mallarmé, Rilke, Joyce, Kafka, and Pirandello: all men who longing to be freed from reason had a kind of bottom supply of it. Neither the English nor the Americans have ever been very good at this sort of thing. Let us say that we have not so much of reason that we can afford to lose any of it; we need it to make our nonsense real as well as genuine; and one would say that in this respect prosody was a form of reason.

Prosody as reason is what the central school of the time characteristically has over and above our two anti-intelligence schools. This is the school of Donne into which the largest number of individual writers of good verse fall when shaken up and let settle. If we generalize them, they are difficult in style, violent in their constructed emotions, private with actual secrecy in meaning. There is in their work a wrestling struggle toward statement, a struggle through paradox and irony (forms of arrogance and self-distrust), and the detritus of convictions. The statements are therefore impossible to make, but the effort to make them is exciting because genuine and because, in the best poems, there is an emotion created in parallel to the undeclarable intent. Their language has flesh and nerves and is recurrently on the verge of voice.

One does what one can. John Ransom and Allen Tate, for example, around the gaps of the unstateable tremendous, are models of the uncontrollable in pseudo-control. John Wheelwright had again and again the frightening stroke of direct wit on the thing itself unsaid, just as Empson can press his meters on the unsayable until it almost bursts into being. Hugh MacDiarmid is another, in his non-political poems, who has the force of immanent statement. Anybody can make his own list, or consult the anthologies; for it is at this point we see the great tide of talent whirl up individual after individual till the unlike is lost in the like.

> What are all those fish that lie gasping on the strand?

The school of Donne: we call it that as a counter in exchange, and a counter of only generally determined value. Like any counter it tells a lie; but it would be a worse lie if we called it the school of Blake. We must tell two lies together. Both intellectually and prosodically we have the right. The general poetry at the center of our time takes the compact and studiable conceit of Donne with the direct eccentricity, vision, and private symbolism of Blake; takes from Hopkins the incalculable and unreliable freedom (which cost him so much, too) of sprung rhythm, and the concentration camp of the single word; and from Emily Dickinson takes spontaneous snatched idiom and wooed accidental inductableness. It is a Court poetry, learned at its fingertips and full of a decorous willfulness called ambiguity. It is, in a mass society, a court poetry without a court. There were some of course who believed there was a court, but they produced very little poetry, or at least very little with the infectiousness of authority. I mean poets like Robert Bridges, Yvor Winters, and Howard Baker. It is not authority one gets from their work but strictures: the impossible effort of the bootstrap-will to remake one's time in accord with one's sense of its defects of sensibility and form. This is the heresy as ancient as that of direct inspiration or (as Winters named it) expressive form: the notion of *a priori* correct form.

Not so much the opposed as the counterpart heresy is William Carlos Williams' notion, which rises from his intense conviction that the only value of sound or sense is in direct perception, that forms are themselves incorrect when they are not unique. To him beauty is absolute and falls like the rain, like the dream of rain in a dry year. He is, if you like, the imagism of 1912 self-transcended. He is contact without tact; he is objectivism without objective; *l'anima semplicetta* run wild, with all the gain in the zest of immediate wonder, with all the loss that strikes when memory and expectation, the double burden of the true music, are both gone. The neo-classicist and the neo-barbarian are alike in this: their vitality is without choice or purpose. *Wind shrieked, and where are they?*

The aghast cry is from Yeats; but the scissors of Eliot or of Pound could have shorn as close. There is in poetry no shearing power so great as the living twist of things called idiom caught on to that qualifying act of perception called style. This, as we hear it, is the music of Lord Tennyson's scissors.

It is a music involved here so that we may remind ourselves how differently, and in what varied voices, it may be heard at one time: all modes being approximations of truth. There are Wallace Stevens, Marianne Moore, and E. E. Cummings, to be invoked here so that we may more richly hear Yeats, Eliot, and Pound. Each, so to speak, is full of syllables where the others are full of words. Each is a kind of dandy, or connoisseur, a true mountebank of behavior made song. I do not know that there is precedence among them; let us say they make an equilateral triangle of three styles hung like a pendant from the three major styles. Each is much interested in prosody at the executive rather than the constructive level: each decorates and expands existing prosody. So with words, each is interested in refinements, recollections, and modifications of major meanings. None of them could ever so penetrate either their prosody or their words that their poems become their own music or their own meaning. It is always a haunting "other" music that you are while the music lasts. That is why each of them has so often been an immediate influence on younger poets and why none of them has ever been a permanent or protracted influence. Each is too remote from the urgency of perception.

Wallace Stevens is a dandy and a Platonist, he darlings the syllables of his ideas: it is the stroke of platonism on prosody that produces Euphues, wit with a secret, ornament on beauty. You need an old dictionary and an old ear to get his beauty: as if he had to find an unfamiliar *name* before the beauty of his perception could emerge; and it is along these lines that you have to think of the French symbolists' influence upon him. They taught Eliot the antipoetic and the conversational style; Stevens they taught the archaic and the rhetorical; that is, Eliot and Stevens saw the one prosody running in opposite directions. But Stevens is in essence of a very old tradition, French and Platonic, working on a modern substance. He is a troubadour, a poet of the Court of Love, and his badge is *Trobar Clus;* he has a bias for the hermetic, for the complex and ornamented protection of complex and violent perception—which is his way of heroizing the sensibility. I would think that he has all his life wanted to make supreme statements discreetly, so that their beauty would show before their force. He should have lived in the age of Pope; with his sensibility and his syllables he could have made rational statements with more beauty than that age was capable of. But as it is, he is "the tranquil jewel in this confusion."

Marianne Moore is a syllabist too, for she has written the most complex syllabic verse of our time: as if she brought French numbers to English rhythms with no principle of equivalence. But she is not the syllabist as dandy but as connoisseur, she is the syllabist of the actual, the metrist of the immediate marvel—the small animal, the close perception, the fragment of phrase; and at her best all these small things move in a momentum, like the El Greco "brimming with inner light" of which one of her poems speaks. But almost everywhere she finds, chooses, refines sophisticated *forms* of simple perceptions which return upon their simplicity and their limits. There is a correspondence here to the coerced heightened perception (the forced close observation) in the painting of still-life. Poetry is to her, as she says, an imaginary garden with real toads in it. She knows all about the toads because she has imagined the garden; as you look suddenly everywhere there is the disengaged leap of a green or a brown toad, all warts, all soft, all leaping, all real. If there is not much other reality there, and there seldom is in a connoisseur's garden, you bring her, or ignore, the life she hasn't got just because what she has got is so real: you bring or ignore as with a shut-in whom you love. While you are with her reading, you wonder what reality can be when her remote refinement of it is so genuine in plain American that cats and dogs can read. You wonder, stop wondering, and are for the moment content with the game and the play that are there.

Perhaps this is the best thing that can be said of E. E. Cummings, too. Certainly when you want to read him for what is there you can neither argue with him nor about him; his emotions, feelings, attitudes have all the direct indignation, the natural blasphemy, the lyric purity, and all the sporadic high jinks of a serious child. He is Dante's *anima semplicetta* running into difficulties, but still running and still singing. He is the child turned poet, the child with *that* terrifying and incomplete dimension. Otherwise put, Cummings is the traditionalist who insists on the literal content of his tradition without re-understanding its sources: this is, of course, the easiest form of eccentricity and the most human form of fanaticism. He is St. Francis turned Unitarian and "candid-shot" honest. Nobody could be more direct and more conventional—and for purity of motive more admirable—in his basic perceptions than he. He has too little a developed self ever to escape from it except waywardly, when you want either to console him or beat him. His verse, oddly, is less direct and even more conventional than his perceptions. He was educated by Edmund Spenser, the English sonneteers, Keats, Swinburne, the funny-papers, and John Bunyan; but perhaps he was most educated by the things that were left out that would have gone to make a structured mind. All he knows is by enthusiasm, habit, and aversion. He refuses the job of the full intelligence, preferring intimacy with what he loves and contempt for what he hates; and he accepts what love and hatred give as if they made the music of a full mind. The gifts are great but they beat as well as console each other; and if he were not part of a going concern larger than he, he would be nothing. Here again is a case where prosody is an instrument of reason. Like the wilder currencies in the age of Veluta (or like the seried marks of Hitler) Cummings' experimental typography depends on the constant presence of the standard it departs from and would be worthless if not measured against it. Indeed it is precisely in the lyric quality which is his highest worth that the old meters break through. Like a roller coaster his thrill lets you drop. It is the mountebank in him that makes the vulgar motions, but it is also the mountebank that plays—the child turned poet—the most serious game in the world.

IV

It is thinking of these others under the aegis of Yeats, Eliot, and Pound that makes us realize the everlasting need of keeping Lord Tennyson's scissors sharp. *What are those fish that lie gasping on the strand?* No doubt they all came out of a common pool, but it is just to observe the order of their apparition, and it is rewarding to guess at those still far from land. The general absence of decorum in metrics and syntax and the general presence of heroized sensibility and private symbolisms only make it plainer (I mean because of the conscious struggle against them) that the work of Yeats, Eliot, and Pound belongs in the full tradition of literature. It is they who stand between the Victorians and Romantics and whatever it is that comes after them. They made form and substance possible. They made possible the further development and release, still inchoate to these observations, of the doomed school of Auden about 1930. The deliberate approach to doggerel through Skelton, the Ballads, the immediate situation, and the multi-valenced distrust of self combined to produce the new flat style on the one hand (as in Auden) and on the other hand (as in Dylan Thomas) what you might call the yelling, swinging style. In between lie many possibilities, not so far satisfied, or if so not so far seen.

Auden alone has all the interest and variety and learning that go with being a true poet, and it would seem that it is something in the age rather than something in himself or the condition of poetry that has kept him from proving the truth. It is as if his crankinesses, his ups and downs, were not what he ate when young but what he picked up on the shore.

> The periwinkle, and the tough dog-fish
> At eventide have got into my dish.

Auden is not yet through; he has had his first rushes, indeed several of them, his rallies and relapses, and his ventures into taxonomies of all sorts. But he remains quick and perceptive even in the flaccid verse of the *Age of Anxiety;* he has an ear as true as any, the beginnings of a style and the earmarks of an idiom. He has the capacities but not yet the achievements of a great poet. But he is in his middle forties: the climacteric is not yet.

It is all the more reason to think so when we look at the generation born between 1913 and 1918: Shapiro, Barker, Schwartz, Thomas, Berryman, Manifold, Lowell, Betjeman, Meredith, and Reed. I would not say that any of these men have managed the full creation, but they have the enormous advantage over their predecessors that there is an idiom ready for them to develop according to their own needs.

> The salt is on the briar rose,
> The fog is on the fir trees.

They have more than a chance—it is half done for them—to develop out of personality the most objective of all creations, the least arbitrary and spontaneous, a style. This they are aware of. They are more open, more freed, nearer both statement and song than their predecessors. They began nearer the prose tradition and the sequence of the musical phrase. We might have a great age out of them yet. What more do you want? Only that it is by prosody alone—by the loving care for the motion of meaning in language—that a poet may prove that he "was blessèd and could bless." That thought is the music of Lord Tennyson's scissors.

NOTE

1. Eliot, thinking of Yeats, once cited La Rochefoucauld's aphorism: If you say of a man that he has quitted his vices, watch out! The vices may have only quitted him.

Robert Penn Warren

PURE AND IMPURE POETRY

Critics are rarely faithful to their labels and their special strategies. Usually the critic will confess that no one strategy—the psychological, the moralistic, the formalistic, the historical—or combination of strategies, will quite work the defeat of the poem. For the poem is like the monstrous Orillo in Boiardo's *Orlando Innamorato.* When the sword lops off any member of the monster, that member is immediately rejoined to the body, and the monster is as formidable as ever. But the poem is even more formidable than the monster, for Orillo's adversary finally gained a victory by an astonishing feat of dexterity: he slashed off both the monster's arms and quick as a wink seized them and flung them into the river. The critic who vaingloriously trusts his method to account for the poem, to exhaust the poem, is trying to emulate this dexterity: he thinks that he, too, can win by throwing the lopped-off arms into the river. But he is doomed to failure. Neither fire nor water will suffice to prevent the rejoining of the mutilated members to the monstrous torso. There is only one way to conquer the monster: you must eat it, bones, blood, skin, pelt, and gristle. And even then the monster is not dead, for it lives in you, is assimilated into you, and you are different, and somewhat monstrous yourself, for having eaten it.

Reprinted from Robert Penn Warren, "Pure and Impure Poetry," in *New and Selected Essays* (New York: Random House, 1989), 3–29.

So the monster will always win, and the critic knows this. He does not want to win. He knows that he must always play stooge to the monster. All he wants to do is to give the monster —the poem—a chance to exhibit again its miraculous power, which is poetry.

With this fable, I shall begin by observing that poetry wants to be pure. And it always succeeds in this ambition. In so far as we have poetry at all, it is always pure poetry; that is, it is not non-poetry. The poetry of Shakespeare, the poetry of Pope, the poetry of Herrick, is pure, in so far as it is poetry at all. We call the poetry "higher" or "lower," we say "more powerful" or "less powerful" about it, and we are, no doubt, quite right in doing so. The souls that form the great rose of Paradise are seated in banks and tiers of ascending blessedness, but they are all saved, they are all perfectly happy; they are all "pure," for they have all been purged of mortal taint. This is not to say, however, that if we get poetry from only one source, say Shakespeare, such a single source ought to suffice us, in as much as we can always appeal to it; or that, since all poetry is equally pure, we engage in a superfluous labor in trying to explore or create new sources of poetry. No, for we can remember that every soul in the great rose is precious in the eyes of God. No soul is the substitute for another.

Poetry wants to be pure, but poems do not. At least, most of them do not want to be too pure. The poems want to give us poetry, which is pure, and the elements of a poem, in so far as it is a good poem, will work together toward that end, but many of the elements, taken in themselves, may actually seem to contradict that end, or be neutral toward the achieving of that end. Are we then to conclude that neutral or recalcitrant elements are simply an index to human frailty, and that in a perfect world there would be no dross in poems, which would, then, be perfectly pure? No, it does not seem to be merely the fault of our world, for the poems include, deliberately, more of the so-called dross than would appear necessary. They are not even as pure as they might be in this imperfect world. They mar themselves with cacophonies, jagged rhythms, ugly words and ugly thoughts, colloquialisms, clichés, sterile technical terms, headwork and argument, self-contradictions, clevernesses, irony, realism—all things which call us back to the world of prose and imperfection.

Sometimes a poet will reflect on this state of affairs, and grieve. He will decide that he, at least, will try to make one poem as pure as possible. So he writes:

> Now sleeps the crimson petal, now the white;
> Nor waves the cypress in the palace walk;
> Nor winks the gold fin in the porphyry font.
> The fire-fly wakens; waken thou with me.

We know the famous garden—the garden in Tennyson's "Princess." We know how all nature conspires here to express the purity of the moment: how the milk-white peacock glimmers like a ghost, and how like a ghost the unnamed "she" glimmers on to her tryst; how earth lies "all Danaë to the stars," as the beloved's heart lies open to the lover; and how, in the end, the lily folds up her sweetness, "and slips into the bosom of the lake," as the lovers are lost in the sweet dissolution of love.

And we know another poet and another garden. Or perhaps it is the same garden, after all, viewed by a different poet, Shelley.

> I arise from dreams of thee
> In the first sweet sleep of night,
> When the winds are breathing low,
> And the stars are shining bright.
> I arise from dreams of thee,
> And a spirit in my feet
> Hath led me—who knows how?
> To thy chamber window, Sweet!

We remember how, again, all nature conspires, how the wandering airs "faint," how the Champak's odors "pine," how the nightingale's complaint "dies upon her heart," as the lover will die upon the beloved's heart. Nature here strains out of nature, it wants to be called by another name, it wants to spiritualize itself by calling itself another name. How does the lover get to the chamber window? He refuses to say how, in his semi-somnambulistic daze, he got there. He blames, he says, "a spirit in my feet," and hastens to disavow any knowledge of how that spirit operates. In any case, he arrives at the chamber window. Subsequent events and the lover's reaction toward them are somewhat hazy. We know only that the lover, who faints and fails at the opening of the last stanza and who asks to be lifted from the grass by a more enterprising beloved, is in a condition of delectable passivity, in which distinctions blur out in the "purity" of the moment.

Let us turn to another garden: the place, Verona; the time, a summer night, with full moon. The lover speaks:

> But, soft! what light through yonder window breaks?
> It is the east . . .

But we know the rest, and know that this garden, in which nature for the moment conspires again with the lover, is the most famous of them all, for the scene is justly admired for its purity of effect, for giving us the very essence of young, untarnished love. Nature conspires beneficently here, but we may remember that beyond the garden wall strolls Mercutio, who can celebrate Queen Mab, but who is always aware that nature has other names as well as the names the pure poets and pure lovers put upon her. And we remember that Mercutio, outside the wall, has just said:

> . . . 'twould anger him
> To raise a spirit in his mistress' circle
> Of some strange nature, letting it there stand
> Till she had laid it and conjured it down.

Mercutio has made a joke, a bawdy joke. That is bad enough, but worse, he has made his joke witty and, worst of all, intellectually complicated in its form. Realism, wit, intellectual complication—these are the enemies of the garden purity.

But the poet has not only let us see Mercutio outside the garden wall. Within the garden itself, when the lover invokes nature, when he spiritualizes and innocently trusts her, and says,

> Lady, by yonder blessed moon I swear,

the lady herself replies,

> O! swear not by the moon, the inconstant moon,
> That monthly changes in her circled orb.

The lady distrusts "pure" poems, nature spiritualized into forgetfulness. She has, as it were, a rigorous taste in metaphor, too; she brings a logical criticism to bear on the metaphor which is too easy; the metaphor must prove itself to her, must be willing to subject itself to scrutiny beyond the moment's enthusiasm. She injects the impurity of an intellectual style into the lover's pure poem.

And we must not forget the voice of the nurse, who calls from within, a voice which, we discover, is the voice of expediency, of half-measures, of the view that circumstances alter cases—the voice of prose and imperfection.

It is time to ask ourselves if the celebrated poetry of this scene, which as poetry is pure, exists despite the impurities of the total composition, if the effect would be more purely poetic were the nurse and Mercutio absent and the lady a more sympathetic critic of pure poems. I do not think so. The effect might even be more vulnerable poetically if the impurities were purged away. Mercutio, the lady, and the nurse are critics of the lover, who believes in pure poems, but perhaps they are necessary. Perhaps the lover can be accepted only in their context. The poet seems to say: "I know the worst that can be said on this subject, and I am giving fair warning. Read at your own risk." So the poetry arises from a recalcitrant and contradictory context; and finally involves that context.

Let us return to one of the other gardens, in which there is no Mercutio or nurse, and in which the lady is more sympathetic. Let us mar its purity by installing Mercutio in the shrubbery, from which the poet was so careful to banish him. You can hear his comment when the lover says:

> And a spirit in my feet
> Hath led me—who knows how?
> To thy chamber window, Sweet!

And we can guess what the wicked tongue would have to say in response to the last stanza.

It may be that the poet should have made early peace with Mercutio, and appealed to his better nature. For Mercutio seems to be glad to cooperate with a poet. But he must be invited; otherwise, he is apt to show a streak of merry vindictiveness about the finished product. Poems are vulnerable enough at best. Bright reason mocks them like sun from a wintry sky. They are easily left naked to laughter when leaves fall in the garden and the cold winds come. Therefore, they need all the friends they can get, and Mercutio, who is an ally of reason and who himself is given to mocking laughter, is a good friend for a poem to have.

On what terms does a poet make his peace with Mercutio? There are about as many sets of terms as there are good poets. I know that I have loaded the answer with the word *good* here, that I have implied a scale of excellence based, in part at least, on degree of complication. I shall return to this question. For the moment, however, let us examine an anonymous sixteenth-century poem whose apparent innocence and simple lyric cry should earn it a place in any anthology of "pure poetry."

> Western wind, when will thou blow,
> The small rain down can rain?
> Christ, if my love were in my arms
> And I in my bed again!

The lover, grieving for the absent beloved, cries out for relief. Several kinds of relief are involved in the appeal to the wind. First, there is the relief that would be had from the sympathetic manifestation of nature. The lover, in his perturbation of spirit, invokes the perturbations of nature. He invokes the beneficent perturbation,

> Western wind, when will thou blow,

as Lear invokes the destructive,

> Blow, winds, and crack your cheeks! rage! blow!

Second, there is the relief that would be had by the fulfillment of grief—the frost of grief, the drought of grief broken, the full anguish expressed, then the violence allayed in the peace of tears. Third, there is the relief that would be had in the excitement and fulfillment of love itself. There seems to be a contrast between the first two types of relief and the third type; speaking loosely, we may say that the first two types are romantic and general, the third type realistic and specific. So much for the first two lines.

In the last two lines, the lover cries out for the specific solace of his case: reunion with his beloved. But there is a difference between the two lines. The first is general, and romantic. The phrase "in my arms" does not seem to mean exactly what it says. True, it has a literal meaning, if we can look close at the words, but it is hard to look close because of the romantic aura—the spiritualized mist about them.[1] But with the last line the perfectly literal meaning suddenly comes into sharp focus. The mist is rifted and we can look straight at the words, which, we discover with a slight shock of surprise, do mean exactly what they say. The last line is realistic and specific. It is not even content to say,

> And I in bed again!

It is, rather, more scrupulously specific, and says,

> And I in *my* bed again!

All of this does not go to say that the realistic elements here are to be taken as canceling, or negating, the romantic elements. There is no ironical leer. The poem is not a celebration of carnality. It is a faithful lover who speaks. He is faithful to the absent beloved, and he is also faithful to the full experience of love. That is, he does not abstract one aspect of the experience and call it the whole experience. He does not strain nature out of nature; he does not overspiritualize nature. This nameless poet would never have said, in the happier days of his love, that he had been led to his Sweet's chamber window by "a spirit in my feet"; and he certainly would not have added the coy disavowal, "who knows how?" But because the nameless poet refused to overspiritualize nature, we can accept the spirituality of the poem.

Another poem gives us another problem.

> Ah, what avails the sceptered race!
>   Ah, what the form divine!
> What every virtue, every grace!
>   Rose Aylmer, all were thine.
>
> Rose Aylmer, whom these wakeful eyes
>   May weep, but never see,
> A night of memories and of sighs
>   I consecrate to thee.

This is another poem about lost love: a "soft" subject. Now, to one kind of poet the soft subject presents a sore temptation. Because it is soft in its natural state, he is inclined to feel that to get at its poetic essence he must make it softer still, that he must insist on its softness, that he must render it as "pure" as possible. At first glance, it may seem that Landor is trying to do just that. What he says seems to be emphatic, unqualified, and open. Not every power, grace, and virtue could avail to preserve his love. That statement insists on the pathetic contrast. And in the next stanza, wakefulness and tearfulness are mentioned quite unashamedly, along with memories and sighs. It is all blurted out, as pure as possible.

But only in the paraphrase is it "blurted." The actual quality of the first stanza is hard, not soft. It is a chiseled stanza, in which formality is insisted upon. We may observe the balance of the first and second lines; the balance of the first half with the second half of the third line, which recapitulates the structure of the first two lines; the balance of the two parts of the last line, though here the balance is merely a rhythmical and not a sense balance as in the preceding instances; the binders of discreet alliteration, repetition, and assonance. The stanza is built up, as it were, of units which are firmly defined and sharply separated, phrase by phrase, line by line. We have the formal control of the soft subject, ritual and not surrender.

But in the second stanza the rigor of this formality is somewhat abated, as the more general, speculative emphasis (why cannot pomp, virtue, and grace avail?) gives way to the personal emphasis, as though the repetition of the beloved's name had, momentarily, released the flood of feeling. The first line of the second stanza spills over into the second; the "wakeful eyes" as subject find their verb in the next line, "weep," and the *wake-weep* alliteration, along with the pause after *weep,* points up the disintegration of the line, just as it emphasizes the situation. Then with the phrase "but never see" falling away from the long thrust of the rhetorical structure to the pause after weep, the poem seems to go completely soft, the frame is broken. But, even as the poet insists on "memories and sighs," in the last two lines he restores the balance. Notice the understatement of "A night." It says: "I know that life is a fairly complicated affair, and that I am committed to it and to its complications. I intend to stand by my commitment, as a man of integrity, that is, to live despite the grief. Since life is complicated, I cannot, if I am to live, spare too much time for indulging grief. I can give *a* night, but not all nights." The lover, like the hero of Frost's poem "Stopping by Woods on a Snowy Evening," tears himself from the temptation of staring into the treacherous, delicious blackness, for he, too, has "promises to keep." Or he resembles the Homeric heroes who, after the perilous passage is made, after their energy has saved their lives, and after they have beached their craft and eaten their meal, can then set aside an hour before sleep to mourn the comrades lost by the way—the heroes who, as Aldous Huxley says, understand realistically a whole truth as contrasted with a half-truth.

Is this a denial of the depth and sincerity of the grief? The soft reader, who wants the poem pure, may be inclined to say so. But let us look at the last line to see what it gives us in answer to this question. The answer seems to lie in the word *consecrate.* The meter thrusts this word at us; we observe that two of the three metrical accents in the line fall on syllables of this word, forcing it beyond its prose emphasis. The word is important and the importance is justified, for the word tells us that the single night is not merely a lapse into weakness, a trivial event to be forgotten when the weakness is overcome. It is, rather, an event of the most extreme and focal importance, an event formally dedicated, "set apart for sacred uses," an event by which other events are to be measured. So the word *consecrate* formalizes, philosophizes, ritualizes the grief; it specifies what in the first stanza has been implied by style.

But here is another poem of grief, grief at the death of a child. It is "Bells for John Whiteside's Daughter," by John Crowe Ransom.[2]

> There was such speed in her little body,
> And such lightness in her footfall,
> It is no wonder her brown study
> Astonishes us all.
>
> Her wars were bruited in our high window.
> We looked among orchard trees and beyond,
> Where she took arms against her shadow,
> Or harried unto the pond
>
> The lazy geese, like a snow cloud
> Dripping their snow on the green grass,
> Tricking and stopping, sleepy and proud,
> Who cried in goose, Alas,
>
> For the tireless heart within the little
> Lady with rod that made them rise
> From their noon apple-dreams, and scuttle
> Goose-fashion under the skies!
>
> But now go the bells, and we are ready;
> In one house we are sternly stopped
> To say we are vexed at her brown study,
> Lying so primly propped.

Another soft subject, softer, if anything, than the subject of "Rose Aylmer," and it presents the same problem. But the problem is solved in a different way.

The first stanza is based on two time-honored clichés: first, "Heavens, won't that child ever be still, she is driving me distracted"; and second, "She was such an active, healthy-looking child, who would've ever thought she would just up and die?" In fact, the whole poem develops these clichés, and exploits, in a backhand fashion, the ironies implicit in their interrelation. And in this connection, we may note that the fact of the clichés, rather than more original or profound observations at the root of the poem, is important; there is in the poem the contrast between the staleness of the clichés and the shock of the reality. Further, we may note that the second cliché is an answer, savagely ironical in itself, to the first: the child you wished would be still *is* still, despite all that activity which had interrupted your adult occupations.

But such a savage irony is not the game here. It is too desperate, too naked, in a word, too pure. And ultimately, it is, in a sense, a meaningless irony if left in its pure state, because it depends on a mechanical, accidental contrast in nature, void of moral content. The poem is concerned with modifications and modulations of this brute, basic irony, modulations and modifications contingent upon an attitude taken toward it by a responsible human being, the speaker of the poem. The savagery is masked, or ameliorated.

In this connection, we may observe, first, the phrase "brown study." It is not the "frosted flower," the "marmoreal immobility," or any one of a thousand such phrases which would aim for the pure effect. It is merely the brown study which astonishes—a phrase which denies, as it were, the finality of the situation, underplays the pathos, and merely reminds one of those moments of childish pensiveness into which the grownup cannot penetrate. And the phrase itself is a cliché—the common now echoed in the uncommon.

Next, we may observe that stanzas two, three, and four simply document, with a busy yet wavering rhythm (one sentence runs through the three stanzas), the tireless naughtiness which was once the cause of rebuke, the naughtiness which disturbed the mature goings-on in the room with the "high window." But the naughtiness is now transmuted into a kind of fanciful story-book dream world, in which geese are whiter than nature, and the grass greener, in which geese speak in goose language, saying "Alas," and have apple-dreams. It is a drowsy, delicious world, in which the geese are bigger than life, and more important. It is an unreal (now unreal because lost), stylized world. Notice how the phrase "the little lady with rod" works: the detached primness of "little lady"; the formal, stiff effect gained by the omission of the article before *rod;* the slightly unnatural use of the word *rod* itself, which sets some distance between us and the scene (perhaps with the hint of the fairy story, a magic wand, or a magic rod—not a common, everyday stick). But the stanzas tie back into the premises of the poem in other ways. The little girl, in her excess of energy, warred against her shadow. Is it crowding matters too hard to surmise that the shadow here achieves a sort of covert symbolic significance? The little girl lost her war against her "shadow," which was always with her. Certainly the phrase "tireless heart" has some rich connotations. And the geese which say "Alas" conspire with the family to deplore the excessive activity of the child. (They do not conspire to express the present grief, only the past vexation—an inversion of the method of the pastoral elegy, or of the method of the first two garden poems.)

The business of the three stanzas, then, may be said to be twofold. First, they make us believe more fully in the child and therefore in the fact of the grief itself. They "prove" the grief, and they show the deliciousness of the lost world which will never look the same from the high window. Second, and contrariwise, they "transcend" the grief, or at least give a hint of a means for transcending immediate anguish: the lost world is, in one sense, redeemed out of time; it enters the pages of the picture book where geese speak, where the untrue is true, where the fleeting is fixed. What was had cannot, after all, be lost. (By way of comparison—a comparison which, because extreme, may be helpful—we may think of the transcendence in *A la Recherche du Temps Perdu*.) The three stanzas, then, to state it in another way, have validated the first stanza and have prepared for the last.

The three stanzas have made it possible for us to say, when

the bell tolls, "we are ready." Some kind of terms, perhaps not the best terms possible but some kind, has been made with the savage underlying irony. But the terms arrived at do not prevent the occasion from being a "stern" one. The transcendence is not absolute, and in the end is possible only because of an exercise of will and self-control. Because we control ourselves, we can say "vexed" and not some big word. And the word itself picks up the first of the domestic clichés on which the poem is based—the outburst of impatience at the naughty child who, by dying, has performed her most serious piece of naughtiness. But now the word comes to us charged with the burden of the poem, and further, as re-echoed here by the phrase "brown study," charged by the sentence in which it occurs: we are gathered formally, ritualistically, sternly together to say the word *vexed*.[3] *Vexed* becomes the ritualistic, the summarizing word.

I have used the words *pure* and *impure* often in the foregoing pages, and I confess that I have used them rather loosely. But perhaps it has been evident that I have meant something like this: the pure poem tries to be pure by excluding, more or less rigidly, certain elements which might qualify or contradict its original impulse. In other words, the pure poems want to be, and desperately, all of a piece. It has also been evident, no doubt, that the kinds of impurity which are admitted or excluded by the various little anthology pieces which have been presented, are different in the different poems. This is only to be expected, for there is not one doctrine of "pure poetry"—not one definition of what constitutes impurity in poems—but many.

And not all of the doctrines are recent. When, for example, one cites Poe as the father of *the* doctrine of pure poetry, one is in error; Poe simply fathered *a* particular doctrine of pure poetry. One can find other doctrines of purity long antedating Poe. When Sir Philip Sidney, for example, legislated against tragicomedy, he was repeating a current doctrine of purity. When Ben Jonson told William Drummond that Donne, for not keeping of accent, deserved hanging, he was defending another kind of purity; and when Dryden spoke to save the ear of the fair sex from metaphysical perplexities in amorous poems, he was defending another kind of purity, just as he was defending another when he defined the nature of the heroic drama. The eighteenth century had a doctrine of pure poetry, which may be summed up under the word *sublimity,* but which involved two corollary doctrines, one concerning diction and the other concerning imagery. But at the same time that this century, by means of these corollary doctrines, was tidying up and purifying the doctrine derived from Longinus, it was admitting into the drama certain impurities which the theorists of the heroic drama would not have admitted.

But when we think of the modern doctrine of pure poetry, we usually think of Poe, as critic and poet, perhaps of Shelley, of the Symbolists, of the Abbe Bremond, perhaps of Pater, and certainly of George Moore and the Imagists. We know Poe's position: the long poem is "a flat contradiction in terms," because intense excitement, which is essential in poetry, cannot be long maintained; the moral sense and the intellect function more satisfactorily in prose than in poetry, and, in fact, "Truth" and the "Passions," which are for Poe associated with the intellect and the moral sense, may actually be inimical to poetry; vagueness, suggestiveness are central virtues, for poetry has for "its object an *indefinite* instead of a *definite* pleasure"; poetry is not supposed to undergo close inspection, only a cursory glance, for it, "above all things, is a beautiful painting whose tints, to minute inspection, are confusion worse confounded, but start out boldly to the cursory glance of the connoisseur"; poetry aspires toward music, since it is concerned with "indefinite sensations, to which music is an *essential,* since the comprehension of sweet sound is our most indefinite conception"; melancholy is the most poetical effect and enters into all the higher manifestations of beauty. We know, too, the Abbé Bremond's mystical interpretation, and the preface to George Moore's anthology, and the Imagist manifesto.

But these views are not identical. Shelley, for instance, delights in the imprecision praised and practiced by Poe, but he has an enormous appetite for "Truth" and the "Passions," which are, except for purposes of contrast, excluded by Poe. The Imagist manifesto, while excluding ideas, endorses precision rather than vagueness in rendering the image, and admits diction and objects which would have seemed impure to Poe and to many poets of the nineteenth century, and does not take much stock in the importance of verbal music. George Moore emphasizes the objective aspect of his pure poetry, which he describes as "something which the poet creates outside his own personality," and this is opposed to the objective emphasis in Poe and Shelley; but he shares with both an emphasis on verbal music, and with the former a distaste for ideas.

But more recently, the notion of poetic purity has emerged in other contexts, contexts which sometimes obscure the connection of the new theories with the older theories. For instance, Max Eastman has a theory. "Pure poetry," he says in *The Literary Mind,* "is the pure effort to heighten consciousness." Mr. Eastman, we discover elsewhere in his book, would ban idea from poetry, but his motive is different from, say, the motive of Poe, and the difference is important: Poe would kick out the ideas because the ideas hurt the poetry, and Mr. Eastman would kick out the ideas because the poetry hurts the ideas. Only the scientist, he tells us, is entitled to have ideas on any subject, and the rest of the citizenry must wait to be told what attitude to take toward the ideas which they are not permitted to have except at second-hand. Literary truth, he says, is truth which is "uncertain or comparatively unimportant." But he does assign the poet a function—to heighten consciousness. In the light of this context we would have to rewrite his original definition: pure poetry is the pure effort to heighten consciousness, but the consciousness which is heightened must not have any connection with ideas, must involve no attitude toward any ideas.

Furthermore, to assist the poet in fulfilling the assigned function, Mr. Eastman gives him a somewhat sketchy doctrine of "pure" poetic diction. For instance, the word *bloated* is not admissible into a poem because it is, as he testifies, "sacred to the memory of dead fish," and the word *tangy* is, though he knows not exactly how, "intrinsically poetic." The notion of a vocabulary which is intrinsically poetic seems, with Mr. Eastman, to mean a vocabulary which indicates agreeable or beautiful objects. So we might rewrite the original definition to read: pure poetry is the pure effort to heighten consciousness, but the consciousness which is heightened must be a consciousness exclusively of agreeable or beautiful objects—certainly not a consciousness of any ideas.

In a recent book, *The Idiom of Poetry,* Frederick Pottle has discussed the question of pure poetry. He distinguishes another type of pure poetry in addition to the types already mentioned. He calls it the "Elliptical," and would include in it symbolist and metaphysical poetry (old and new) and some work by poets such as Collins, Blake, and Browning. He observes—without any pejorative implication, for he is a critical relativist and scarcely permits himself the luxury of evaluative judgments—that the contemporary product differs from older examples of the elliptical type in that "the modern poet goes much farther in employing private experiences or ideas than would formerly have been thought legitimate." To the common reader, he says, "the prime characteristic of this kind of poetry is not the nature of its imagery but its obscurity: its urgent suggestion that you add something to the poem without telling you what that something is." This omitted "something" he interprets as the prose "frame"—to use his word—the statement of the occasion, the logical or narrative transitions, the generalized application derived from the poem, etc. In other words, this type of pure poetry contends that "the effect would be more powerful if we could somehow manage to feel the images fully and accurately without having the effect diluted by any words put in to give us a 'meaning'—that is, if we could expel all the talk *about* the imaginative realization and have the pure realization itself."[4]

For the moment I shall pass the question of the accuracy of Mr. Pottle's description of the impulse of Elliptical Poetry and present the question which ultimately concerns him. How pure does poetry need to be in practice? That is the question which Mr. Pottle asks. He answers by saying that a great degree of impurity may be admitted, and cites our famous didactic poems, *The Faerie Queene, Essay on Man, The Vanity of Human Wishes, The Excursion*. That is the only answer which the relativist, and nominalist, can give. Then he turns to what he calls the hardest question in the theory of poetry: What kind of prosaism is acceptable and what is not? His answer, which he advances very modestly, is this:

> . . . the element of prose is innocent and even salutary when it appears as—take your choice of three metaphors—a background on which the images are projected, or a frame in which they are shown, or a thread on which they are strung. In short, when it serves a *structural* purpose. Prose in a poem seems offensive to me when . . . the prosaisms are sharp, obvious, individual, and ranked coordinately with the images.

At first glance this looks plausible, and the critic has used the sanctified word *structural*. But at second glance we may begin to wonder what the sanctified word means to the critic. It means something rather mechanical—background, frame, thread. The structure is a showcase, say a jeweler's showcase, in which the little jewels of poetry are exhibited, the images. The showcase shouldn't be ornamental itself ("sharp, obvious, individual," Mr. Pottle says), for it would then distract us from the jewels; it should be chastely designed, and the jewels should repose on black velvet and not on flowered chintz. But Mr. Pottle doesn't ask what the relation among the bright jewels should be. Not only does the showcase bear no relation to the jewels, but the jewels, apparently, bear no relation to each other. Each one is a shining little focus of heightened interest, and all together they make only such a pattern, perhaps, as may make it easier for the eye to travel from one little jewel to the next, when the time comes to move on. Structure becomes here simply a device of salesmanship, a well-arranged showcase.

It is all mechanical. And this means that Mr. Pottle, after all, is himself an exponent of pure poetry. He locates the poetry simply in the images, the nodes of "pure realization." This means that what he calls the "element of prose" includes definition of situation, movement of narrative, logical transition, factual description, generalization, ideas. Such things, for him, do not participate in the poetic effect of the poem; in fact, they work against the poetic effect, and so, though necessary as a frame, should be kept from being "sharp, obvious, individual."[5]

I have referred to *The Idiom of Poetry,* first, because it is such an admirable and provocative book, sane, lucid, generous-spirited, and second, because, to my mind, it illustrates the insidiousness with which a doctrine of pure poetry can penetrate into the theory of a critic who is suspicious of such a doctrine. Furthermore, I have felt that Mr. Pottle's analysis might help me to define the common denominator of the various doctrines of pure poetry.

That common denominator seems to be the belief that poetry is an essence that is to be located at some particular place in a poem, or in some particular element. The exponent of pure poetry persuades himself that he has determined the particular something in which the poetry inheres, and then proceeds to decree that poems shall be composed, as nearly as possible, of that element and of nothing else. If we add up the things excluded by various critics and practitioners, we get a list about like this:

1. ideas, truths, generalizations, "meaning"
2. precise, complicated, "intellectual" images
3. unbeautiful, disagreeable, or neutral materials
4. situation, narrative, logical transition
5. realistic details, exact descriptions, realism in general
6. shifts in tone or mood
7. irony
8. metrical variation, dramatic adaptations of rhythm, cacophony, etc.
9. meter itself
10. subjective and personal elements.

No one theory of pure poetry excludes all of these items, and, as a matter of fact, the items listed are not on the same level of importance. Nor do the items always bear the same interpretation. For example, if one item seems to be central to discussions of pure poetry, it is the first: "ideas," it is said, "are not involved in the poetic effect, and may even be inimical to it." But this view can be interpreted in a variety of ways. If it is interpreted as simply meaning that the paraphrase of a poem is not equivalent to the poem, that the poetic gist is not to be defined as the statement embodied in the poem with the sugar-coating as bait, then the view can be held by opponents as well as exponents of any theory of pure poetry. We might scale down from this interpretation to the other extreme interpretation that the poem should merely give the sharp image in isolation. But there are many complicated and confused variations possible between the two extremes. There is, for example, the interpretation that "ideas," though they are not involved in the poetic effect, must appear in poems to provide, as Mr. Pottle's prosaisms do, a kind of frame, or thread, for the poetry—a spine to support the poetic flesh, or a Christmas tree on which the baubles of poetry are hung.[6] T. S. Eliot has said something of this sort:

> The chief use of the "meaning" of a poem, in the ordinary sense, may be (for here again I am speaking of some kinds of poetry and not all) to satisfy one habit of the reader, to keep his mind diverted and quiet, while the poem does its work upon him: much as the imaginary burglar is always provided with a bit of nice meat for the house-dog.

Here, it would seem, Mr. Eliot has simply inverted the old sugar-coated-pill theory: the idea becomes the sugar-coating and the "poetry" becomes the medicine. This seems to say that the idea in a poem does not participate in the poetic effect, and seems to commit Mr. Eliot to a theory of pure poetry. But to do justice to the quotation, we should first observe that the parenthesis indicates that the writer is referring to some sort of provisional and superficial distinction and not to a fundamental one, and second observe that the passage is out of its context. In the context, Mr. Eliot goes on to say that some poets "become impatient of this 'meaning' [explicit statement of ideas in logical order] which seems superfluous, and perceive possibilities of intensity through its elimination." This may mean either of two things. It may mean that ideas do not participate in the poetic effect, or it may mean that, though they do participate in the poetic effect, they need not appear in the poem in an explicit and argued form. And this second reading would scarcely be a doctrine of pure poetry at all, for it would involve poetic casuistry and not poetic principle.

We might, however, illustrate the second interpretation by glancing at Marvell's "Horatian Ode" on Cromwell. Marvell does not give us narrative; he does not give us an account of the issues behind the Civil War; he does not state the two competing ideas which are dramatized in the poem, the idea of "sanction" and the idea of "efficiency." But the effect of the poem does involve those two factors; and the reserved irony, scarcely resolved, which emerges from the historical situation, is an irony derived from unstated materials and ideas. It is, to use Mr. Pottle's term again, a pure poem in so far as it is elliptical in method, but it is anything but a pure poem if by purity we mean the exclusion of idea from participation in the poetic effect. And Mr. Eliot's own practice implies that he believes that ideas do participate in the poetic effect. Otherwise, why did he put the clues to his ideas in the notes at the end of *The Waste Land* after so carefully excluding any explicit statement of them from the body of the poem? If he is regarding those ideas as mere bait—the "bit of nice meat for the house-dog"—he has put the ideas in a peculiar place, in the back of the book—like giving the dog the meat on the way out of the house with the swag, or giving the mouse the cheese after he is in the trap.

All this leads to the speculation that Marvell and Mr. Eliot have purged away statement of ideas from their poems, not because they wanted the ideas to participate less in the poetry, but because they wanted them to participate more fully, intensely, and immediately. This impulse, then, would account for the characteristic types of age, types in which precision, complication, and complicated intellectual relation to the theme are exploited; in other words, they are trying—whatever may be their final success—to carry the movement of mind to the center of the process. On these grounds they are the exact opposite of poets who, presumably on grounds of purity, exclude the movement of mind from the center of the poetic process—from the internal structure of the poem—but pay their respects to it as a kind of footnote, or gloss, or application coming at the end. Marvell and Eliot, by their cutting away of frame, are trying to emphasize the participation of ideas in the poetic process. Then Elliptical Poetry is not, as Mr. Pottle says it is, a pure poetry at all; the elliptical poet is elliptical for purposes of inclusion, not exclusion.

But waiving the question of Elliptical Poetry, no one of the other theories does—or could—exclude all the items on the list above. And that fact may instruct us. If all of these items were excluded, we might not have any poem at all. For instance, we know how some critics have pointed out that even in the strictest Imagist poetry idea creeps in—when the image leaves its natural habitat and enters a poem, it begins to "mean" something. The attempt to read ideas out of the poetic party violates the unity of our being and the unity of our experience. "For this reason," as Santayana puts it, "philosophy, when a poet is not mindless, enters inevitably into his poetry, since it has entered into his life; or rather, the detail of things and the detail of ideas pass equally into his verse, when both alike lie in the path that has led him to his ideal. To object to theory in poetry would be like objecting to words there; for words, too, are symbols without the sensuous character of the things they stand for; and yet it is only by the net of new connections which words throw over things, in recalling them, that poetry arises at all. Poetry is an attenuation, a rehandling, an echo of crude experience; it itself a theoretic vision of things at arm's length."

Does this not, then, lead us to the conclusion that poetry does not inhere in any particular element but depends upon the set of relationships, the structure, which we call the poem?

Then the question arises: what elements cannot be used in such a structure? I should answer that nothing that is available in human experience is to be legislated out of poetry. This does not mean that anything can be used in *any* poem, or that some materials or elements may not prove more recalcitrant than others, or that it might not be easy to have too much of some things. But it does mean that granted certain contexts, any sort of material, a chemical formula, for instance, might appear functionally in a poem. It also may mean that, other things being equal, the greatness of a poet depends upon the extent of the area of experience which he can master poetically.

Can we make any generalizations about the nature of the poetic structure? First, it involves resistances, at various levels. There is the tension between the rhythm of the poem and the rhythm of speech (a tension which is very low at the extreme of free verse and at the extreme of verse such as that of "Ulalume," which verges toward a walloping doggerel); between the formality of the rhythm and the informality of the language; between the particular and the general, the concrete and the abstract; between the elements of even the simplest metaphor; between the beautiful and the ugly; between ideas (as in Marvell's poem); between the elements involved in irony (as in "Bells for John Whiteside's Daughter" or "Rose Aylmer"); between prosaisms and poeticisms (as in "Western Wind").

This list is not intended to be exhaustive; it is intended to be merely suggestive. But it may be taken to imply that the poet is like the jujitsu expert; he wins by utilizing the resistance of his opponent—the materials of the poem. In other words, a poem, to be good, must earn itself. It is a motion toward a point of rest, but if it is not a resisted motion, it is motion of no consequence. For example, a poem which depends upon stock materials and stock responses is simply a toboggan slide, or a fall through space. And the good poem must, in some way, involve the resistances; it must carry something of the context of its own creation: it must come to terms with Mercutio.

This is another way of saying that a good poem involves the participation of the reader; it must, as Coleridge puts it, make the reader into "an active creative being." Perhaps we can see this most readily in the case of tragedy: the determination of good or evil is not a "given" in tragedy, it is something to be earned in the process, and even the tragic villain must be "loved." We must kill him, as Brutus killed Caesar, not as butchers but as sacrificers. And all of this adds up to the fact that the structure is a dramatic structure, a movement through action toward rest, through complication toward simplicity of effect.

In the foregoing discussion, I have deliberately omitted reference to another type of pure poetry, a type which tends to become dominant in an age of political crisis and social disorientation. Perhaps the most sensible description of this type can be found in an essay by Herbert Muller:

> If it is not the primary business of the poet to be eloquent about these matters [faith and ideals], it still does not follow that he has more dignity or wisdom than those who are, or that he should have more sophistication. At any rate the fact is that almost all poets of the past did freely make large, simple statements, and not in their prosy or lax moments.

Mr. Muller then goes on to illustrate by quoting three famous large, simple statements:

> *In la sua volontade è nostra pace*

and

> We are such stuff
> As dreams are made on; and our little life
> Is rounded with a sleep.

and

> The mind is its own place, and in itself
> Can make a heaven of hell, a hell of heaven.

Mr. Muller is here attacking the critical emphasis on ironic tension in poetry. His attack really involves two lines of argument. First, the poet is not wiser than the statesman, philosopher, or saint, people who are eloquent about faith and ideals and who say what they mean, without benefit of irony. This Platonic line of argument is, I think, off the point in the present context. Second, the poets of the past have made large, simple affirmations, have said what they meant. This line of argument is very much on the point.

Poets have tried very hard, for thousands of years, to say what they mean. Not only have they tried to say what they mean, they have tried to prove what they mean. The saint proves his vision by stepping cheerfully into the fires. The poet, somewhat less spectacularly, proves his vision by submitting it to the fires of irony—to the drama of his structure—in the hope that the fires will refine it. In other words, the poet wishes to indicate that his vision has been earned, that it can survive reference to the complexities and contradictions of experience. And irony is one such device of reference.

In this connection let us look at the first of Mr. Muller's exhibits. The famous line occurs in Canto III of the *Paradiso*. It is spoken by Piccarda Donati, in answer to Dante's question as to why she does not desire to rise higher than her present sphere, the sphere of the moon. But it expresses, in unequivocal terms, a central theme of the *Commedia,* as of Christian experience. On the one hand, it may be a pious truism, fit for sampler work, and on the other hand, it may be a burning conviction, tested and earned. Dante, in his poem, sets out to show how it has been earned and tested.

One set of ironic contrasts which centers on this theme concerns, for instance, the opposition between the notion of human justice and the notion of divine justice. The story of Paolo and Francesca is so warm, appealing, and pathetic in its human terms, and their punishment so savage and unrelenting, so incommensurable, it seems, with the fault, that Dante, torn by the conflict, falls down as a dead body falls. Or Farinata, the enemy of Dante's house, is presented by the poet in terms of his human grandeur, which now, in Hell, is transmuted into a superhuman grandeur,

com' avesse l'inferno in gran dispitto.

Ulysses remains a hero, a hero who should draw special applause from Dante, who defined the temporal end of man as the conquest of knowledge. But Ulysses is damned, as the great Brutus is damned, who hangs from the jaws of the fiend in the lowest pit of traitors. So divine justice is set over against human pathos, human dignity, human grandeur, human intellect, human justice. And we recall how Virgil, more than once, reminds Dante that he must not apply human standards to the sights he sees. It is this long conflict, which appears in many forms, this ironic tension, which finally gives body to the simple eloquence of the line in question; the statement is meaningful, not for what it says, but for what has gone before. It is earned. It has been earned by the entire poem.

I do not want to misrepresent Mr. Muller. He does follow his quotations by the sentence: "If they are properly qualified in the work as a whole, they may still be taken straight, they are [he italicizes the word] taken so in recollection as in their immediate impact." But how can we take a line "straight," in either "recollection" or "immediate impact," unless we ignore what "properly qualified" the line in "the work as a whole"? And if we do take it so, are we not violating, very definitely, the poet's meaning, for the poet means the *poem,* he doesn't mean the line.

It would be interesting to try to develop the contexts of the other passages which Mr. Muller quotes. But in any case, he is simply trying, in his essay, to guard against what he considers to be, rightly or wrongly, a too narrow description of poetry; he is not trying to legislate all poetry into the type of simple eloquence, the unqualified statement of "faith and ideals." But we have also witnessed certain, probably preliminary, attempts to legislate literature into becoming a simple, unqualified, "pure" statement of faith and ideals. We have seen the writers of the 1920s called the "irresponsibles." We have seen writers such as Proust, Eliot, Dreiser, and Faulkner called writers of the "death drive." Why are these writers condemned? Because they have tried, within the limits of their gifts, to remain faithful to the complexities of the problems with which they are dealing, because they have refused to take the easy statement as solution, because they have tried to define the context in which, and the terms by which, faith and ideals may be earned.

This method, however, will scarcely satisfy the mind which is hot for certainties; to that mind it will seem merely an index to lukewarmness, indecision, disunity, treason. The new theory of purity would purge out all complexities and all ironies and all self-criticism. And this theory will forget that the hand-me-down faith, the hand-me-down ideals, no matter what the professed content, is in the end not only meaningless but vicious. It is vicious because, as parody, it is the enemy of all faith.

NOTES

1. It may be objected here that I am reading the phrase "in my arms" as a twentieth-century reader. I confess the fact. Certainly, several centuries have passed since the composition of the little poem, and those centuries have thickened the romantic mist about the words, but it is scarcely to be believed that the sixteenth century was the clear, literal Eden dawn of poetry when words walked without the fig leaf.

2. From *Selected Poems,* by John Crowe Ransom. Copyright 1924, 1945, by Alfred A. Knopf, Inc. Used by permission.

3. It might be profitable, in contrast with this poem, to look at "After the Burial," by James Russell Lowell, a poem which is identical in situation. But in Lowell's poem the savagery of the irony is unqualified. In fact, the whole poem insists, quite literally, that qualification is impossible: the scheme of the poem is to set up the brute fact of death against possible consolations. It insists on "tears," the "thin-worn locket," the "anguish of deathless hair," "the smallness of the child's grave," the "little shoe in the corner." It is a poem which, we might say, does not progress, but ends where it begins, resting in savage irony from which it stems; or we might say that it is a poem without any "insides," for the hero of the poem is not attempting to do anything about the problem which confronts him—it is a poem without issue, without conflict, a poem of unconditional surrender. In other words, it tries to be a pure poem, pure grief, absolutely inconsolable. It is a strident poem, and strident in its rhythms. The fact that we know this poem to be an expression of a bereavement historically real makes it an embarrassing poem, as well. It is a naked poem.

4. F. W. Bateson, in *English Poetry and the English Language,* discusses the modern elliptical practice in poetry. Tennyson, he points out in connection with "the Sailor Boy," dilutes his poetry by telling a story as well as writing a poem, and "a shorter poem would have spoilt his story." The claims of prose conquer the claims of poetry. Of the Victorians in general: "The dramatic and narrative framework of their poems, by circumventing the disconcerting plunges into *medias res* which are the essence of poetry, brings it down to a level of prose. The reader knows where he is; it serves the purpose of introduction and note." Such introductions and notes in the body of the poem are exactly what Mr. Pottle says is missing in Elliptical Poetry. Mr. Bateson agrees with Poe in accepting intensity as the criterion of the poetic effect, and in

accepting the corollary that a poem should be short. But he, contradicting Poe, seems to admire precise and complicated incidental effects.

5. Several other difficulties concerning Pottle's statement may suggest themselves. First, since he seems to infer that the poetic essence resides in the image, what view would he take of meter and rhythm? This statement, strictly construed, would mean that these factors do not participate in the poetic effect, but are simply part of the frame. Second, what view of dramatic poetry is implied? It seems again that a strict interpretation would mean that the story and the images bear no essential relation to each other, that the story is simply part of the frame. That is, the story, characters, rhythms, and ideas are on one level, and the images, in which the poetry inheres, are on another. But Caroline Spurgeon, G. Wilson Knight, and other critics have given us some reason for holding that the images do bear some relation to the business of the other items. In fact, all of the items, as Jacques Maritain has said, "feelings, ideas, representations, are for the artist merely materials and means, still symbols." That is, they are all elements in a single expressive structure.

6. Such an interpretation seems to find a parallel in E. M. Forster's treatment of plot in fiction. Plot in his theory becomes a mere spine and does not really participate, except in a narrow, formal sense, in the fictional effect. By his inversion of the Aristotelian principle the plot becomes merely a necessary evil.

ELDER OLSON

THE LYRIC

Most of us become acquainted with poetry of one sort or another in our early childhood. At some point in our education we are told about the "forms" of poetry: epic, tragedy, ballad, elegy, pastoral, sonnet, lyric and the rest. And most of us remain content with such supposed knowledge. As a rule we do not reflect on the fact that of these "forms" some, like epic and tragedy, are genuine forms; some, like sonnet and triolet, merely verse patterns; and some, like pastoral and ballad, merely sets of conventions which can be used in varying forms. We talk with confidence about the lyric, as we do about the novel and the drama. We talk about the nature of poetry, the nature of the lyric, of the novel, of the drama. And usually we talk thus with perfect safety, even if we are professional students of literature. It is only when we fall into the hands of a shrewd and persistent questioner that, like the Athenians questioned by Socrates, we come to doubt whether we really know what we think we know. Fortunately or unfortunately, such questioners are rare.

Why should we bother to discriminate literary forms—why bother to define them accurately? Let me admit immediately that for many modes of criticism, for many critical problems, there is no reason whatsoever to bother; for such

Reprinted from Elder Olson, "The Lyric," in *On Value Judgments in the Arts and Other Essays* (Chicago: University of Chicago Press, 1976), 212–19.

modes and such problems the questions of specific form are either insignificant or irrelevant. But, on the other hand, there are other modes and other problems for which such questions are crucial. It is sometimes dangerous to talk of things as being the same or alike when they are in fact different. Furthermore, a poet may have a gift for one kind of poetry and not for another; the criteria which are appropriate to one kind may not be appropriate to another; a good judge of one kind may not necessarily be a good judge of another.

Besides, all of us do differentiate, at one level or another—it is only a matter of how general or how specific we wish to be. We talk about poetry, after all; and merely to mention the word "poetry" is of course to differentiate poetry from something else. A great many of us even attempt to define poetry—to say what it is. John Stuart Mill, writing in 1833, observed: "It has often been asked, What is Poetry? And many and various are the answers which have been returned." The question has been asked even more frequently since 1833, and the answers have multiplied in number and variety. We make definitions, none of them satisfactory, and some very bad indeed. Evidently, then, whatever we say, we do think the problem worth thinking about. If it is worth thought, thought ought to be worthy of it. And this our thought has scarcely been.

Consider, for example, the upshot of our various attempts to define the lyric. What is a lyric? A brief poem? How brief? The epigram and the aphorism are briefer; and some lyrics, like Shelley's "Adonais," are very long. Is it a poem of intense emotion? Shall we say the emotion in lyrics is more intense than that in *King Lear?* And in any case, do all lyrics involve intense emotion? What is so intense about "Full fathom five thy father lies?" Is the lyric a poem expressing the poet's innermost feelings? If so, how is it that we recognize as lyrics thousands of poems, the very identity of whose author is unknown to us, let alone his innermost feelings? Conversely, what were Yeats's innermost feelings about old age? He has left us a good number of lyrics on old age, expressing a variety of quite incompatible "innermost feelings." Does, in fact, our recognition of lyric form or the pleasure we derive from it in any way depend upon our reflection on the poet and his innermost feelings? Is the lyric a poem capable of being sung or set to music? Any discourse, verse or prose, is capable of being sung or set to music; you could sing or set to music William of Ockham's *Summa totius logicae* if you wanted to, or for that matter, Webster's Dictionary, or the city telephone directory. Well, then: a poem characterized by lyrical quality? That is a vicious circle. Et cetera. I find all such pseudo-definitions senseless trash, the only significance of which is that their makers neither knew what a lyric nor what a definition is. T. S. Eliot, by the way, seems to have felt much as I do, although his distinction between the three voices of poetry is hardly more helpful.

I do not propose in this paper to attempt definitions or the statement of principles or the construction of a poetics. I propose something far more simple, far more modest: to see whether we can establish, so to speak, a geography of the lyric; to delineate its boundaries, so that we may at least know where it begins and where it leaves off. And it occurs to me that a certain kind of procedure might be very useful in this connection. In things that exist by nature we observe that some possess relatively simple, some relatively complex structures. No one doubts that the amoeba is among the simpler organisms, whereas man is among the most complex. It is evident, too, that a greater or less complexity exists also in the poetic arts. The lyric consists of a single utterance, usually brief; epic and tragedy usually involve many characters, in manifold interaction in many incidents, uttering many speeches. Between these extremes, moreover, we find such things as one-act plays, epic episodes, and the like, obviously more complex than the lyric, and less complex than epic or tragedy. It seems that it might be possible, thus, to arrange the structures of poetry, beginning with the very simplest, in the order of increasing complexity, and to see whether we can locate the lyric among them.

What, then, is the simplest form of poetry? While there is no necessary correlation of mere length with complexity of structure, it is clear on the other hand that something may be too brief to be very complex. Homer could not have written the *Iliad,* or Shakespeare *Hamlet,* in ten words or less. It seems reasonable, thus, to look for the simple forms of poetry in some area of discourse in which expression is severely restricted. Naturally one thinks at once of the more stringent verse-forms, the haiku particularly.

Here is a haiku by Issa, called "Spring Day":

Departing, the spring day
Lingers
Where there is water.

Is this a poem? Certainly. A lyric poem? Surely. Is it the simplest kind of poem? It must be: it conveys only a single perception; if we try to divide that into parts, we have nothing. But if this is true, we have already established one boundary of lyric poetry; it begins with the very simplest kind. Not that I want to argue, mind you, that everything in the haiku pattern of five syllables plus seven plus five is a poem. I was amused to see a sign, gold-lettered on scarlet background on the Hong Kong ferry:

Notice
Smoking and spitting
Are strictly prohibited
On these premises.

That has the verse-pattern, but I do not think it is a poem. Nor do I wish to contend that every haiku is a lyric. I merely think this one of Issa's is. We said it involved only a single perception; now, perception is not merely an exercise of sense, but a mental activity of a certain kind. Are there other elementary mental activities? Certainly, there must be absolutely elementary and indivisible activities of every sort—recollecting, recognizing, inferring, expecting, imagining, and the like, as well as of every emotional response. It would be wearisome to illustrate them all; perhaps we need merely observe that the anonymous "O Westron Wind" involves a single wish for spring, so that the lover can return to his beloved at home. And we may also observe that each of them, if it enters into a *poem* as the wish enters into "O Westron Wind," will produce a *lyric* poem.

It now occurs to me that these elements can be used as elements in a more complex poem; for example, in a sequence of perceptions. Are there such poems? I think at once of Theodore Roethke's fine poem, "The Heron"; it is nothing other than a sequence of such perceptions. Any such sequence, of course, must have a certain unity and continuity; but if it results in a poem, that poem is a lyric poem. Is this possible for all the other elementary activities? Certainly. And again, if a poem results, it is a lyric. Nor is it necessary that the activities be all of the same kind; for example, a perception may lead to an emotion and that to recollection and that to another emotion.

Let us observe something else. The "speaker," if I may use that word, in Issa's poem is hardly characterized at all; he is simply someone capable of that perception and whatever it may imply. We know something more about the speaker in "O Westron Wind": he is a lover, separated from his love by winter (we are not even sure that "he" is a *he*). Of his moral character we know nothing; we do not even know whether the love is licit or illicit, or anything further. But, while emotions and desires and choices and wishes are common to all mankind, *what* moves, *what* is desired, chosen, or wished may characterize men indeed, as to their state of mind, disposition, or moral character. It is obvious, then, that the character of the "speaker" in a lyric poem may range from one absolutely universal to one very much particularized. Consider the difference, for example, between Issa's speaker and Browning's in "Soliloquy of the Spanish Cloister."

We might note, also, that this sequence of ours can be of various kinds; that it can, for instance, proceed in a straight line, or involve a turning point, or several turning points; "Lycidas" and Keats's "Ode to a Nightingale" involve turning points; but I shall pass over such matters. What really concerns us is this: that events and activities of the mind, if rendered into poems complete as such and no more, will always result in lyric poems. I shall not define "poetry" for you; you know the difference between Issa's haiku and the "haiku" on the Hong Kong ferry. Now reflect that what goes on in the mind is purely private; you can only know what goes on in the mind of another, even your husband or wife, if it is somehow expressed. *Expression* is a word we knock about a good deal; I shall strictly define it as—whatever form it takes—the *external* manifestation of activities and events in the mind that would otherwise remain private. *Internal.* So—granted we have poetry—there is a poetry of *expression*. And it is lyric poetry. At once we see, in the absurdity of the definition of lyric poetry as "the *poet's* innermost thoughts and feelings" a grain of truth: a lyric poetry of *private* thoughts and feelings, unknown unless expressed. *Whose* private thoughts and feelings? It does not matter; it matters very much what the thoughts and feelings are and how they are expressed. Unless of course, by "whose" you mean, not Yeats or Keats, but the person in the poem. And notice that *External* events are here simply the circumstances of the internal or private events.

At this point I recall a poem somewhat unduly celebrated some thirty years ago: Marvell's "To His Coy Mistress." It is a superb poem although I personally cannot—no doubt through poetic insensibility—read into it all of the profundities that better sensibilities have found in it. Whatever the case may be, there is no doubt about one thing: it is not simply an *expression,* as I defined the term, of internal conditions of a lover; it is an act (true, a verbal act, and these are no less real than physical acts, as some of you may have reason to know)—an act performed upon another person or persons. Let us not deceive ourselves here: Tennyson's "Ulysses" looks like an act but is not: it is merely *expression* masking as an act; Marvell's lover means business, and is operating upon his coy mistress precisely insofar as she is willing but coy, that is to say, temporizing; and like a sensible fellow, he addresses himself to the topic of Time. But, in any case, we must regard here, not an interior condition, but an external *act.* Is "To His Coy Mistress" a lyric poem? Why not? It has been so regarded by everyone. It follows that there is a lyric poem of the verbal act. There may be many verbal acts: of persuading, beseeching, commanding, informing, betraying, and so on. But we have an *act*. How did the coy mistress *react?* We have no idea, unless we suppose (illicitly) that she could not have resisted. Who is she? She is a mere circumstance of the act. Indeed, we ask nothing further of her; we are satisfied with the poem as it is.

We have seen that the elementary activities of mind in the private sphere might be extended in sequence. Basically, that is elementarily, Marvell's lover offers nothing but plea and reason; it is possible to imagine a *sequence* of such pleas, the lady in no way responding. This would give us a sequence of lyric poems. We can also suppose that the lover, here characterized as ardent and witty, can be generalized to the point where he is ardent simply, as in Marlowe's "Come live with me and be my love"; we can also suppose him to be particularized in character. It makes no difference; we are still within the areas of what we should call lyric poems. True, we might call them, as Browning did, "dramatic lyrics"; but all this means is that we have particularized character and circumstance. And here we may note something further: out of such elements alone, no matter how compounded, we should never be able to achieve the kind of construction we call *plot*. The same observation, of course, applies to the private experiences of which we have spoken.

Let us call this second major stage the *address*—the act—regardless of the verbal form it takes. So we have two major divisions, thus far: expression and address. Suppose we add a third: suppose the coy mistress *replies*. At once we have something different: not the expression of the private mental activity, not the act, (which may, by the way, be morally characteristic or not) in itself, but act and response or reaction. That is, *interaction*. At once we have a very different element; such elements, compounded, are capable of producing what we call a *plot*. As individual perception and passion and thought are swallowed up, so to speak, in act, individual act is here swallowed up in interaction; what results is a contexture of interaction. Yet there are lyric poems of interaction: for example, "The Nut-Brown Maid." So, it seems, we are approaching the limits of lyric.

We must, therefore, be very careful here. Such interplay or

inter-action (suppose we call it *colloquy*) can take various forms: utterances in turn, like lovers pledging mutual love; question and answer; demand and response; and things beside. All these may be found, of course, in plays as well as in lyrics. When do they overpass the bounds of lyric and become something else? Precisely when external circumstances and events cease to be mere *occasions* for individual action as purely individual action and become something prior; when the continuity of the external overrules the internal continuity of individual action and reaction; when, for example, the consequences of former actions or the working out of Nemesis or the changes of circumstance take priority over the individual. Under such conditions the individual action is intelligible and effective primarily in terms of what it subserves. But if external circumstances and events remain *secondary,* as ingredients in the individual act, the case is the reverse. If a poem results, it remains lyric. We can even use colloquies as elements, again, as elements in a sequence; and the elements can merely be juxtaposed or involve some type of progression such as addition (the one adding to the other) or repetition, or contrast, or dialectical progression, or opposition, or conflict. If the poet proceeds in this way, at the most he will produce something approaching a dramatic scene, as Browning does in "The Bishop Orders His Tomb at St. Praxed's Church" (though here the colloquy is represented through one speaker only); he will not produce a plot.

There is one further possibility. We may note that a framework of action—some sort of general action not serving as plot, but as successive *occasions* for lyric poems—is possible. To give instances: Meredith's "Modern Love," Wilfrid Scawen Blunt's "Esther," Eugene Lee-Hamilton's "Mima Bella," William Ellery Leonard's "Two Lives," Edna St. Vincent Millay's "Fatal Interview." There are of course other possibilities of organization—for example, as illustrating the various aspects of love. Whatever the organization, so long as it merely provides *occasions* for lyrics, the poem will remain lyrical.

Suppose we sum up. We have three basic lyrical phases: that of the private sphere, which involves the continuity of expression; that of the verbal act, which involves the continuity of address; and that of the colloquy, which involves the continuity of interchange or inter-action. All of these may entail the momentary (or elementary) or the sequential. They remain lyrical so long as their form is unaffected by any contexture in which they may be placed; for example, Shakespeare's lyrics in the plays are lyrics so long as their independence as wholes is not affected. In other words, lyric poetry presents individual action and reaction as wholes, unaffected by their context; the contexture of external events remains, not as conditions affecting them, but as occasions. Again, while they may contain within themselves a considerable narrative or dramatic portion, that portion is subordinate to the lyrical whole; thus the narrative of the wreck of the Deutschland, in the poem of that name, remains subservient to a lyrical whole, and Hopkins rightly remarked that his poem was not a narrative but an ode. Once we pass the bounds of that independence, however, once expression and address and colloquy become subservient to a further end as affecting their form as complete and whole in themselves, we have gone beyond the bounds of the lyric, and find ourselves in other and more complex forms.

Obviously private happenings in the mind, verbal acts, and colloquy or dialogue are not peculiar to the lyric forms; they may be found everywhere in the longer and more complex narrative and dramatic forms. But here they are parts, not wholes; they are subservient to some more comprehensive principle, such as *plot;* and, serving a function beyond themselves, they are seldom intelligible by themselves (a speech from a play is not intelligible by itself) or developed as they would be in lyrical treatment. The train of thought or passion and the verbal act are constantly subject to interruption or deflection from their course by external forces such as the speeches and actions of others; the colloquy is similarly subject. The difference, if I may use a somewhat homely comparison, is that between a balloon inflated to its proper shape, nothing affecting it but the internal forces of the gas, and a balloon subjected to the pressure of external forces which counteract the internal. Thus, as we move from simpler to more complex forms, the speech which might have been whole and complete in itself takes the form demanded by the scene; the scene takes the form demanded by the episode; the episode, the form demanded by the plot or some other comprehensive principle. As the principle becomes more and more comprehensive, the subservient parts are subject to further and further determination.

We may note a similar progression. In the lyric of mental experience or activity, that experience or activity is primary. In the lyric of the verbal act, it is no longer primary but merely a factor of the act. In the lyric of colloquy, the verbal act is no longer primary but a factor in the colloquy. And so on: each is sublated in the next.

We have found, I think, the boundaries of lyric territory, but we are far from knowing everything these boundaries contain. It should be clear even from this much consideration that there are different forms ruled by different principles, so that we can no longer speak, with any strictness at least, of *the* lyric in the sense of a single form. And we have not even touched upon such matters as the serious and the comic (for lyrics can be comic—"Soliloquy of the Spanish Cloister" is comic); matters which, since they are differentiations affecting form, will enter into the definitions of these forms. A further thing is clear—that it is futile to attempt a definition of lyric, if we mean by definition a statement of the nature or essence of something; for things of different natures cannot have one nature or definition. A corollary of this is that it is also futile to attempt to define poetry in general; for the same principle applies, and if lyric cannot be defined, neither can poetry.

ROBERT HAYDEN

"HOW IT STRIKES A CONTEMPORARY"

REFLECTIONS ON POETRY AND THE ROLE OF THE POET

I call him the Inquisitor, though he is more like Chekhov's Black Monk than anything else. He has appeared in my study on several occasions—once or twice during the sixties and most recently a few weeks ago.

Each of his visits has been unannounced, if not entirely unexpected.

I cannot say that I wholly dislike the Inquisitor, though neither can I say that I enjoy his company. But his attitudes toward me and my work do have a stimulating effect, and, I have come to believe, an ultimately salutary influence. Nevertheless, I wonder sometimes if the remedy isn't worse than the disease. I can value him at certain moments as a sort of Reader over your Shoulder—to use Robert Graves's term. He often reminds me of the tough old woman I once knew who said to me, "Boy, what you messin' round with all that poetry stuff for? Ain't no percentage in *that*."

Quite often this Devil's Advocate looks and sounds like certain acquaintances of mine who feel it is their duty to see that I keep both feet on the ground. Or like certain professors I have endured who have tried in vain to convince me that Shakespeare said it all and therefore I should accept the fact

---

Reprinted from Robert Hayden, "'How It Strikes a Contemporary': Reflections on Poetry and the Role of the Poet," in *Collected Prose,* ed. Frederick Glaysher (Ann Arbor: University of Michigan Press, 1984), 3–16.

that I was born with too little too late. Yes, he is very similar at times to these self-appointed guardians of poetry. Not to mention his resemblance to certain "criticasters" for whom my blackness is so dense they can never see their way through or beyond it to me as a poet.

On his most recent visit, the Inquisitor seemed, I thought, more cynical and querulous than ever. But far less original. What he said then I have heard him say before. Most of his comments were simply repetitions of the misconceptions about poets and poetry current nowadays. And they brought out the unwilling didact in me.

I was writing when the Inquisitor entered the room. He seated himself on my worktable and began talking in his usual, peremptory fashion:

INQ.: Long time no see. How's the poetry business these days?

POET: You know how it irritates me to have you ask about "the poetry business."

INQ.: But it's such fun to needle you. All you poets take yourselves much too seriously. What're you writing?

POET: A talk I'm to give as my final performance at the Library of Congress. I'm having a hard time getting it into shape. I don't like lecturing anyway. I'm not good at it.

INQ.: Yes, I know. I've heard you.

POET: I'm not *that* bad.

INQ.: I've heard worse.

POET: Look here—I've more interesting things to do than listen to your snide remarks. Anyhow, we've been through something like this before.

INQ.: When did we last meet, by the way?

POET: During the late sixties. A couple of midnight sessions, as I recall.

INQ.: It was when you were trying to define the role of the poet in twentieth-century America—your own in particular; or some such nonsense. Did you succeed?

POET: I thought I had. But I've changed my mind since then, several times. I see the question differently now and rather feel that . . .

INQ.: Later, later. We'll get to your diatribe later, if you'll be so kind. Now this talk of yours . . .

POET: Just some of my own thoughts about poets and poetry.

INQ.: Well, you've always been one to take foolish risks. Got a title yet?

POET: Sure. "How It Strikes a Contemporary."

INQ.: Hey, ain't that from old Bob Browning?

POET: From *Robert* Browning, yes. One of my favorite poets, if you remember. I'm using the title of one of his poems. It's the one where he sees the poet as God's confidant:

> We had among us, not so much a spy,
> As a recording chief-inquisitor,
> The town's true master if the town but knew!
> We merely kept a governor for form,
> While this man walked about and took account
> Of all thought, said and acted, then went home,
> And wrote it fully to our Lord the King. . . .

INQ.: You can't make me. You know you can't get rid of me until I choose to leave. Remember last time when I made you so mad? Now that I've hit a nerve I'm going to stay here and enjoy seeing you squirm.

POET: Don't count on it. I've heard this kind of blather a good many times by now, and I shouldn't react to it, but I guess I always do. I'm old enough to know there's no defense against mean-spirited ignorance except to keep away from it. I know that but still react. You're implying that standards are different for me from what they are for other American poets. You're saying I must be granted considerations not on the basis of my work, but purely in terms of racial quotas, politics, and sociology.

INQ.: Well, not entirely, maybe. But you will admit, won't you, that people are less interested in you as a poet than as a *black poet?*

POET: Yes, I have reason to believe that's partly true—and true on *both* sides of the American color line today. But it's not *my* problem—my problem is to go on trying to be the poet I think I may some day become.

INQ.: But, look, you can't just ignore the social context—the, er, social situation your people are in. Don't you feel any responsibility toward *them?*

POET: You know very well, if you know anything about me at all, that I do, that I'm fully conscious, and sometimes painfully conscious, of their and my situation. But I assert my right to approach it in my own way as a poet. I deal with it as I feel it, and not as people like you think I should. After all, as a poet I am trying to come to grips with reality, yes, to define reality, as I can perceive it. Isn't that what every poet worthy of the name is attempting to do? Why does a particular racial identity make me any the less aware of life, life as human beings live it? What is a poet but a human being speaking to other human beings about things that matter to all of us? And of course some of these concerns are social and political—racial or ethnic, to use a currently fashionable word. But there are other matters that are also important. Sermons in stones—that sort of thing. To put it succinctly, I feel that Afro-American poets ought to be looked at as poets first, if that's what they truly are. And as one of them I dare to hope that if my work means anything, if it's any good at all, it's going to have a human impact, not a narrowly racial or ethnic or political and overspecialized impact. But, as Fats Waller said for all time, "One never *know, do* one?"

INQ.: You always put too much importance on poetry. All you verse-makers do. Wasn't it Oscar Wilde who said that all art is quite useless?

POET: I think it was. And then W. H. Auden wrote in his elegy on Yeats that poetry makes nothing happen. I disagree with both points of view.

INQ.: So what else is new? I recall your having some inflated notions about poetry being a spiritual act. And you once argued that a poet was a kind of priest—was at least the conscience of his culture. To all of which I say nonsense. Poets are just guys or dames who sit around playing with words like kids with brightly colored building blocks. They fool around long enough, they make something that looks like a poem. And poems are nothing but artifacts like blocks or chairs.

POET: And for the sake of argument, let us say that chairs are useful, aren't they? And necessary and sometimes beautiful.

INQ.: This is taking a funny turn. But, *touché, touché.*

POET: You're giving in? It's not like you.

INQ.: Twinges. I'm not myself tonight. I'm getting old. And so are you, incidentally.

POET: You recall Browning's lines: "Grow old along with me; / The best is yet to be . . ."

INQ.: Oh, please, no more, no more. Sententious doggerel of a pompous old burgher. Let's get back to the subject. I was saying poetry is . . .

POET: You can't define it any better than I can. But I would make so bold as to say it's probably best defined by the poems a poet writes. For me that's the most fruitful attempt at a definition. Actually, I'd much rather spend my time writing poetry than worrying over what it is or isn't. A matter of feeling anyway, a matter of sensibility. I haven't much patience, hardly any in fact, with theories of poetry. They're all *after* the fact. It's the practice that gives rise to theory anyway, wouldn't you agree, however grudgingly?

INQ.: I'm sure I wouldn't. Does it matter whether I do or not?

POET: No.

At this point, the Inquisitor left abruptly. I was glad to be rid of him. Still, though he had angered and disconcerted me, as he usually does, he had also left me with some ideas that might be developed for my talk, even if only in a negative way. I took some scratch paper and scrawled several pages of notes:

1. *The nature and function of poetry:* Poetry as the illumination of experience through language. (The Inquisitor would surely accuse me of cribbing again; this time from Virginia Woolf, etc.) Poetry has always dealt with fundamental human concerns. Could we think of it as a species of Primal Scream? Did it not grow out of primitive mysteries? And does it not remain, despite all we know about it, rather mysterious?

2. *Poetry as a medium, an instrument for social and political change:* Poetry *does* make something happen, for it changes sensibility. In the early stages of a culture it helps to crystallize language and is a repository for value, belief, ideals. The *Griot* in African tribes keeps names and legends and pride alive. Among the Eskimos the shaman or medicine man is a poet. In ancient Ireland and Wales the bard was a preserver of the culture. Academicians and purists to the contrary notwithstanding, great poets of the past as well as the present have often been spokesmen for a cause, have been politically involved. A point to consider: What would I as a poet do if my people were rounded up like the Jewish people in Germany under the Nazis? Claude McKay's sonnet "If We Must Die"; the poems of the Greek poet Yannis Ritsos that were recited and sung by men and women fighting in the streets for the freedom of their country; Pablo Neruda, William Butler Yeats, Emily Sachs, Muriel Rukeyser, Gwendolyn Brooks, Walt Whitman; they stand out as poets

even if you dislike their politics. To be a poet, it seems to me, is to care passionately about justice and one's fellow beings. Sometimes this is not true. Ezra Pound, for instance. Also note that much political or protest or socially conscious poetry is bad, not because of the poet's loyalties or affiliations but owing to lack of talent; sometimes to a pragmatist's contempt for art as a means of understanding: and race.

3. *Poetry as therapy:* A great many people are writing poetry today—I do not call them poets—who are not so much concerned with art or craft as they are with achieving some kind of emotional or psychic release. I'm sure this is good for them, and there is no questioning the therapeutic value of poetry, of the arts in general. But if therapy is all one is after I hardly consider it justifies one considering himself a poet. But of course they do. They are, I am well aware, often seeking escape from the anonymity that threatens us all. They are seeking affirmation of their being, their uniqueness, through poetry or other forms of art. But self-expression becomes an end in itself; questions of craftsmanship, form, style are likely to be dismissed as "elitist" and therefore irrelevant. I would not object to the self-expressionists but for the fact that their efforts result in delusions of poetic grandeur. When I discussed Mr. X's poetry with him in the Poetry Office one day, I soon recognized him as the counterpart of Miss Y, who invaded my office at the University of Michigan with a sheaf of mediocre verses—all terribly *fraught,* as an old friend used to say of such efforts. Both would-be poets were visibly annoyed when I pointed out weaknesses in diction, imagery, and grammar, because they thought these things of minor consequence, since the poems expressed their feelings. And, oh, the sine qua non of all sine qua nons: their poems were *spontaneous* (not labored over like yours, sir). "No, I never rewrite my poems; I let them come as they will and do not revise. I've been writing for about a year, and all my friends are after me to publish a book. Tell me how to get my work published."

Well, you do what you can with these hopeless cases. You send up a silent prayer that time and hard-nosed poetry editors will show these people the error of their ways.

4. *Poetry as the art of saying what cannot be said or at least not said quite so effectively in any other form:* Maybe I've worn this statement out, I've used it so many times, and should give It a long rest. But somehow I can't resist repeating it. What I have said in my poems I am sure I could not otherwise have said. Indeed, I might have said too much. A poem is built on silences as well as on sounds. And it imposes a silence audible as a laugh, a sigh, a groan.

A few nights ago, I was looking over these notes and wondering how on earth I'd work them into the talk when the Inquisitor arrived. Shall I pretend I was not glad for the interruption?

INQ.: I know why I've been so groggy lately that I let you get the better of the argument sometimes. I know what's wrong, yesiree.

POET: Then tell me. The suspense is unbearable.

INQ.: I'm tired of poets and poetry, worn out by all the rapping I've had to endure regarding the role of the poet, the function of poetry in this society.

POET: You're one of the chief instigators. And you've never been exactly our friend. You've always . . .

INQ.: Don't interrupt. All this palavering about the American poet's role. What else is it but to be a poet and write verses? A useless function at best, but never mind. You don't hear electricians and plumbers bellyaching the way you versifiers do.

POET: They've got unions.

INQ.: Well, your crowd has too, in a manner of speaking; you're all professors nowadays, most of you at any rate. You're all safely inside the ivy-covered walls of Academe, grousing, or as you say when you're being cute, *kvetching.* No two ways about it, you're a sorry bunch. All you characters calling yourselves poets, oh, but playing it safe, observing the rules, conforming to what is expected of you as responsible citizens. Baudelaire and Rimbaud would laugh their heads off if they could see you. You and your faculty club teas, your polite conversation and mildly vicious gossip. No passion, no wildness, no risking anything. What a bunch of phonies you are. And, oh, those carefully contrived little poems you write about life in outer suburbia.

POET: Stop it already. Why don't you say something original for a change, even if you can't distinguish between truth and appearances. You're stereotyping us because you're intellectually too lazy to be discriminating. I grant you that the university is not necessarily the best environment for poets, because energies that should go into creative work too often are dissipated by routine and academic drudgery of one kind or another. Still, it's less enervating than picking cotton or working in a factory. And I guess as teachers we must be making some contribution to students, giving them what they couldn't get from anyone else. Few of us, and it's a very small few, earn enough from our books and our poetry readings to live on. So we have to do the impossible and somehow manage as best we can to pursue what are really two full-time jobs, two demanding careers.

INQ.: Careers, careers! You poets today think too much about your careers. You're so busy being seen by the right people at the right time in the right place, you're so greedy for publicity and fame, you're so busy promoting yourselves I wonder that you ever find time to do what poets are supposed to do—write poems. I'm fed up with the whole flipping lot of you. Nothing but hustlers.

POET: If we are, it's because of you and your crowd.

IQ.: Let your poems do the hustling.

POET: And let your fingers do the walking, I suppose.

INQ.: That's clever, that is. I'll die laughing.

POET: Let your poems do the hustling, indeed!

INQ.: That's what I said. Worry about writing well. That's all that's important.

POET: As if you gave a tinker's damn about poetry. You're only saying it because you know it gets me worked up. And you'll be telling me next to live in a garret and go hungry so's to produce a masterpiece.

INQ.: Why don't some of you birds give it a try?

POET: Because we're none of us characters in *La Bohème*. And because some of us know what real poverty is. Food and shelter and a few amenities have never prevented a real poet from writing real poetry.

INQ.: Enough of this blather. I told you I'm tired of talking about poetry.

POET: Well, you started it, Buster, and I'm not going to let you have the last word. You flout the value, the importance of poetry and you heap ridicule on poets. But there are thousands tonight who except for us would have no one to speak in a human voice for them. Who more earnestly than poets have warned of the dangers of abstraction and anonymity to the human spirit?

INQ.: He's off and running.

POET: Let there be poets and more poets—just as long as they are poets. For poets too are the keepers of a nation's conscience, the partisans of freedom and justice, even when they eschew political involvement. By the very act of continuing to function as poets they are affirming what is human and eternal. And as I have contemplated the almost bewildering diversity of American poetry, I have come to see a vital relationship between the poetic endeavor and freedom of speech in this country. In the monolithic dictatorships poets are silenced unless they repeat the clichés of the state. The dangers of censorship in our own country are certainly present, and

> although I would not overstate the case by saying it is poets who are chiefly keeping the lines of verbal communication open, I will say that we know the dangers of censorship and we are therefore part of the advance guard in the struggle. When poets are silenced then tyranny has won.

Well, maybe the Inquisitor did have the last word, for he disappeared while I was still talking. It was quite late, way past midnight, and I was exhausted, but I stayed up to make a few notes. I wouldn't have slept even if I had gone to bed, because I was thinking of all the things I should have said to that old curmudgeon but had not had the presence of mind or sufficient wit to say. I reached for a notebook and scribbled some of them down. Perhaps I could use them in my talk.

Delmore Schwartz

THE ISOLATION OF MODERN POETRY

The characteristic of modern poetry which is most discussed is of course its difficulty, its famous obscurity. Certain discussions, usually by contemporary poets, have done much to illuminate the new methods and forms of contemporary poetry. Certain other discussions have illustrated an essential weakness inherent in all readers, the fact that the love of one kind of writing must often interfere with the understanding of another kind. Wordsworth was undoubtedly thinking of this weakness when he wrote, in his justly well-known preface, that

> It is supposed that by the act of writing in verse an Author makes a formal engagement that he will gratify certain known habits of association; that he not only apprises the reader that certain classes of ideas and expression will be found in his book, but that others will be carefully excluded.

This seems to me to be a perfect statement of the first barrier which intervenes between the reader and any kind of writing with which he is not familiar. But it is far from being sufficient as a defense of modern poetry. Wordsworth was engaged in defending his poetry against the habitual expectations of the reader accustomed to Dryden, Pope, and Johnson.

Reprinted from Delmore Schwartz, "The Isolation of Modern Poetry," in *Selected Essays of Delmore Schwartz*, ed. Donald A. Dike and David H. Zucker (Chicago: University of Chicago Press, 1970), 3–13.

It is necessary now to defend the modern poet against the reader accustomed to Wordsworth. The specific difference between such a poet as Wordsworth and the typical modern poet requires a specific explanation.

There is another defense of the modern poet which seems utterly insufficient to me. It is said that the modern poet must be complex because modern life is complicated. This is the view of Mr. T. S. Eliot, among others. "It appears likely," he says, "that poets in our civilization, as it exists at present, must be *difficult*. Our civilization comprehends great variety and complexity, and this variety and complexity, playing upon a refined sensibility, must produce various and complex results." Mr. Eliot's explanation seems to me not so much wrong as superficial. I need hardly say that Mr. Eliot is seldom superficial in any regard; here, however, I think he is identifying the surface of our civilization with the surface of our poetry. But the complexity of modern life, the disorder of the traffic on a business street or the variety of reference in the daily newspaper is far from being the same thing as the difficulties of syntax, tone, diction, metaphor, and allusion which face the reader in the modern poem. If one is the product of the other, the causal sequence involves a number of factors on different levels, and to imply, as I think Mr. Eliot does, that there is a simple causal relationship between the disorder of modern life and the difficulty of modern poetry is merely to engender misunderstanding by oversimplification.

Now obscurity is merely one of the peculiar aspects of modern poetry. There are others which are just as important. Nothing could be more peculiar than the fact that modern poetry is lyric poetry. Almost without exception there is a failure or an absence of narrative or dramatic writing in verse. With the possible exception of Hardy and Robinson, it is impossible to think of any modern poet who will be remembered for his writing in any form other than that of the lyric.

It is obvious by contrast that the major portion of the poetry of the past, of poetry until we reach the latter half of the nineteenth century, is narrative and dramatic as well as lyrical in its most important moments; and it is equally evident that all of that poetry is never obscure in the modern sense.

I need not mention further characteristics of modern poetry which coexist with its obscurity and its limitation to the lyric form. The two characteristics seem to me to be closely related to each other and to spring from the essential condition of the modern poet. The way in which this condition, if that is the adequate word for what I mean, the way in which this essential circumstance affects the modern poet is a rather involved matter, but had better be stated bluntly and crudely at this point. The modern poet has been very much affected by the condition and the circumstance that he has been separated from the whole life of society. This separation has taken numerous forms and has increased continually. It is a separation which occurs with an uneven development in all the matters with which the modern poet must concern himself. Different poets have been differently affected, and their efforts to cope with this separation have been various. But there is a common denominator which points to a common cause.

The beginning of the process of separation, if one can rightly discern a beginning in such things, is the gradual destruction of the world picture which, despite many changes, had for a long time been taken for granted by the poet. Amid much change, development, and modification, the Bible had provided a view of the universe which circumscribed the area in which anyone ventured to think, or use his imagination. It would of course be a serious mistake to suppose that this view of the universe had not been disturbed in numerous ways long before the modern poet arrived upon the scene. But it is doubtful if the poet before the time of Blake felt a conflict between two pictures of the world, the picture provided by the Bible and the one provided by the physical sciences.

In Blake's rage against Newton and Voltaire, in his interest, as a poet, in the doctrine of Swedenborg, and in his attempt to construct his own view of the universe, we come upon the first full example of this difficulty of the poet. There is a break between intellect and sensibility; the intellect finds unreasonable what the sensibility and the imagination cannot help but accept because of centuries of imagining and feeling in terms of definite images of the world. Milton's use of a Ptolemaic cosmology, though he knew that the Copernican one was mathematically superior, is an example from a still earlier period; it shows with exactitude the extent to which the poet depended upon the traditional world picture of Western culture. After Blake, the Romantic poets are further instances; not only were they intensely interested in new conceptions of the world, new philosophies; but in turning to Nature as they did, they displayed their painful sense that the poet no longer belonged to the society into which he was born, and for which, presumably, he was writing his verse.

But these authors are not modern poets. And it was not until the middle of the nineteenth century that the progress of the physical sciences brought forth a body of knowledge which was in serious and open conflict with the picture of the world which had been in use for so long a time. This conflict had been going on, of course, for centuries, but it was not until we come to an occasion like the publication of the Darwinian theory that the conflict becomes so radical and so obvious that no poet of ambition can seriously avoid it. I am not referring to any conflict between religious doctrine and scientific knowledge, for this conflict, if it actually exists, is hardly the direct concern of the poet at any time. It is a question of the conflict between the sensibility of the poet, the very images which he viewed as the world, and the evolving and blank and empty universe of nineteenth century science.

The development of modern culture from Darwin and Huxley to Freud, Marx, and the author of *The Golden Bough,* has merely extended, hastened, and intensified this process of removing the picture of the world which the poet took for granted as the arena of his imagination, and putting in its place another world picture which he could not use. This is illustrated broadly in the career of such poets as Yeats. Hearing as a young man that man was descended from the ape, Yeats occupied himself for many years with theosophy, black magic, and the least respectable forms of psychical research, all in the effort to gain a view of the universe and of man which would restore dignity and importance to both man and the universe. We may invent an illustration at this point and suppose that when Yeats or any other modern poet of similar interests heard of how many million light years the known regions of the universe comprise, he felt a fundamental incongruity between his own sense of the importance of human lives and their physical smallness in the universe. This is merely a difficulty in imagining—one has an image of a very small being in an endless world; but that's just the point, the difficulty with images. The philosopher and the theologian know that size is not a particularly important aspect of anything; but the poet must see, and what he has had to see was this incongruity between the importance man attributes to himself and his smallness against the background of the physical world of nineteenth century science.

Now this is only one aspect of the poet's isolation: it is the aspect in which the sensibility of the poet has been separated from the theoretical knowledge of his time. The isolation of the modern poet has, however, taken an even more difficult form, that of being separated by poetry from the rest of society. Here one must guard against a simple view of what this separation has amounted to in any particular context. It is not a simple matter of the poet lacking an audience, for that is an effect, rather than a cause, of the character of modern poetry. And it is not, on the other hand, the simple matter of the poet being isolated from the usual habits and customs and amusements of his time and place; for if this were the trouble, then the poet could perhaps be justly accused of retiring to his celebrated ivory tower; and it would then be quite reasonable to advise the poet as some have done: to tell him that he ought to get "experience," see the world, join a political party, make sure that he participates in the habitual activities of his society.

The fundamental isolation of the modern poet began not with the poet and his way of life; but rather with the whole way of life of modern society. It was not so much the poet as it was poetry, culture, sensibility, imagination, that were isolated. On the one hand, there was no room in the increasing industrialization of society for such a monster as the cultivated man; a man's taste for literature had at best nothing to do with most of the activities which constituted daily life in an industrial society. On the other hand, culture, since it could not find a place in modern life, has fed upon itself increasingly and has created its own autonomous satisfactions, removing itself further all the time from any essential part in the organic life of society.

Stated thus, this account may seem abstract and even implausible. It would be best before going further to mention certain striking evidences of what has taken place. There is, for instance, the classic American joke about how bored father is at the opera or the concert; the poet too has been an essentially comic figure, from time to time. But this homely instance may seem merely the product of vulgarity and lack of taste. A related tendency which has been much observed by foreigners is the belief in America that women were supposed to be interested in literature, culture, and "such things," while men had no time for such trivial delights because they were busy with what is called *business*. But this instance may seem local in that it is American and inconclusive since it has to do with the poet's audience rather than with the poet himself. There is then a third example, one which seems almost dramatic to me, the phenomenon of American authors of superior gifts going to Europe and staying there. Henry James is the most convincing case; one can scarcely doubt that he lived in Europe because there the divorce between culture and the rest of life, although it had begun, had by no means reached the point which was unavoidable in America. George Santayana, Ezra Pound, and T. S. Eliot are cases which come later in time; we do not know exactly why these men went to Europe; the significant fact is that they do not come back to America. I do not merely wish to suggest a critical view of the role of culture in American life, for the same process was occurring in Europe, though at a slower rate and with local modifications. The important point is the intuitive recognition on the part of both the artist and the rest of the population that culture and sensibility—and thus the works by means of which they sustained their existence—did not belong, did not fit into the essential workings of society.

At this point, it might be objected that culture has never played a very important part in the life of any society; it has only engaged the attention and devotion of the elect, who are always few in number. This view seems utterly false to me, and for the sake of showing briefly how false it has been historically, I quote one of the greatest living classical scholars on the part that dramatic tragedy played in the life of Periclean Athens. Werner Jaeger writes that

> After the state organized the dramatic performances held at the festival of Dionysus, tragedy more and more evoked the interest and participation of the entire people. . . . Its power over them was so vast that they held it responsible for the spirit of the whole state . . . it is no exaggeration to say that the tragic festival was the climax of the city's life. (*Paideia,* pp. 245–246.)

No contrast could be more extreme than this one between the function of the Greek dramatist and that of the modern poet in their respective societies.

One significant effect of this divorce has been the poet's avowal of the doctrine of Art for Art's Sake, a doctrine which is meaningful only when viewed in the context in which it is always announced, that is, to repeat, a society which had no use and no need for Art, other than as a superfluous amusement or decoration. And another significant and related effect is the sentiment of the poet, and at times his convinced belief, that he has no connection with or allegiances to anything else. Nowhere is this belief stated with more clarity than in the following prose poem by Baudelaire, who in so many ways is either the first or the typical modern poet:

> "Whom do you love most of all, enigmatic man, tell me?
> Your father, your mother, your brother, or your sister?"
> "I have neither father, mother, brother, nor sister."
> "Do you love your friends then?"

> "You have just used a word whose meaning remains unknown to me to this very day."
>
> "Do you love your country, then?"
>
> "I ignore the latitude in which it is situated."
>
> "Then do you love Beauty?"
>
> "I love her with my whole will; she is a goddess and immortal."
>
> "Do you love gold?"
>
> "I hate it as you hate God."
>
> "Well then: extraordinary stranger, what do you love?"
>
> "I love the clouds . . . the clouds which pass . . . far away . . . far away . . . the marvelous clouds!"

It would be possible to take this stranger who is the modern poet with less seriousness, if he were merely affecting a pose, attempting to dramatize himself or be clever. The shocking passages in modern poetry have sometimes been understood in this way as Bohemianism, and the conventional picture or caricature of the poet has been derived from this Bohemianism, considered as a surface. But the sentiments which Baudelaire attributes to his stranger are the deepest feelings of the modern poet. He does feel that he is a stranger, an alien, an outsider; he finds himself without a father or mother, or he is separated from them by the opposition between his values as an artist and their values as respectable members of modern society. This opposition cannot be avoided because not a government subsidy, nor yearly prizes, nor a national academy can disguise the fact that there is no genuine place for the poet in modern life. He has no country, no community, insofar as he is a poet, and his greatest enemy is money, since poetry does not yield him a livelihood. It is natural then that he should emphasize his allegiance, his devotion to Beauty, that is to say, to the practice of Art and the works of art which already exist. And thus it is that Baudelaire's stranger announces that what he loves most of all is to look at the clouds, that is, to exercise his own sensibility. The modern poet has had nothing to do, no serious activity other than the cultivation of his own sensibility. There is a very famous passage in Walter Pater advising just this course.

From this standpoint, the two aspects of modern poetry which I marked at the start can be seen as natural and almost inevitable developments. In cultivating his own sensibility, the modern poet participated in a life which was removed from the lives of other men, who, insofar as they could be considered important characters, were engaged in cultivating money or building an industrial society. Thus it became increasingly impossible for the poet to write about the lives of other men; for not only was he removed from their lives, but, above all, the culture and the sensibility which made him a poet could not be employed when the proposed subject was the lives of human beings in whom culture and sensibility had no organic function. There have been unsuccessful efforts on the part of able poets to write about bankers and about railroad trains, and in such examples the poet has been confronted by what seems on the surface a technical problem, the extraordinary difficulty of employing poetic diction, meter, language, and metaphor in the contexts of modern life. It is not that contemporary people do not speak or think poetically; human beings at any time in general do not speak or think in ways which are immediately poetic, and if they did there would be no need for poetry. The trouble has been that the idiom of poetic style and the normal thought and speech of the community have been moving in opposite directions and have had little or no relationship to each other. The normal state of affairs occurs when poetry is continually digesting the prose of its time, and folk art and speech are providing sustenance for major literary efforts.

Since the only life available to the poet as a man of culture has been the cultivation of his own sensibility, that is the only subject available to him, if we may assume that a poet can only write about subjects of which he has an absorbing experience in every sense.[1] Thus we find that in much modern poetry, the poet is writing about other poetry, just as in modern painting the art works and styles of the past have so often become the painter's subject. For writing about other poetry and in general about works of art is the most direct way of grasping one's sensibility as a subject. But more than that, since one can only write about one's sensibility, one can only write lyric poetry. Dramatic and narrative poetry require a grasp of the lives of other men, and it is precisely these lives, to repeat, that are outside the orbit of poetic style and poetic sensibility. An analogous thing has, of necessity, happened in the history of the novel; the development of the autobiographical novel has resulted in part from the inability of the novelist to write about anyone but himself or other people in relation to himself.

From this isolation of poetic sensibility the obscurity of modern poetry also arises. The poet is engaged in following the minutest movements, tones, and distinctions of his own being as a poetic man. Because this private life of his sensibility is the chief subject available to him, it becomes increasingly necessary to have recourse to new and special uses of language. The more the poet has cultivated his own sensibility, the more unique and special has his subject, and thus his method, become. The common language of daily life, its syntax, habitual sequences, and processes of association, are precisely the opposite of what he needs, if he is to make poetry from what absorbs him as a poet, his own sensibility.

Sometimes, indeed, the poet has taken this conflict between sensibility and modern life as his subject. The early fiction of Thomas Mann concerns itself repeatedly with the opposition between the artist and the bourgeoisie, and in such a story as "Tonio Kröger" we see the problem most explicitly; the artist feels at home nowhere and he suffers from an intense longing to be normal and bourgeois himself. Again, there is the famous device of modern poetry which was invented by Laforgue and used most successfully by T. S. Eliot, the ironic contrast between a past in which culture was an important part of life and the present in which the cultural monument sits next to vulgarity and insensitivity. This has been misunderstood very often as a yearning to go back to a past idyllically conceived. It is nothing of the kind; it is the poet's conscious experience of the isolation of culture from the rest of society.

I would like to cite one more instance of this condition. Four years ago one of the very best modern poets lectured and read his own poetry at Harvard. As a normal citizen, this man is an executive of an important corporation. It may reasonably be presumed that most of his writing is done on holidays and vacations. At the conclusion of his reading of his own poetry, this poet and businessman remarked to one of the instructors who had welcomed him: "I wonder what the boys at the office would think of this."

But I have spoken throughout as if this isolation was in every sense a misfortune. It is certainly a misfortune so far as the life of the whole community is concerned; this is evident in the character of popular taste, in the kind of fiction, play, and movie which is successful, as compared with the popular authors of the nineteenth century, who were very often the best authors also. But on the other hand, it seems to me that the period of modern poetry, the age which begins with Baudelaire, is undoubtedly one in which the art of poetry has gained not only in the number of fine poets, but in technical resources of all kinds. If the enforced isolation of the poet has made dramatic and narrative poetry almost impossible, it has, on the other hand, increased the uses and powers of languages in the most amazing and the most valuable directions.

I have also spoken as if this isolation of the poet had already reached its conclusion. Whether it has or not, and whether it would be entirely desirable that it should, may be left as unanswered and perhaps unanswerable questions. It is true, at any rate, that during the past ten years a new school of poets has attempted to free itself from the isolation of poetry by taking society itself as the dominant subject.[2] The attempt has been a brilliant and exciting one in many ways; the measure of its success is not yet clear, particularly since it has been inspired by the present crisis of society; and its relative popularity may also be limited to contemporary and transient interests. But the very nature of the effort testifies in its own way to the isolation which haunts modern poetry, and from which these poets have been trying to escape.

NOTES

1. The connection between the way in which an author lives and his writing is of course a complicated one. But how close the connection is and how effective can be seen if we ask ourselves: would Eliot have written *The Waste Land* as we know it, if he had not lived in London? would Pound have written the later Cantos, if he had not lived on the Italian Riviera? would either have written, using culture as they have, if they were not expatriate Americans? Certainly Joyce might not have written *Finnegans Wake* if he had not taught in a Berlitz school and Perse could not have written *Anabase* if he had not been sent to Asia as a diplomat, and Yeats might not have written his later poetry, if he had lived on Lady Gregory's estate.

2. These are the poets who, significantly enough, have invented the recurrent figure of "the island," as a symbol of isolation. From the point of view of this essay, the leading themes of the Agrarian-Regionalist poets, such as Tate and Ransom, would represent another, very different effort to get back to the center of the community and away from the poet's isolation.

Randall Jarrell

POETS, CRITICS, AND READERS

People often ask me: "Is there any poet who makes his living writing poetry?" and I have to say: "No." The public has an unusual relationship to the poet: it doesn't even know that he is there. Our public is a rich and generous one; if it knew that the poet was there, it would pay him for being there. As it is, poets make their living in many ways: by being obstetricians, like William Carlos Williams; or directors of Faber and Faber, like T. S. Eliot; or vice-presidents of the Hartford Accident and Indemnity Company, like Wallace Stevens. But most poets, nowadays, make their living by teaching. Kepler said, "God gives every animal a way to make its living, and He has given the astronomer astrology"; and now, after so many centuries, He has given us poets students. But what He gives with one hand He takes away with the other: He has taken away our readers.

Yet the poet can't help looking at what he has left, his students, with gratitude. His job may be an impossible one—there are three impossible tasks, said Freud: to teach, to govern, and to cure—but what is there so grateful as impossibility? and what is there better to teach, more nearly impossible to teach, than poems and stories? As Lord Macaulay says: "For how can

Reprinted from Randall Jarrell, "Poets, Critics, and Readers," in *Kipling, Auden & Co.: Essays & Reviews, 1935–1964* (New York: Farrar, Straus & Giroux, 1980), 305–18.

man live better / Than facing fearful odds / For the poems of his fathers—"

I seem to have remembered it a little wrong, but it's a natural error. And, today, when we get people to read poems—to read very much of anything—naturally and joyfully, to read it not as an unnatural rightness but as a natural error: what people always have done, always will do—we do it against fearful odds. I can't imagine a better way for the poet to make his living. I certainly can't imagine his making his living by writing poems—I'm not that imaginative. I'm used to things as they are.

But there is a passage in Wordsworth that I read, always, with a rueful smile. He is answering the question, *Why write in verse?* He gives several reasons. His final reason, he writes, "is all that is *necessary* to say upon this subject." Here it is, all that it is *necessary* to say upon this subject: "Few persons will deny, that of two descriptions, either of passions, manners, or characters, each of them equally well executed, the one in prose and the other in verse, the verse will be read a hundred times where the prose is read once."

One sees sometimes, carved on geology buildings: *O Earth, what changes thou hast seen!* When a poet finishes reading this passage from Wordsworth, he thinks in miserable awe: *O Earth, what changes thou hast seen!* Only a hundred and fifty years ago *this* is what people were like. Nowadays, of course, the prose will be read a thousand times where the verse is read once. And this seems to everybody only natural; the situation Wordsworth describes seems unnatural, improbable, almost impossible. What Douglas Bush writes is true: we live in "a time in which most people assume that, as an eminent social scientist once said to me, 'Poetry is on the way out.'" To most of us verse, any verse, is so uncongenial, so exhaustively artificial, that I have often thought that a man could make his fortune by entirely eliminating from our culture verse of any kind: in the end there would *be* no more poems, only prose translations of them. This man could begin by publishing his Revised Standard Version of *Mother Goose:* without rhyme, meter, or other harmful adulterants; with no word of anything but honest American prose, prose that cats and dogs can read.

A friend of mine once took a famous Italian scholar on a tour of New Haven. She specialized in objects of art and virtue —samplers, figureheads, paintings of women under willows, statues of General Washington—but no matter what she showed him, the man would only wave his hand in the air and exclaim: *Ridickalus!* And shouldn't we feel so about things like *Mother Goose?*

Early to bed and early to rise
Makes a man healthy, wealthy, and wise.

Ridickalus! Why say it like a rocking horse? why make it jingle so? and *wise*—who wants to be wise?

Which sibling is the well-adjusted sibling?
The one that gets its sleep.

That is the way the modern *Mother Goose* will put it. I don't expect the modern *Mother Goose* to be especially popular with little children, who have not yet learned not to like poetry; but it is the parents who buy the book.

Isn't writing verse a dying art, anyway, like blacksmithing or buggy-making? Well, not exactly: poets are making as many buggies as ever—good buggies, fine buggies—they just can't get anybody much to ride in them. As for blacksmithing: I read the other day that there are twice as many blacksmith shops in the United States as there are bookstores. Something has gone wrong with that comparison too. No, I'm doing what poets do, complaining; and if I exaggerate a little when I complain, why, that's only human—surely you want me to exaggerate a little, in my misery. Goethe says, when he is talking about slum children: "No person ever looks miserable who feels that he has the right to make a demand on you." This right is not anything that anyone can confer upon himself; it is the public, society, all of us, that confer this right. If the poet looks miserable, it is because we have made him feel that he no longer has the right to make a demand on us. It is no longer a question of what he wants, or of what he ought to be given—he takes what he gets, and complains about getting it, and he hears the echo of his complaint, and then the silence settles around him, a little darker, a little deeper.

What does he want? To be read. Read by whom? Critics? men wise enough to tell him, when they have read the poem, what it is and ought to be, what its readers feel and ought to feel? Well, no. A writer cannot learn about his readers from his critics: they are different races. The critic, unless he is one in a thousand, reads to criticize; the reader reads to read.

Freud talks of the "free-floating" or "evenly-hovering" attention with which the analyst must listen to the patient. Concentration, notetaking, listening with a set—a set of pigeonholes—makes it difficult or impossible for the analyst's unconscious to respond to the patient's; takes away from the analyst the possibility of learning from the patient what the analyst doesn't already know; takes away from him all those random guesses or intuitions or inspirations which come out of nowhere—and come, too, out of the truth of the patient's being. But this is quite as true of critics and the poems that are *their* patients: when one reads as a linguist, a scholar, a New or Old or High or Low critic, when one reads the poem *as a means to an end,* one is no longer a pure reader but an applied one. The true reader "listens like a three years' child: / The Mariner hath his will." Later on he may write like a sixty-three-year-old sage, but he knows that in the beginning, unless ye be converted, and become as little children, ye shall not enter into the kingdom of art. Hofmannsthal says, with awful finality: "The world has lost its innocence, and without innocence no one creates or enjoys a work of art"; but elsewhere he says more hopefully, with entire and not with partial truth, that each of us lives in an innocence of his own which he never entirely loses.

Is there a public for poetry that is still, in this sense of the word, innocent? Of course, there are several publics for poetry—small, benighted, eccentric publics—just as there are publics for postage stamps and cobblers' benches; but this is such a disastrous change from the days of *Childe Harold* and *In Memoriam* and *Hiawatha,* when the public for poetry was, simply, the reading public, that you can see why poets feel the miserable astonishment that they feel. The better-known poets feel it more than the lesser-known, who—poor things—lie under the table grateful for crumbs, pats, kicks, anything at all that will let them be sure they really exist, and are not just a dream someone has stopped dreaming. A poet like Auden says that nobody reads him except poets and young men in cafeterias—his description of the young men is too repellent for me to repeat it to you.

Literally, Auden is wrong: we read Auden, this is no cafeteria; but, figuratively, Auden is right—the poet's public's gone. Frederick the Great translated Voltaire, and trembled as the poet read the translation; Elizabeth—Elizabeth the First—and Henry the Eighth and Richard the Lion-Hearted wrote good poems and read better; and I cannot resist quoting to you three or four sentences from Frans Bengtsson's novel *The Long Ships,* to show you what things were like at the court of Harald Bluetooth, King of Denmark in the year 1000. A man gets up from a banquet table: "His name was Björn Asbrandsson, and he was a famous warrior, besides being a great poet to boot . . . Although he was somewhat drunk, he managed to improvise some highly skilful verses in King Harald's honor in a meter known as *Timestöglag.* This was the latest and most difficult verse-form that the Icelandic poets had invented, and indeed the poem was so artfully contrived that little could be understood of its content. Everybody, however, listened with an appearance of understanding, for any man who could not understand poetry would be regarded as a poor specimen of a warrior; and King Harald praised the poet and gave him a gold ring."

Auden is a descendant of just such poets as this one; but if Auden, when he next visits the University of your state, makes up an incomprehensible poem, in a difficult new meter, in honor of the President of the University, will all its football players pretend they understand the poem, so as not to be thought poor specimens of football players? and will the President give Auden a gold ring?

In the days when his readers couldn't read, the poet judged his public by his public: the gold ring or the scowl the king gave him was as concrete as the labored, triumphant faces of his hearers. But nowadays King Harald and his warriors are represented by a reviewer, next year, in *The New York Times;* a critic, nine years later, in *The Sewanee Review.* "Ah, better to sing my songs to a wolf pack on the Seeonee than to a professor on the *Sewanee*!" the poet blurts, baring his teeth; but then—what choice has he?—he lets the Reality Principle do its worst, and projects or extends or extrapolates a critic or two, a dozen reviewers, into the Public; into Posterity. Critics, alas! are the medium through which the poet darkly senses his public. Nor is it altogether different for the public: Harald and his Vikings, lonely in their split-levels, do not even remember the days when, as they listened, they could look into one another's faces and know without looking what they would find there. Now they too look into the *Times;* wish that they could replace that scowl with a gold ring, that gold ring with a scowl; reconstruct from the exclamations on dust jackets, quotations in advertisements, the fierce smiles on the faces of the warriors.

So if we are to talk about the poet and his poems and his public, what each is to the others, we must spend much of our time—too much of our time—talking about his critics. Criticism is necessary, I suppose; I know. Yet criticism, to the poet, is no necessity, but a luxury he can ill afford. Conrad cried to his wife: "I don't want criticism, I want praise!" And it is praise, blame, tears, laughter, that writers want; when Columbus comes home he needs to be cheered for finding a new way to India, not interned while the officials argue about whether it is Asia, Africa, or Antarctica that he has discovered. Really, of course, it's America—and if they agreed about it this would be helpful to Columbus; he could say to himself, in awe: "So it was America I discovered!" But how seldom the critics do agree! A gray writer seems black to his white critics, white to his black critics: the same poem will seem incomprehensible modernistic nonsense to Robert Hillyer, and a sober, old-fashioned, versified essay to the critics of some little magazine of advanced tastes. Ordinary human feeling, the most natural tenderness, will seem to many critics and readers rank sentimentality, just as a kind of nauseated brutality (in which the writer's main response to the world is simply to vomit) will seem to many critics and readers the inescapable truth. We live in a time in which Hofmannsthal's "Good taste is the ability continuously to counteract exaggeration" will seem to most readers as false as it seems tame. "Each epoch has its own sentimentality," Hofmannsthal goes on, "its specific way of overemphasizing strata of emotion. The sentimentality of the present is egotistic and unloving; it exaggerates not the feeling of love but that of the self."

Everyone speaks of the "negative capability" of the artist, of his ability to lose what self he has in the many selves, the great self of the world. Such a quality is, surely, the first that a critic should have; yet who speaks of the negative capability of the critic? How often are we able to observe it? The commonest response to the self of a work of art is the critic's assertion that he too has a self. What he writes proves it. I once saw, in an essay by a psychoanalyst, the phrase *the artist* and *his competitor, the critic.* Where got he that truth? Out of an analysand's mouth? I do not know; but that it is an important and neglected truth I do know. All mediators become competitors: the exceptions to this rule redeem their kind.

Critics disagree about almost every quality of a writer's work; and when some agree about a quality, they disagree about whether it is to be praised or blamed, nurtured or rooted out. After enough criticism the writer is covered with lipstick and bruises, and the two are surprisingly evenly distributed. There is *nothing* so plain about a writer's books, to some critics, that its opposite isn't plain to others. Kafka is original? Not at all, according to Edmund Wilson. A fine critic of poetry, Ezra Pound, writes: "In the writer So-and-So you have an embroidery of language, a talk *about* the matter, not presentation; you have grace, richness of language, etc., as much as you like, but you have nothing that isn't replaceable by something else, no ornament that wouldn't have done just as well in some other connection, or that for which some other figure of rhetoric or fancy couldn't have served, or which couldn't have been distilled from literary antecedents." About whom is Pound speaking? About Shakespeare. Anyone who has read at all widely has come across thousands of such judgments, and it is easy for him to sympathize with the artist when the artist murmurs: "We wish to learn from our critics, but it is hard for us even to recover from them. A fool's reproach has an edge like a razor, and his brother's praise is small consolation. Critics are like bees: one sting lasts longer than a dozen jars of honey."

The best thing ever said about criticism—I am not, now, speaking as a critic—was said, as is often the case, by Goethe: "Against criticism we can neither protect nor defend ourselves; we must act in despite of it, and gradually it resigns itself to this." The great Goethe suffered just as we little creatures do, and he spoke about it, as we don't, in imperishable sentences: "All great excellence in life or art, at its first recognition, brings with it a certain pain arising from the strongly felt inferiority of the spectator; only at a later period, when we take it into our own culture, and appropriate as much of it as our capacities allow, do we learn to love and esteem it. Mediocrity, on the other hand, may often give us unqualified pleasure; it does not disturb our self-satisfaction, but rather encourages us with the thought that we are as good as another . . . Properly speaking, we learn only from those books we cannot judge. The author of a book that I am competent to criticize would have to learn from me." Goethe says over and over: "Nothing is more terrible than ignorance in action . . . It is a terrible thing when fools thrive at the expense of a superior man." You and I will agree—and then we will have to decide whether we're being thriven at the expense of, or thriving. Goethe says in firm doggerel: "However clear and simple be it / Finder and doer alone may see it." No, Goethe didn't have too much use for critics, since he thought that critics weren't of too much use.

And why am I quoting all this to you? Have critics hurt me so that I want to pull down the temple upon their heads, even if I too perish in the ruins?—for I too am a critic. No, it's not that; critics have done their best for me, and their best has been, perhaps, only too good; when I myself criticize, I am willing for you to believe what I say; but I am trying to explain why it is that critics are of so little use to writers, why it is that they are such a poor guide to the opinions of the next age—and I am explaining in an age which has an unprecedented respect for, trust in, criticism.

All of us have read pieces of criticism—many pieces of criticism—which seem worthy both of delighted respect and cautious trust. All of us have read criticism in which the critic takes it for granted that what he writes about comes first, and what he writes comes second—takes it for granted that he is writing as a reader to other readers, to be of use to them; criticism in which the critic works, as far as he is able, in the spirit of Wordsworth's "I have endeavored to look steadily at my subject." All of us have some favorite, exceptional critic who might say, with substantial truth, that he has not set up rigid standards to which a true work of art must conform, but that he has tried instead to let the many true works of art—his experience of them—set up the general expectations to which his criticism of art conforms; that he has tried never to see a work of art as mere raw material for criticism, data for generalization; that he has tried never to forget the difference between creating a work of art and criticizing a work of art; and that he has tried, always, to remember what Proust meant when he said, about writers like Stendhal, Balzac, Hugo, Flaubert, the great creators called "romantics": "The classics have no better commentators than the 'romantics.' The romantics are the only people who really know how to read the classics, because they read them as they were written, that is to say, 'romantically' and because if one would read a poet or a prose writer properly one must be, not a scholar, but a poet or a prose writer." It might be put a little differently: if one would read a poet or a prose writer properly one must be, not a scholar or a poet or a prose writer, but a reader: someone who reads books as they were written, that is to say, "romantically." Proust's grandmother was not a poet or a prose writer, but she read Madame de Sévigné properly. To be, as she was, a reader, is a lofty and no longer common fate.

The best poetry critic of our time, T. S. Eliot, has said about his criticism: "I see that I wrote best about poets whose work had influenced my own, and with whose poetry I had become thoroughly familiar, long before I desired to write about them, or had found the occasion to do so . . . The best of my literary criticism . . . is a by-product of my private poetry-workshop." But perhaps something of this sort is always true: perhaps true criticism is something, like sincerity or magnanimity, that cannot be aimed at, attained, directly; that must always be, in some sense, a by-product, whether of writing or reading, of a private poetry-workshop or a private reading-room.

We all realize that writers are inspired, but helpless and fallible beings, who know not what they write; readers, we know from personal experience, are less inspired but no less helpless and fallible beings, who half the time don't know what they're reading. Now, a critic is half writer, half reader: just as the vices of men and horses met in centaurs, the weaknesses of readers and writers meet in critics. A good critic—we cannot help seeing, when we look back at any other age—is a much rarer thing than a good poet or a good novelist. Unless you are one critic in a hundred thousand, the future will quote you only as an example of the normal error of the past, what everybody was foolish enough to believe then. Critics are discarded like calendars; yet, for their year, with what trust the world regards them!

Art is long, and critics are the insects of a day. But while he survives, it is the work of art he criticizes which is the critic's muse, or daemon, or guardian angel: it is a delight to the critic to think that sometimes, in moments of particular good fortune, some poem by Rilke or Yeats or Wordsworth has hovered above him, whispering what to say about it in his ear. And, in the moments of rash ambition which can come even to such humble—rightly humble—things as critics, the critic can imagine some reader, in the midst of his pleasure at a poem or story the critic has guided him to, being willing to think of some paragraph of the critic's work in terms of a sentence of Goethe's: "There is a sensitive empiricism that ultimately identifies itself with the object and thereby becomes genuine theory."

In other moments the critic can imagine the reader's thinking of him in terms of a paragraph that Proust once wrote. That miraculous writer and great critic, distressed at someone's having referred to Sainte-Beuve as one of the "great guides," exclaimed: "Surely no one ever failed so completely as did he in performing the functions of a guide? The greater part of his *Lundis* are devoted to fourth-rate writers, and whenever, by chance, he does bring himself to speak of somebody really important, of Flaubert, for instance, or Baudelaire, he immediately atones for what grudging praise he may have accorded him by letting it be understood that he writes as he does about them simply because he wants to please men who are his personal friends . . . As to Stendhal, the novelist, the Stendhal of *La Chartreuse,* our 'guide' laughs out of court the idea that such a person ever existed, and merely sees in all the talk about him the disastrous effects of an attempt (foredoomed to failure) to foist Stendhal on the public as a novelist . . . It would be fun, had I not less important things to do, to 'brush in' (as Monsieur Cuvillier Fleury would have said), in the manner of Sainte-Beuve, a 'picture of French literature in the nineteenth century,' in such a way that not a single great name would appear and men would be promoted to the position of outstanding authors whose books today have been completely forgotten."

A portion of any critic, as he reads these sentences, turns white; and if another portion whispers, "Ah, but *you* needn't be afraid; certainly *you're* not as bad a critic as Sainte-Beuve," it is not a sentence to bring the color back into his cheeks, unless he blushes easily.

Wordsworth said, as Proust said after him, that "every writer, in so far as he is great and at the same time *original,* has the task of creating the taste by which he is to be enjoyed: so is it, so will it continue to be." But *taste,* he goes on to say, is a vicious and deluding word. (And surely he is right; surely we should use, instead, a phrase like *imaginative judgment.*) Using such a word as *taste* helps to make us believe that there is some passive faculty that responds to the new work of art, registering the work's success or failure; but actually the new work must call forth in us an active power analogous to that which created it—the reader "cannot proceed in quiescence, he cannot be carried like a dead weight," he must "exert himself" to feel, to sympathize, and to understand. "*There,*" as Wordsworth says, "lies the true difficulty." He is right: *there* lies the difficulty for us, whether we are critics or readers; so is it, so will it continue to be.

You may say, "Of course this is true of great and original talents, but how does it apply to the trivial, immature, and eccentric writers with whom our age, like any other, is infested?" It applies only in this way: some of these trivial, immature, and eccentric writers *are* our great and original talents. The readers of Wordsworth's age said, "Of course what he says is true of great and original talents, but it is absurd when applied to a trivial and eccentric creature like Wordsworth"; and the critics of Wordsworth's age, applying the standards of the age more clearly, forcibly, and self-consciously, could condemn him with a more drastic severity. The readers read to read, the critics read to judge—both were wrong, but the critics were more impressively and rigorously and disastrously wrong, since they confirmed most readers in their dislike of Wordsworth and scared most of the others out of their liking.

We all see that the writer cannot afford to listen to critics when they are wrong—though how is he, how are we, to know when they are wrong? Can he afford to listen to them when they are right?—though how is he, how are we, to know when they are right? and right for this age or right for the next?[1] The writer cannot afford to question his own essential nature; he must have, as Marianne Moore says, "the courage of his peculiarities." But often it is this very nature, these very peculiarities—originality always seems peculiarity, to begin with—that critics condemn. There must be about the writer a certain spontaneity or naïveté or somnambulistic rightness: he must, in some sense, move unquestioning in the midst of his world—at his question all will disappear.

And if it is slighter things, alterable things which the critics condemn, should the poet give in, alter them, and win his critics' surprised approval? "No," says Wordsworth, "where the understanding of an author is not convinced, or his feelings altered, this cannot be done without great injury to himself: for his own feelings are his stay and support, and, if he set them aside in this one instance, he may be induced to repeat this act till his mind shall lose all confidence in itself, and become utterly debilitated. To this it may be added, that the critic ought never to forget that he is himself exposed to the same errors as the Poet." Let me repeat this: we ought never to forget that the critic is himself exposed to the same errors as the poet. We all know this—yet, in a deeper sense, we don't know it. We all realize that the poet's beliefs are, first of all, *his:* our books show how his epoch, his childhood, his mistresses, and his unconscious produced the beliefs; we know, now, the "real" reasons for his believing what he believed. Why do we not realize what is equally true (and equally false)?—that the critic's beliefs are, first of all, *his;* that we can write books showing how his epoch, his mistresses, and his unconscious produced the beliefs; that we can know, now, the "real" reasons for his believing what he believed. The work of criticism is rooted in the unconscious of the critic just as the poem is rooted in the unconscious of the poet. I have had the pleasure and advantage of knowing many poets, many critics, and I have not found one less deeply neurotic than the other.

When the critic is also an artist—a T. S. Eliot—we find it easier to remember all this, and to distrust him; but when the critic is an Irving Babbitt—that is to say, a man who, tenanted by all nine of the muses, still couldn't create a couplet—we tend to think of his beliefs as somehow more objective. "Surely," we feel, "a man with so little imagination couldn't be making up something—couldn't be *inspired.*" We are wrong. Criticism is the poetry of prosaic natures (and even, in our time, of some poetic ones); there is a divinity that inspires the most sheep-like of scholars, the most tabular of critics, so that the man too dull to understand *Evangeline* still can be possessed by some theory about *Evangeline,* a theory as just to his own being as it is unjust to *Evangeline*'s. The man is entitled to his inspiration; and yet . . . if only he would leave out *Evangeline*! If only he could secede from Literature, and set up some metaliterary kingdom of his own!

The poet *needs* to be deluded about his poems—for who can be sure that it is delusion? In his strongest hours the public hardly exists for the writer: he does what he ought to do, has to do, and if afterwards some Public wishes to come and crown him with laurel crowns, well, let it! If critics wish to tell people all that he isn't, well, let them—he knows what he is. But at night when he can't get to sleep it seems to him that it is what he is, his own particular personal quality, that he is being disliked for. It is this that the future will like him for, if it likes him for anything; but will it like him for anything? The poet's hope is in posterity, but it is a pale hope; and now that posterity itself has become a pale hope . . .

The writer—I am still talking about the writer-not-yet-able-to-go-to-sleep—is willing to have his work disliked, if it's bad; is ready to rest content in dislike, if it's good. But which is it? *He* can't know. He thinks of all those pieces of his that he once thought good, and now thinks bad; how many of his current swans will turn out to be just such ducklings? All of them? If he were worse, would people like him better? If he were better, would people like him worse? If—He says to himself, "Oh, go to sleep!" And next morning, working at something the new day has brought, he is astonished at the night's thoughts—he does what he does, and lets public, critics, posterity worry about whether it's worth doing. For to tell the truth, the first truth, the poem is a love affair between the poet and his subject, and readers come in only a long time later, as witnesses at the wedding . . .

But what would the ideal witnesses—the ideal public—be? What would an ideal public do? Mainly, essentially, it would just read the poet; read him with a certain willingness and interest; read him imaginatively and perceptively. It needs him, even if it doesn't know that; he needs it, even if he doesn't know that. It and he are like people in one army, one prison, one world: their interests are great and common, and deserve a kind of declaration of dependence. The public might treat him very much as it would like him to treat it. It has its faults, he has his;

but both "are, after all," as a man said about women, "the best things that are offered in that line." The public ought not to demand the same old thing from the poet whenever he writes something very new, nor ought it to complain, *The same old thing!* whenever he writes something that isn't very new; and it ought to realize that it is not, unfortunately, in the writer's power to control what he writes: something else originates and controls it, whether you call that something else the unconscious or Minerva or the Muse. The writer writes what he writes just as the public likes what it likes; he can't help himself, it can't help itself, but each of them has to try: most of our morality, most of our culture are in the trying.

We readers can be, or at least can want to be, what the writer himself would want us to be: a public that reads a *lot*—that reads widely, joyfully, and naturally; a public whose taste is formed by acquaintance with the good and great writers of many ages, and not simply acquaintance with a few fashionable contemporaries and the fashionable precursors of those; a public with broad general expectations, but without narrow particular demands, that the new work of art must satisfy; a public that reads with the calm and ease and independence that come from liking things in themselves, for themselves.

This is the kind of public that the poet would like; and if it turned out to be the kind of public that wouldn't like him, why, surely that is something he could bear. It is not his poems but poetry that he wants people to read; if they will read Rilke's and Yeats's and Hardy's poems, he can bear to have his own poems go unread forever. He knows that their poems are good to read, and that's something he necessarily can't know about his own; and he knows, too, that poetry itself is good to read—that if you cannot read poetry easily and naturally and joyfully, you are cut off from much of the great literature of the past, some of the good literature of the present. Yet the poet could bear to have people cut off from all that, if only they read widely, naturally, joyfully in the rest of literature: much of the greatest literature, much of the greatest poetry, even, is in prose.

If people read this prose—read even a little of it—generously and imaginatively, and felt it as truth and life, as a natural and proper joy, why, that would be enough.

A few months ago I read an interview with a critic; a well-known critic; an unusually humane and intelligent critic. The interviewer had just said that the critic "sounded like a happy man," and the interview was drawing to a close; the critic said, ending it all: "I read, but I don't get time to read at whim. All the reading I do is in order to write or teach, and I resent it. We have no TV, and I don't listen to the radio or records, or go to art galleries or the theater. I'm a completely negative personality."

As I thought of that busy, artless life—no records, no paintings, no plays, no books except those you lecture on or write articles about—I was so depressed that I went back over the interview looking for some bright spot, and I found it, one beautiful sentence: for a moment I had left the gray, dutiful world of the professional critic, and was back in the sunlight and shadow, the unconsidered joys, the unreasoned sorrows, of ordinary readers and writers, amateurishly reading and writing "at whim." The critic said that once a year he read *Kim;* and he read *Kim,* it was plain, at whim: not to teach, not to criticize, just for love—he read it, as Kipling wrote it, just because he liked to, wanted to, couldn't help himself. To him it wasn't a means to a lecture or an article, it was an end; he read it not for anything he could get out of it, but for itself. And isn't this what the work of art demands of us? The work of art, Rilke said, says to us always: *You must change your life.* It demands of us that we too see things as ends, not as means—that we too know them and love them for their own sake. This change is beyond us, perhaps, during the active, greedy, and powerful hours of our lives; but during the contemplative and sympathetic hours of our reading, our listening, our looking, it is surely within our power, if we choose to make it so, if we choose to let one part of our nature follow its natural desires. So I say to you, for a closing sentence: *Read at whim! Read at whim!*

NOTE

1. "When the great innovation appears, it will almost certainly be in a muddled, incomplete, and confusing form. To the discoverer himself it will be only half-understood; to everybody else it will be a mystery. For any speculation which does not at first glance look crazy, there is no hope."—F. L. Dyson, *Innovation in Physics*

John Ciardi

HOW DOES A POEM MEAN?

"Bitzer," said Thomas Gradgrind, "your definition of a horse."

"Quadruped. Gramnivorous. Forty teeth, namely twenty-four grinders, four eye-teeth, and twelve incisive. Sheds coat in the spring; in marshy countries sheds hoofs too. Hoofs hard, but requiring to be shod with iron. Age known by marks in mouth." Thus (and much more) Bitzer.

"Now girl number twenty," said Mr. Gradgrind, "you know what a horse is."

—CHARLES DICKENS, *Hard Times*

The School of Hard Facts over which Mr. Gradgrind presided was a school of fixed answers. Mr. Gradgrind would have agreed with a recent anthologist who wrote that the inspection of a poem should be as certain as a chemical analysis. Mr. Gradgrind would have assured himself that he was a first-class critic, of poetry as of horses. "Now girl number twenty," he would have said looking up from his analysis, "you know what a poem is."

Today, a century later than Mr. Gradgrind's School of Hard Facts, the idea is still current that the methods of measurement evolved by the physical sciences can be applied to all human

Reprinted from John Ciardi, "How Does a Poem Mean?" in *How Does a Poem Mean?* Part Three of *An Introduction to Literature,* ed. Herbert Barrows, et al. (Boston: Houghton Mifflin Company, 1959), 665–77.

processes. And there still lingers the belief that a dictionary definition is a satisfactory description of an idea or of an experience.

There are many grounds on which dictionary definitions can be disputed, but only one need concern us here. Bitzer's definition of a horse was a dictionary definition. Note that it is put almost exclusively in terms of classification. In those terms, it may do as a table of physical characteristics of *Equus caballus.* But what can it possibly say of the experience one has had of the living animal? No horseman ever rode a "gramnivorous quadruped." No gambler ever bet on one. No sculptor ever dreamed one out of a block of stone. For horseman, gambler, and sculptor are involved in a living relation to a living animal, *and the kind of relation is expressed in the language each has evolved for his experience.* ("A good winded bay," says the horseman, "but he has a mouth like iron and won't answer to the bit. He's had bad schooling." Or the gambler: "A good four-year-old. Better than his performance to date. And a good mudder. He's due to win, especially on a wet track. And at nice odds." Or the sculptor: "The set of the stone suggested a rearing posture: the line of force curving down the haunches repeated in the straining line of the neck with the mouth held hard-down by the bit.") Whatever the "gramnivorous quadruped" may be to the biologist, these three ways of speaking are three experiences of the living horse. As Tip O'Neill once wrote in a fine sarcastic line: "There's not a wedding in the world that's worth a running horse." Now try the line revised: "There is not a marriage ceremony in existence worthy of comparison with a gramnivorous quadruped of the genus *Equus caballus* in rapid motion."

The point is that *the language of experience is not the language of classification.* A boy burning with ambition to become a jockey does not study a text on zoology. He watches horses, he listens to what is said by those who have spent their lives around horses, he rides them, trains them, feeds them, curries them, pets them. He lives with intense feelings toward them. He may never learn how many incisors a horse has, nor how many yards of intestines. What does it matter? He is concerned with a *feel,* a response-to, a sense of the character and reaction of the living animal. And zoology cannot give him that. Not all the anatomizing of all the world's horses could teach a man horse-sense.

So for poetry. The concern is not to arrive at a definition and to close the book, but to arrive at an experience. There will never be a complete system for "understanding" or for "judging" poetry. Understanding and critical judgment are admirable goals, but neither can take place until the poem has been experienced, and even then there is always some part of every good work of art that can never be fully explained or categorized. It still remains true that the reader who has experienced most fully will finally be the best judge.

Poetry has only a remote place in the gross of our culture. As has, for example, the opera. Therefore, Americans generally need to be taught in school how to experience both poetry and the opera. In Milan, on the other hand, no one need go to school in order to learn how to experience an opera: the Milanese do not study opera, they *inhale* it. They would have to go to school to learn, for example, how to watch a baseball game in an experienceable way. Certainly no one in The Bronx need go to that school: in The Bronx it is baseball that is inhaled as a living thing, and opera and poetry that have to be learned.

If the reader cared enough for poetry, he would have no need to study it. He would *live into it*. As the Milanese citizen becomes an encyclopedia of opera information, and as even retarded boys in The Bronx are capable of reciting endlessly detailed baseball statistics, so the passionate reader of poetry becomes alive to it by natural process.

Any teaching of the poem by any other method owes the poem an apology. What greater violence can be done to the poet's experience than to drag it into an early morning classroom and to go after it as an item on its way to a Final Examination? The apology must at least be made. It is the experience, not the Final Examination, that counts. Though one must note with care—as in the case of the baseball fan—that passionate learning is full of very technical stuff. Why else would baseball statistics give rise to such heated argument as one can hear throughout the season?

And in poetry there is the step beyond: once one has learned to experience the poem as a poem, there inevitably arrives a sense that one is also experiencing himself as a human being. It must certainly have been this second experience (to put it in another way, the point at which Art for Art's sake becomes Art for Life's sake) that Matthew Arnold had in mind when he wrote: "The grand power of poetry is its interpretative power . . . the power of so dealing with things as to awaken in us a wonderfully full, new, and intimate sense of them, and of our relations with them." But the grand power of a good sermon is also its interpretative power, and a sermon, it must be remembered, is not a poem.

Paradise Lost is, in one sense, a rhymed sermon written to justify God's ways to man. So is Michael Wigglesworth's *The Day of Doom*. Wigglesworth was a Puritan clergyman of the Massachusetts Bay Colony and for over two centuries Puritan children memorized large sections of his poem as part of their church training. Wigglesworth's theology is every bit as sound and as comprehensive as Milton's. Yet today *The Day of Doom* is all but unknown except as a scholar's curio. The difference is not in content but in the fact that Milton wrote a poem whereas Wigglesworth wrote only doggerel. Poetry, it follows, is more than simply "something to say." Nor is it simply an elaborate way of saying something or nothing.

W. H. Auden was once asked what advice he would give a young man who wished to become a poet. Auden replied that he would ask the young man why he wanted to write poetry. If the answer was "because I have something important to say," Auden would conclude that there was no hope for that young man as a poet. If on the other hand the answer was something like "because I like to hang around words and overhear them talking to one another," then that young man was at least interested in a fundamental part of the poetic process and there was hope for him.

When one "message-hunts" a poem (i.e., goes through the

poem with no interest except in its paraphraseable content) he is approaching the writing as did the young man with "something important to say." He is giving it the Wigglesworth treatment. The common question from which such an approach begins is "WHAT DOES THE POEM MEAN?" His mind closed on that point of view, the reader tends to "interpret" the poem rather than to experience it, seeking only what he can make over from it into a prose statement (or examination answer) and forgetting in the process that it was originally a poem. Thus, students are too often headed by their teachers in the direction of reciting, almost like Bitzer: "Keats. 'When I have fears that I may cease to be.' Sonnet. Irregular. Consisting of three quatrains and a couplet, the third quatrain consisting of very close rhymes, thus: 'hour, more, power, shore.' Written on the theme of the vanity of earthly wishes, but given a strong romantic coloration of individualistic aspiration for the good pleasures of the world."

Poor Keats!

For WHAT DOES THE POEM MEAN? is too often a self-destroying approach to poetry. A more useful way of asking the question is HOW DOES A POEM MEAN? Why does it build itself into a form out of images, ideas, rhythms? How do these elements become the meaning? How are they inseparable from the meaning? As Yeats wrote:

> O body swayed to music, o quickening glance,
> How shall I tell the dancer from the dance?

What the poem is, is inseparable from its own performance of itself. The dance is in the dancer and the dancer is in the dance. Or put in another way: where is the "dance" when no one is dancing it? and what man is a "dancer" except when he is dancing?

Above all else, poetry is a performance. Keats' overt subject in his sonnet was his own approaching death. But note this about poetry: Keats took the same *self-delighting pains* in writing about his death as he took in poems on overtly happy subjects, such as "On First Looking into Chapman's Homer" or the "Ode to a Nightingale." Here is the complete sonnet:

When I have fears that I may cease to be
Before my pen has gleaned my teeming brain,
Before high piled books, in charactery,
Hold like rich garners the full ripened grain,
When I behold upon the night's starred face,
Huge cloudy symbols of a high romance,
And think that I may never live to trace
Their shadows with the magic hand of chance;
And when I feel, fair creature of an hour,
That I shall never look upon thee more,
Never have relish in the faery power
Of unreflecting love;—then on the shore
Of the wide world I stand alone, and think
Till love and fame to nothingness do sink.

If this sonnet means "the vanity of human wishes given a strong romantic coloration, etc.," why did Keats take the trouble to bring his rhythms to a stop at the end of the fourth and eighth lines and in the middle of the twelfth? Sonnets normally divide into "octet" (the first eight lines) and "sestet" (the final six lines). Note that Keats' divisions occur in a very nearly symmetrical pattern. Why did Keats spend so much care on symmetry? What has symmetry to do with "the vanity of earthly wishes"? Why, too, did Keats bother to compare his mind to a field of grain, and the books he felt himself able to write, to storage bins? An elaborate figure. Why did Keats bother to construct it? Why did he search out such striking phrases as "the magic hand of chance"? If Keats were really convinced that all human wishes are vain, why did he wish to phrase his idea with such earthly care? If *nothingness* is all, why bother to make *the something* a poem is?

Robert Frost provided a valuable clue when he spoke of "the pleasure of taking pains." The paradox here is simply verbal. Frost meant precisely what the German critic Baumgarten meant when he spoke of the central impulse toward poetry (and toward all art) as the *Spieltrieb,* the play impulse.

An excellent native example of the play impulse in poetry is the child clapping its hands in response to a Mother Goose rhyme. What does a child care for "meaning"? What on earth is the "meaning" of the following poem?

> High Diddle diddle
> The cat and the fiddle
> The cow jumped over the moon;
> The little dog laughed
> To see such craft
> And the dish ran away with the spoon.

"Preposterous," says Mr. Gradgrind. But the child is wiser: he is busy having a good time with the poem. The poem pleases and involves him. He responds to it in an immediate muscular way. He recognizes its performance at once and wants *to act with it.*

This is the first level of play. As rhythm is the first element of music. The child claps hands, has fun, and the play involves practically no thoughtful activity. Beyond this level of response, there begins the kind of play whose pleasure lies for the poet in overcoming meaningful and thoughtful (and "feelingful") difficulties, and for the reader in identifying with the poet in that activity.

Nor is the word "difficulty" one to be afraid of. Chess is a play-activity, yet it is play only because the players deliberately make the game difficult in order to overcome the difficulties. The equation is simple: no difficulty, no fun. No chess player finds any real pleasure in playing an obviously inferior opponent. *Every game ever invented by mankind is a way of making things hard for the fun of it. The great fun, of course, is in making the hard look easy.* Too much difficulty is painful. The Freshman football coach does not send his squad to play last year's Rose Bowl winner. Neither does he send it to play grammar school teams. He tries to find opponents who will give his players a real chance to extend themselves, win or lose, and he hopes bit by bit to develop them for harder play.

Learning to experience poetry is not a radically different process from that of learning any other kind of play. The way to develop a poetic sense is by using it. And one of the real joys of the play-impulse is in the sudden discovery that one is getting better at it than he had thought he would be.

It is this self-delighting play impulse that the literalist and message-hunter overlooks, just as Mr. Gradgrind overlooked the living fun it is to ride a horse, even an undefined horse.

To summarize these same points in more formal terms: *no matter how serious the overt message of a poem, the unparaphraseable and undiminishable life of the poem lies in the way it performs itself through the difficulties it imposes upon itself.* The way *in which* it means is *what* it means.

What for example does a dance "mean"? Or what does music "mean"? Or what does a juggler "mean" when we watch him with such admiration of his skill? All of these forms—and poetry with them—have meaning only as they succeed in being good performances.

One sees a wizard of a poet tossing his words in the air and catching them and tossing them again—what a grand stunt! Then suddenly one may be astonished to find that the poet is not simply juggling cups, saucers, roses, rhymes and other random objects, but the very stuff of life. And discovering that, one discovers that seeing the poet's ideas flash so in the air, seeing them performed under such control, is not only a reward in itself, but a living experience that deepens every man's sense of life. One finds himself more alert to life, surer of his own emotions, wiser than he would have been without that experience.—And he thought he was just watching a show!

But only a poem can illustrate how a poem works. One of the purposes of this volume is to provide beginning students with a reasonable bulk of poems from the great tradition of English and American poetry. But great as are the virtues of wide reading, they amount to nothing unless the reading goes deep as well as wide. It is good to read much. It is even more important to read a little in greater depth, for every poem one reads closely will teach him something about how to read another poem.

What should such a close reading take into consideration?

Here is a poem, one of the master lyrics of American poetry, perhaps the best known poem by an American poet:

STOPPING BY WOODS ON A SNOWY EVENING[1]

Whose woods these are I think I know.
His house is in the village though;
He will not see me stopping here
To watch his woods fill up with snow.

My little horse must think it queer
To stop without a farmhouse near
Between the woods and frozen lake
The darkest evening of the year.

He gives his harness bells a shake
To ask if there is some mistake.
The only other sound's the sweep,
Of easy wind and downy flake.

The woods are lovely, dark and deep.
But I have promises to keep,
And miles to go before I sleep,
And miles to go before I sleep.

—*Robert Frost*

Note that the poem begins as a simple description of events, but that it ends in a way that suggests meanings far beyond the specific description. This movement *from the specific to the general* is one of the basic formulas of poetry. Such a poem, as Yvor Winters's "Before Disaster" (p. 1005), and Holmes's "The Chambered Nautilus" (p. 742) follow exactly this progression from the specific to the general, but the generalization in these poems is, in a sense, divided from the specific description or narration, and even seems additional to the specific action rather than intrinsically part of it. It is this sense of division that is signified when one speaks of "a tacked-on moral." Frost, however, is painstakingly careful to avoid the tacked-on moral. Everything in the poem pretends, on one level, to be part of the incident narrated. Yet one cannot miss the feeling that by the end of the poem, Frost has referred to something much more far-reaching than stopping by woods or than driving home to go to bed. There can be little doubt, in fact, that part of Frost's own pleasure in this poem was in making the larger intent *grow out* of the poem rather than in tacking it on. It is in the poem's own performance of itself that the larger meaning is made to emerge from the specific incident. A careful look at that performance will teach a great deal about the nature of poetry.

The poem begins with a situation. A man—knowing Robert Frost, we know it is a Vermont or New Hampshire man—is on his way somewhere at night-fall. It is snowing and as he passes a patch of woods he stops to watch the easy down-drift of the snow into the dark woods. We are told two other things: first that the man is familiar with these parts (he knows who owns these woods and where he lives) and second that no one sees him stop. More could be read into this opening (for example: why doesn't he say what errand he is on? why does he say he knows whose woods these are? what is the significance of watching another man's woods in this way?). Such questions can be multiplied almost endlessly without losing real point, but for present purposes let us assume that we have identified scene one of the poem's performance without raising these questions.

Note that the scene is set in the simplest possible terms. We have no trouble sensing that the man stopped because the scene moved him, but he neither tells us that it is beautiful nor that it moved him. A student writer, always ready to overdo, might have said that he was moved to stop and "to fill his soul with the slow steady stately sinking of that crystaline loveliness into the glimmerless profundities of the hushed primeval wood." Frost prefers to avoid such a spate of words, and to speak the incident in the simplest terms.

His choice illustrates two basic principles of writing of which every sensitive reader should be aware. Frost stated the first principle himself in "The Mowing" (p. 812) when he wrote "Anything *more* than the truth would have seemed too *weak*."

(italics mine) Understatement is one of the principal sources of power in English poetry.

The second principle here illustrated is to let the action speak for itself. A good novelist who wishes us to know a character does not tell us that character is good or bad and leave it at that. Rather, he introduces the character, shows him in action, and lets his actions speak for him. This process is spoken of as *characterization in action*. One of the skills of a good poet is to enact his experiences rather than to talk about having had them. "*Show* it, don't *tell* it," he says, "make it happen, don't talk about its happening."

One part of this poem's performance, in fact, is *to act out* (and thereby to make us act out—*i.e., feel out—i.e., identify with*) just why the speaker did stop. The man is the principal actor of this little "drama of why" and in scene one he is the only character. In scene two (starting with the beginning of stanza two), however, a "foil" is introduced. In drama, a "foil" is a character who "plays against" a more important character; by presenting a different point of view or an opposed set of motives, the foil moves the more important character to react in ways that might not have found expression without such opposition. The more important character is thus more fully revealed, to the reader and to himself. The foil here is the horse.

The horse forces the first question in the drama of why. Why did the man stop? Until he comes to realize that his "little horse must think it queer" to stop this way, he has not asked himself why he stopped; he simply did. But he senses that the horse is confused by the stop. He imagines how the horse must feel about it—what *is* there to stop for out here in the cold, away from bin and stall and all that any self-respecting horse would value on such a night?

In imagining the horse's question, the man is of course led to examine his own reasons. In stanza two this question arises only as a feeling within the man. In stanza three, however, the horse acts definitely. He gives his harness bells a shake. "What's wrong," he seems to say, "what are we doing here?"

By now, obviously, the horse, without losing its identity as a horse has also become a symbol. A symbol is something that stands for something else. That something else may, perhaps, be taken as the order of life that does not understand why a man stops in the wintry middle of nowhere to watch snow come down. (Could the dark and the snowfall symbolize a death wish? that hunger for the last rest that man may feel, but not a beast?) So there is the man, there is that other order of life, and there is the third presence—the movement of the inanimate wind and snow (the all-engulfing?) across both their lives—with the difference that the man knows the second darkness of the dark while the horse does not.

The man has no ready answer to this combination of forces. They exist and he feels them—all three of them, himself included. We sense that he would like to remain here longer to ponder these forces, perhaps to yield to their total. But a fourth force prompts him. That fourth force can be given many names. It is almost certainly better, in fact, to give it many names than attempt to limit it to one. Social obligation, responsibility, personal commitment, duty, or just the realization that a man cannot indulge a mood forever—all of these things and more. He has a long way to go and it is time to be getting there (so there's something to be said for the horse, too). We find the man's inner conflict dramatized to this point by the end of scene two (which coincides with the end of stanza three).

Then and only then—his feelings dramatized in the cross tug of motives he has given form to—does the poet, a little sadly, venture on the comment of his final scene. "The woods are lovely, dark and deep." The very sound of the syllables lingers over the thought. But there is something to do yet before he can yield to the lovely dark-and-deep. "Not yet," he seems to say, "not yet." He has a long way to go—miles to go before he can sleep. Yes, miles to go. He repeats the line and the performance ends.

But why the repetition? The first time Frost writes "And miles to go before I sleep" there can be little doubt that he means, "I have a long way to go yet before I can get to bed tonight." The second time he says it, however, "miles to go" and "sleep" are suddenly transformed into symbols. What is the "something else" these symbols stand for? Hundreds of people have asked Mr. Frost that question in one form or another, and Mr. Frost has always turned the question away with a joke. He has turned it away primarily *because he cannot answer it*. He could answer some part of it. But some part is not enough.

For a symbol is like a rock dropped into a pool: it sends out ripples in all directions, and the ripples are in motion. Who can say where the last ripple disappears? One may have a sense that he at least knows approximately the center point of all those ripples, the point at which the stone struck the water. Yet even then he has trouble marking it precisely. How does one make a mark on water? Oh, very well—the center point of "miles to go" is probably approximately in the neighborhood of being close to meaning, perhaps, "the road of life," and "before I sleep" is maybe that close to meaning "before I take my final rest." (That rest-in-darkness that seemed so temptingly "lovely dark-and-deep" for the moment of the mood.) But the ripples continue to move and the light to change on the water and the longer one watches the more changes he sees. And such shifting-and-being-at-the-same-instant is of the very sparkle and life of poetry. Of poetry and of life itself. For the poem is a dynamic and living thing. One experiences it as one experiences life —as everybody but Mr. Gradgrind experiences life. One is never done with it: every time he looks he sees something new, and it changes even as he watches. And that very sense of continuity in fluidity is one of the kinds of knowledge, one of the ways of knowing, that only the arts can teach, poetry foremost among them.

Frost himself certainly did not ask what the lines "meant." They came to him and he received them; he "felt right" about them. And what he "felt right about" may perhaps be called their "meaning," but it is far more to the point to describe it as "their long possibility of meaning." For the poem is not a statement but a performance of forces, not an essay on life but a reenactment, and just as men must search their lives over and over again for the meaning of their deepest experiences, so the performance of a true poem is endless in being not a meaning but an act of existence.

Now look at the poem in another way. Did Frost know what he was going to do when he began? Considering the poem simply as a piece of juggling one cannot fail to respond to the magnificent turn at the end where, with one flip, seven of the simplest words in the language suddenly dazzle full of never-ending waves of thought and feeling; or—more precisely—of felt-thought. Certainly an equivalent stunt by a juggler—could there be such an equivalent—would bring the house down. Was it to cap his performance with that grand stunt that Frost wrote the poem?

Far from it: the fact that must not be overlooked is that *Frost did not know he was going to write those lines until he wrote them.* Then a second fact must be registered: *he wrote them because, for the fun of it, he had got himself into trouble.*

Let us start by saying that Frost began by playing a game with himself. The most usual way of writing a four line stanza with four feet to the line, is to rhyme the third line with the first, and the fourth line with the second. Even that much rhyme is so difficult that many poets and almost all the anonymous ballad makers do not bother to rhyme the first and third lines at all, settling for two rhymes in four lines. For the fact is that English is a rhyme-poor language. In Italian and in French, for example, so many words end with the same sounds that rhyming is relatively easy. English, being a more agglomerate language, has far more final sounds, hence fewer of them rhyme. When an Italian poet writes a line ending with "vita" (life) he has literally hundreds of possible rhyme words available. When an English poet writes "life" at the end of a line, he can summon "strife, wife, knife, fife, rife" and then he is in trouble. Now "life-strife," and "life-rife" and "life-wife" seem to offer a combination of ideas that are possibly related by more than rhyme. Inevitably, therefore, the poets have had to work, re-work, and over-work these combinations until the sparkle has gone out of them. Readers are normally tired of these combinations. When one encounters "life-strife" he is certainly entitled to suspect that the poet did not really want to say "strife"—that if there had been in English such a word as, say, "hife" meaning "infinite peace and harmony," he would gladly have used that word instead of "strife." So one feels that the writing is haphazard: that the rhyme is making the poet say things he doesn't really feel, and which, therefore, the reader does not feel. One likes to see the rhymes fall into place, but he must end up with the belief that it is the poet who is deciding what is said and not the rhyme scheme.

So rhyme is a kind of game, and an especially difficult one in English. As in every game, the fun of rhyme is to set one's difficulties high and then to meet them skillfully. As Frost himself once defined freedom, it consists of "moving easy in harness."

In "Stopping by Woods on a Snowy Evening" Frost took a long chance. He decided to rhyme not two lines, but three in each stanza. Not even Frost could have sustained that much rhyme in a long poem (as Dante, for example, with the advantage of writing in Italian sustained triple rhyme for thousands of lines in *The Divine Comedy*). He would have known instantly, therefore, when he took that first chance, that he was going to write a short poem. He would have had that much foretaste of it. So the first stanza emerged rhymed aaba. And with the certain sense that this was to be a short poem, Frost decided to take a chance and redouble: in English three rhymes in four lines is enough—there is no need to rhyme the fourth line. For the fun of it, however, Frost set himself to pick up that loose rhyme and weave it into the pattern—thereby accepting the all but impossible burden of quadruple rhyme.

The miracle is that it worked. Despite that enormous freight of rhyme the poem not only came out as a neat pattern, but managed to do so with no sense of strain. It is this unstrained fulfillment of one's difficulties Frost means by "moving easy in harness." Despite all his self-imposed restrictions the poem *seems* to go effortlessly. Every word falls into place as naturally as if there were no rhyme restricting the choice.

That ease is part of the success of the performance. One watches the skill-man juggle two balls, then three, then four—

and every addition makes the trick more wonderful, but unless he makes the hard trick *seem* as easy as the easy one, then all is lost.

The real point, however, is not only that Frost took on a hard rhyme-trick and made it look easy. It is rather as if a juggler, carried away, had tossed up one more ball than he could really handle—and then amazed himself by actually handling it. So with the real triumph of this poem. Frost could not have known what a stunning effect his repetition of the last line was going to produce. He could not even have known he was going to repeat the line. He simply found himself up against a difficulty he probably had not foreseen: in picking up the rhyme from the third line of stanza one and carrying it over into stanza two, he had created an endless chain-link form. Each stanza left a hook sticking out for the next stanza to catch. So by stanza four, feeling the poem rounding to its end, Frost had to do something about his third-line rhyme.

He might have tucked it back in a third line rhyming with "know/though/snow" of stanza one. That would have worked out to the mathematical symmetry of using each rhyme four times. But though such a device might be defensible in theory, a rhyme repeated after eleven lines is so far from its original rhyme sound that its feeling as rhyme must certainly be lost, and what good is theory if the reader is not moved by the writing?

It must have been in some such quandary that the final repetition suggested itself—a suggestion born of the very difficulty of what the poet had set out to do. So the point beyond mere ease in handling a hard thing: that the very difficulty of the restrictions the poet imposed upon himself offered the opportunity to do better than he had imagined. What—aside from having that happen to oneself—could be more self-delighting than to participate in its happening by one's reader-identification with the poem?

You will observe one further point: that the human-insight of the poem, and the technicalities of the poetic devices are inseparable. Each feeds the other. This interplay is the poem's meaning, a matter not of WHAT IT MEANS (nobody can say entirely what a good poem means) but HOW IT MEANS—a process one can come much closer to discussing.

Is it too frivolous to have compared this process to the act of juggling? Consider the following parable based on a short story by Anatole France, "The Juggler of Notre Dame."

The juggler wandered France from fair to fair and whenever he saw a chance to earn a few pennies he unrolled his rug, lay on his back, and juggled his paraphernalia with his hands and feet. It was all he knew how to do, he did it well, and he was happy in the doing.

As he grew older, however, misfortunes crowded him. One winter's day, ill and tired, he took refuge in a monastery and by the time he had recovered he decided to remain there. It was a pleasant monastery dedicated to the Virgin and each of the monks and brothers set himself a special task in her honor. One illuminated manuscripts to offer her, another decorated her altar, another raised flowers. Only the juggler had no productive art, only he produced nothing that could be set in place before her and stay tangibly in place. (This rendering takes a few liberties with the original for the sake of making a point.)

Finally, in despair, the juggler took to stealing into the chapel when no one else was about. There he would unroll his rug and juggle before the Virgin's statue. It was all he had to offer, the one thing he could do well.

One day a passing brother discovered the juggler at work before the statue and summoned the other monks in horror to witness the profanation of the chapel. Soon all the windowsills were lined with the heads of outraged monks come to verify the horrible report. They were just about to rush in and put an end to the sacrilege, when before their eyes the Virgin descended smiling from her pedestal and wiped the sweat from the juggler's brow. The offering was acceptable.

A note to the residual Gradgrinds: This parable is not a religious excursion. It is an allegory. An allegory is a story in which each character and element is more important as a symbol (as something else) than as its presumably-literal self. Then all these symbols-put-together acquire further meanings by their interaction upon on another.—What does the Virgin stand for in poetic terms? What do the monks stand for? The juggler? How does juggling relate to Frost's definition of freedom (in poetry)? Why should juggling produce the miracle? How does the parable mean what it means?

NOTE

1. From *Complete Poems of Robert Frost.* Copyright 1930, 1949, by Henry Holt and Company, Inc. Copyright 1936, by Robert Frost. By permission of the publishers.

Bibliography

Blackmur, R. P. *The Double Agent: Essays in Craft and Elucidation*. New York: Arrow, 1935.

———. "Lord Tennyson's Scissors: 1912–1950." In *Form and Value in Modern Poetry,* 369–88. New York: Anchor, 1957.

———. *Poems of R. P. Blackmur.* Princeton, N.J.: Princeton University Press, 1977.

Bogan, Louise. *Collected Poems, 1923–1953*. New York: Noonday, 1954.

———. *A Poet's Alphabet: Reflections on the Literary Art and Vocation*. Edited by Robert Phelps and Ruth Limmer. New York: McGraw, 1970.

———. "Some Notes on Popular and Unpopular Art." In *Selected Criticism,* 238–51. New York: Noonday, 1955.

Burke, Kenneth. *Collected Poems 1915–1967*. Berkeley: University of California Press, 1968.

———. "Freud—and the Analysis of Poetry." In *The Philosophy of Literary Form,* 3d ed., 258–92. Berkeley: University of California Press, 1973.

———. *Language as Symbolic Action: Essays on Life, Literature, and Method*. Berkeley: University of California Press, 1966.

Ciardi, John. *Dialogue with an Audience.* New York: Lippincott, 1963.

———. "How Does a Poem Mean?" *How Does a Poem Mean? An Introduction to Literature.* Boston: Houghton Mifflin Company, 1959.

———. *Selected Poems.* Fayetteville: University of Arkansas Press, 1984.

Hayden, Robert. "'How It Strikes a Contemporary': Reflections on Poetry and the Role of the Poet." In *Collected Prose,* edited by Frederick Glaysher, 3–16. Ann Arbor: University of Michigan Press, 1984.

———. *Robert Hayden: Collected Poems.* Edited by Frederick Glaysher. New York: Liveright, 1985.

———, ed. *Kaleidoscope: Poems by American Negro Poets.* New York: Harcourt, 1967.

Jarrell, Randall. *The Complete Poems.* New York: Farrar, 1969.

———. *Poetry and the Age.* New York: Knopf, 1953. London: Faber, 1955.

———. "Poets, Critics, and Readers." In *Kipling, Auden & Co.,* 305–18. New York: Farrar, 1980.

———. *A Sad Heart at the Supermarket: Essays and Fables.* New York: Atheneum, 1962.

———. *The Third Book of Criticism.* New York: Farrar, 1969.

Olson, Elder. *Collected Poems.* Chicago: University of Chicago Press, 1963.

———. *Last Poems.* Chicago: University of Chicago Press, 1984.

———. "The Lyric." In *On Value Judgments in the Arts and Other Essays,* 212–19. Chicago: University of Chicago Press, 1976.

Ransom, John Crowe. *The New Criticism.* Norfolk: New Directions, 1941.

———. *Selected Essays of John Crowe Ransom.* Edited by Thomas Daniel Young and John Hindle. Baton Rouge: Louisiana State University Press, 1984.

———. *Selected Poems.* Revised and enlarged ed. New York: Ecco Press, 1978.

———. "Wanted: An Ontological Critic." In *Beating the Bushes: Selected Essays 1941–1970,* 1–46. New York: New Directions, 1972.

———. *The World's Body.* New York: Scribners, 1938.

Schwartz, Delmore. "The Isolation of Modern Poetry." In *Selected Essays of Delmore Schwartz,* edited by Donald A. Dike and David H. Zucker, 3–13. Chicago: University of Chicago Press, 1970.

———. *Last and Lost Poems of Delmore Schwartz.* Edited by Robert Phillips. New York: Vanguard, 1979.

———. *Summer Knowledge: New and Selected Poems, 1938–1958.* Garden City: Doubleday, 1959.

Tate, Allen. *Collected Poems 1919–1976.* New York: Farrar, 1977.

———. *Memoirs & Essays Old and New, 1926–1974.* Chicago: Swallow, 1975.

———. "Tension in Poetry." In *Essays of Four Decades,* 56–71. Chicago: Swallow, 1968.

Warren, Robert Penn. "Pure and Impure Poetry." In *New and Selected Essays,* 3–29. New York: Random House, 1989.

———. *Selected Essays.* New York: Random House, 1958.

Warren, Robert Penn, and Cleanth Brooks Jr. *Understanding Poetry.* New York: Holt, 1938.

Winters, Yvor. *The Anatomy of Nonsense.* Norfolk: New Directions, 1943.

———. "The Audible Reading of Poetry." In *The Function of Criticism,* 79–100. Norfolk: New Directions, 1943.

———. *In Defense of Reason.* New York: Swallow, 1947.

———. *The Poetry of Yvor Winters.* Athens: Swallow, 1980.